Dear Reader,

I loved Ray Stedman! And I am unashamed to tell you that tears exploded from my eyes as I read several passages of this book by Mark Mitchell. I literally sobbed with joy and gratitude to God for this one life—this God-centered, Christ-honoring, Spirit-filled life.

What I remember most about Ray Stedman: Ray was humorous. He was filled with the joy of the Lord. Ray was a real man. He was a man's man in every way. Ray was authentic. He loved you enough to firmly rebuke you when needed. His practical application of Scripture quickly shook your conscience. Ray Stedman made biblical exposition seem utterly simple! Over and over he used these three principles: observation, interpretation, application.

While serving as one of Ray Stedman's first two interns (Charles Swindoll was the other), I also grew to value his unique way of counseling. I remember Ray telling me: "Get past the façade, the smoke screen, and go straight for the soul. All man's problems stem from the ego—pride. The answers, of course, to the ego are Jesus Christ and Scripture, principle and truth—so lead them there." I have practiced that advice for years on TV, radio, and in personal counseling.

Ray loved his daughters to the point of tears of pain. He always believed they would one day walk with God in amazing ways. Ray's wife, Elaine, made Jesus Christ, their daughters, and the ministry her first priority. Ray never took that for granted.

Ray lived out the resurrected indwelling life of a Christian unlike any man I have known, and he taught us well.

Were there any weaknesses in Ray Stedman's life? Sure, he was human!! But of this I am quite certain: Ray Stedman was a faithful servant of Jesus Christ throughout his lifetime and will enjoy the Lord's "Well done!" for all eternity.

— Luis Palau

Discovery House Publishers

Books, music, and videos that feed the soul with the Word of God

Box 3566 Grand Rapids, MI 49501

Portrait *of* Integrity

The Life of Ray C. Stedman

MARK S. MITCHELL

Discovery House Publishers is affiliated with RBC Ministries,
Grand Rapids, Michigan 49512

Discovery House books are distributed to the trade exclusively by
Barbour Publishing, Inc., Uhrichsville, Ohio 44583

Designed by Sherri L. Hoffman

Library of Congress Cataloging-in-Publication Data

Mitchell, Mark.
    Portrait of integrity : the life of Ray C. Stedman / by Mark
Mitchell.
        p. cm.
    ISBN 1-57293-116-7
    Stedman, Ray C. 2. Peninsula Bible Church—Clergy—Biography.
I. Title.
    BX9999.P46M58 2004
    280'.4'092—dc22   2003022184

Printed in the United States of America
04 05 06 07 08 09 / CHG / 10 9 8 7 6 5 4 3 2 1

To my wife, Lynn,
the one and only love of my life,
and a portrait of integrity.

CONTENTS

FOREWORD

EVERY YOUNG MAN WHO survives the challenge of a lonely child-hood secretly embraces a hope that one day he will meet a soul brother, a kindred spirit, another guy who sees life the same way he does. So when I met Ray Stedman on the post-WWII campus of Dallas Theological Seminary, the two of us bonded immediately. In His all-knowing wisdom God sometimes designs a rocky path for spunky little boys, a maze of twists and turns with dark shadows and blank walls. When a man finally emerges, he spots another grown-up doggie right away.

From opposite sides of the North American continent, Ray and I melded together our permanent heart connection. Both of us were sure of where we wanted to go, and here was a comrade for the journey. We were marching in a war-weary world that was done with victory parades and memorial monuments. Our generation was asking, "Now what?"

Ray brought his western outdoorsmanship, honed with military exposure and Pentecostal roots. I contributed my eastern conservatism polished with college disciplines and Presbyterian flavoring. Together we sat in classrooms absorbing ancient biblical truth; together we leaned against tree trunks and squatted in the shade of campus pecan branches to sort out what it all meant for the spiritual mixmaster where we found ourselves.

We hacked away at theological mysteries and proposed our solutions, pounding and kneading them, only then to discard them and start all over again the next day with altered assumptions. Our theological wrestling matches always ended with a win-win verdict. Each of us was clarifying in his mind what we knew God wanted in the years ahead. As graduation approached, our focus narrowed and we agreed to a split teamwork. Ray would go back to the West Coast and I would stay someplace east of the Rockies. Together we would trust God to incubate a new batch of young leaders to show mid-century USA the power of biblical belief and practice.

Now, it's been more than a decade since God called Ray home to heaven. His departure left a cavernous hole in my heart. I have missed him more than words can ever express. Our visceral linkage never detached, but always vibrated with a mutual love. Though we lived many miles distant from each other, every phone call or visit or hastily scribbled note started as if the previous one had simply ended with a comma and this was the continuation.

Ray's exceptional contribution was not only to me personally, but to his constantly expanding world. The life-changing message of God's grace in Christ had ignited his inner confidence in such a way that every fiber of his being was devoted to translating an accurate representation of Jesus Christ to our ever-more-secularized world. Consequently, every message he delivered was a carefully prepared feast for hungry hearts. He did his exegetical homework with diligence, but just as intently he scrutinized his society. And thus he engaged his listeners with logic and irrefutable data so compelling that any hearer had to respond. Whether he addressed two or three informally, or several thousand in a large meeting, Ray was always the same—conversational, confident, and magnetic.

Ray defied every stereotype. He was totally approachable, never wanting to be known as a condescending cleric. He spoke as an ordinary man, but his words seared permanently like a tattoo. He was affable, warm, yet exacting, but he never scarred an earnest seeker. He was spiritual but never churchy; he was impatient with pretense, angry with arrogance, but always at ease with the awkwardness of a crippled sheep seeking spiritual shelter.

Ray was rough-hewn but never abrasive; he was always a gentleman, never coarse or crude. He loved to laugh and learned to lay his deepest sorrows on his Lord, so that in the midst of disappointment he could still rejoice. His eye was fixed on an eternal objective.

I am a rich man for having had a companionship with Ray Stedman. My heart beats with anticipation to catch up with him in heaven. For those who know only the sweet aroma of his lasting fragrance, Mark Mitchell has crafted a remarkable literary likeness of Ray. Read it to meet one of the most attractive men who ever walked this earth. Like Abel, *". . . by faith he still speaks, even though he is dead."*

Ray was unique, impossible to encapsulate in words, but he was a man through whom God's Spirit brought light to darkened minds, a man totally devoted to serving our Savior, and solid proof that it is not the man but the message that makes the difference.

Howard G. Hendricks
Distinguished Professor
Chairman, Center for Christian Leadership
Dallas Theological Seminary
January 2004

INTRODUCTION

―◦―

The writer of Hebrews charges every new generation with the task of remembering past leaders: "Remember your leaders who first taught you the word of God. Think of all the good that has come from their lives, and trust the Lord as they do" (Hebrews 13:7 NLT).

Ray Stedman was one of the great pastors and leaders of a generation of evangelicals that is quickly passing away. From a secular standpoint, Tom Brokaw calls this "the greatest generation." Whether or not Ray Stedman's generation of evangelicals was the greatest, they certainly leave a legacy that today's generation cannot afford to neglect.

When asked why a biography of Ray Stedman should be written, Ray's longtime friend Howard Hendricks responded, "We're living in a generation in which the pedestals are empty. . . . One of the disadvantages of our generation is that it's called the 'Now Generation' because the past is irrelevant, the future is uncertain; therefore they live for the present. The result is they have historical amnesia and need to know the men of the last generation, upon whose shoulders we stand today. Ray certainly qualifies, I believe. He was a much more important leader in evangelicalism than most Christians would know, because of his incredible humility. He was never a self-promoter. He never sought high positions. But everywhere I go, to this day when I mention Ray Stedman's name I get an incredible response. . . . He would be a candidate, in my mind, for a position on the Mount Rushmore of evangelicals."[1]

J. I. Packer also recognized Ray as one of those great leaders. In an endorsement of an expositional commentary written by Kent Hughes, Packer made the following reference to Stedman:

"Throughout the Christian centuries, from Crysostom and Augustine through Luther, Calvin, and Matthew Henry, to Martin Lloyd-Jones and Ray Stedman, working pastors have been proving themselves to be the best of all Bible expositors."[2]

Is Packer right in placing Stedman among the likes of Augustine, Luther, and Calvin? Consider his legacy:

In 1948, when Ray Stedman came to what was then called Peninsula Bible Fellowship (later to become Peninsula Bible Church), he began what became a prototype for the first "seeker sensitive" church. When I arrived at Peninsula Bible Church (PBC) as a new Christian in 1974, it was packed with teenagers. Having been raised in a Roman Catholic home, this was the first Protestant church I had ever entered; yet I felt immediately at home. The building was simple, and the style of the worship service was casual. Blue jeans were the norm, and contemporary music filled the place with praise. Ray encouraged people to stand up and share about their struggles and sins so the body could "bear one another's burdens, and thus fulfill the law of Christ."[3]

In one important sense, however, Ray's ministry was unlike the modern seeker-sensitive movement, which often abandons biblical exposition in favor of topical preaching that seeks relevancy by focusing on "felt needs." Ray believed that nothing could be more exciting and more relevant to the needs of people than the Scriptures being taught as they should be. Throughout his ministry, he remained committed to biblical exposition, but did so in a way that communicated clearly even to those without any religious background. When Ray preached, unchurched people felt he was talking to them. In other words, Ray believed biblical exposition is the most seeker-sensitive thing a preacher can do!

Stedman's high regard for the Word of God and biblical exposition was at the heart of what he believed the church is all about. "I'm very much persuaded that the power of preaching is, by God's design, the most powerful motivation of a congregation that you will ever see," he said. "Nothing turns people on like God's truth, and when they see the remarkable plan of God for the functioning of His people, they can hardly wait to find opportunity to put it into practice. And much of the artificial prods that we use today to get people going are simply a confession on our part that we have not found the way to motivate people by the power of the preaching of the Word of God."[4]

Though conservative in his theology, Ray Stedman was a radical in the area of ecclesiology. At PBC, Ray birthed many of the things we take for granted in the evangelical church today and chronicled it all in *Body Life,* his seminal book on the church. In this book, which has sold thousands of copies since it was first published in 1972, Ray applied the New Testament vision of the church as the body of Christ to a new generation. He believed the work of the ministry should be done by people in the pews rather than by professionals and that the role of pastors is to equip the saints to use their spiritual gifts. In keeping with this conviction, Ray deplored all things ecclesiastical, even refusing to be called the senior pastor of PBC. He avoided anything that promoted hierarchical separation in the church, and he insisted that the church be led by servant-leaders (called elders) who were responsible to Christ, the Living Head of the body.

Ray's commitment to equipping the saints also extended to the training of pastors. He loved mentoring young men who desired to teach the Scriptures, and he believed that pastors should be trained in the local church rather than in the seminary. Along with David Roper, Ray started Scribe School, a two-year internship program with heavy emphasis on biblical languages, where many pastors were trained over the years. Ray's vision to train pastors also found expression in a successful pastors' conference where for years he and his colleagues taught the principles of Body Life to hundreds of Christian leaders. It is a testimony to the success of Ray's vision that when he retired there was no need to hire a pastor to replace him. Several men already on staff were well prepared to preach and lead the church. And today, many Scribe School graduates, including myself, minister throughout the nation and the world.

One of the men profoundly influenced by Ray Stedman was Charles Swindoll. At one point in his life, after he and several pastors had met with Ray, Swindoll reflected, "As we said good-bye to Ray, I walked a little slower. I thought about the things he had taught me without directly instructing me and about the courage he had given me without deliberately exhorting me. I wondered how it happened. I wondered why I had been so privileged to have my 'face' reflected in his 'water' or my 'iron' sharpened by his 'iron'... I found myself wanting to run back to his car and tell him how much I love and admire him. But it was late, and after all I'm a fifty-five-year-old man. A husband. A father. A grandfather. A pastor.... But as I stood there alone in the cold night air, I suddenly realized what I wanted to be most when I grow up."[5]

It is my hope that this biography of Ray Stedman will provide a new generation of evangelicals a refreshing and relevant model of what to be when they grow up.

ACKNOWLEDGMENTS

I WISH TO ACKNOWLEDGE the invaluable assistance and encouragement of Elaine Stedman, wife of Ray Stedman, and their four daughters, Sheila, Susan, Linda, and Laurie. This biography was written with their permission and support.

The Ray C. Stedman Library, maintained by Discovery Publishing on the Peninsula Bible Church Web site (www.pbc.org) and containing many of Ray's sermons and four of his books in their entirety, was also a tremendous source of information about Ray Stedman and his ministry.

Joanie Burnside's unpublished history of Peninsula Bible Church from 1948 to 1998, "A Stone's Throw," was an invaluable resource, as was Wade Whitcomb's unpublished homiletic biography on Ray Stedman, "Passing of the Torch."

I also wish to acknowledge Ruth N. Brandon for her tireless work in preparing the dissertation stage of this manuscript, as well as her assistance with the bibliography of Ray Stedman's writings.

I am grateful to Haddon Robinson for his encouragement and counsel in this project and for presenting the manuscript to Discovery House. And many thanks to Judith Markham at Discovery House for her skillful editorial work.

Thank you also to Jim Arthur and the kind people of Winifred, Montana, who gave me a deeper understanding of Ray Stedman's roots. It would have been hard to understand Ray without a visit to Winifred.

Gratitude also to those who were so generous with their time in granting interviews and/or helpful information via e-mail: Lambert Dolphin, Bev Forsyth, Doug Goins, Jim and Marian Heaton, Howard and Jeanne Hendricks, Bill Lawrence, Brian Morgan, Ray

Ortlund, Jr., Luis Palau, Bob Roe, David and Carolyn Roper, David Smith, Wendell Sheets, Alan Stedman, Jimmy Stewart, and Steve Zeisler.

I am grateful to the people of Central Peninsula Church, whom I have served as Teaching Pastor since 1986, for giving me the freedom to pursue this project and putting up with endless sermon illustrations from the life of Ray Stedman. It is a joy to serve Christ with you.

Finally, I am deeply grateful to my family for their support, encouragement, good humor, and unconditional love. I wish to thank my wife, Lynn, and my three children: Anne-Marie, Kimberly, and Matthew. Thanks also go to my father, Stewart W. Mitchell, for always believing in me and encouraging me to set the highest goals.

—Mark S. Mitchell
February 2004

ONE

A Father to Me

IN FORTY YEARS OF PREACHING at Peninsula Bible Church, Ray
Stedman rarely mentioned his parents. One could easily have got-
ten the impression that Ray showed up on this earth much like
Adam: lovingly formed by his heavenly Father and placed in a garden called Montana, but without an earthly father or mother to nurture him along the way. Ray certainly had parents, but his
childhood, like many, was not idyllic.

Ray's father, Charles Leslie Stedman, was born to Guy Samuel
and Mary Jane Stedman in Woodstock, Minnesota, on July 21,
1889. Charles was the eighth of fourteen children. Traveling by
covered wagon, the Stedman family relocated in Blunt, South
Dakota, and eventually in Temvik, North Dakota, where they
homesteaded and built a sod house. Then, in January 1907, Mary
Jane died. Most of the details of Charles's early life are unknown
to us, except for the fact that he was a young teenager when his
mother died, and that about that time Charles went to work building barns, some of which still stand today.

On October 16, 1912, at age twenty-three, Charles married
Mabel Clara Allen of Loyalton, South Dakota. Their first son,
Alan Le Roy, was born on August 12, 1913, in Kapowsin, Wash-
ington; Raymond Charles Stedman was born in Temvik, North
Dakota, on October 5, 1917; and Donald Homer Stedman was
born in Denver, Colorado, on February 6, 1922.

We have little information about Ray's mother, but in recent years Ray's nephew, Alan Stedman, learned that she was a talented and published poet. Her poem "The Pines" was published January 13, 1924, in *The Young People's Friend*. Her other poetry was published in newspapers or in a poetry club publication. This was an interesting discovery, because Ray himself always loved poetry.

Life was not easy for the Stedman family. Charles worked as a carpenter, a mechanic, and a railroad worker, but was often unemployed and frequently moved his family from place to place. At different times, the Stedmans lived in North Dakota, Washington, New Mexico, and Colorado. Ray's single memory of his father was of a completely withdrawn man who came home from work and read the newspaper in silence. His mother battled chronic asthma all her life; and some people considered her a hypochondriac.[1] Between his father's emotional detachment and his mother's distraction, Ray did not receive the nurturing a young child needs from his parents.[2]

One startling incident reveals the lack of stability and care in the Stedman home. When Ray was three years old, he and his seven-year-old brother, Alan, traveled alone on a train from Miles City, Montana, to Cimarron, New Mexico, a thousand miles away, to join their parents, who had been living in New Mexico for several months "in quest of health." We don't know where or with whom the two boys stayed in Miles City while they waited to join their parents, but this likely was just one leg of a move the entire family made from Washington. When the train reached Denver, it was held up because of flooding further south, and the two children had to leave the train. Fortunately, Fred W. Johnson, the district passenger agent for the American Railway Express, was at the station to help them. Alan and Ray's mother had asked Mr. Johnson to watch over the boys during the trip, so he took them home with him. He and his wife cared for them until they were able to continue their journey. At the time, a Denver newspaper reported

LADS, ON THOUSAND-MILE TRIP ALONE, CARED FOR BY EXPRESS OFFICIAL WHEN STRANDED HERE

Youngsters From Montana, Held Up by Flood, Are Entertained in Home of Fred W. Johnson As Part of Company's Service.

(By W. H. GRATTAN.)

On a thousand-mile trip alone, Allan Stedman, 7 years old, and his brother, Raymond, 3 years old, reached Denver last Sunday night, bound for Cimarron, N. M., from Miles City, Mont.

Raymond Stedman (on the left) and Allan Stedman, who are in Denver on their way to Cimarron, New Mexico, from Miles City, Montana. Until the flood conditions improve the boys will be kept in Denver at the home of Fred W. Johnson, district passenger agent of the American Express company, who is keeping them at his home.

And then the youngsters found that further progress toward their waiting parents in the southern state was blocked.

"Floods!" said the kindly train officers.

Allen and Raymond were stranded. The case already had won the attention of Fred W. Johnson, district passenger agent for the American Railway Express company. The boys were traveling under the auspices of the American Railway Express and Mr. Johnson had agreed to meet them here.

"Hm!" mused Mr. Johnson just for an instant. "I guess this situation calls for service."

So he took the youngsters to his home at 1546 Cook street. There they have remained since, shown every kindness by Mr. Johnson and his wife. The younger lad follows the express company official around and calls him "papa."

"They are about the best-behaved children I have ever seen," said Mr. Johnson. "It's really a privilege to take care of them. It is just American Railway Express company service. I promised the mother to see the boys got every care on their way to New Mexico and they are getting it. The end of this week E. Pentecost, chief agent for the American Railway Express here, will take the boys for a few days and keep them at his home, 2164 South Grant street."

Mr. and Mrs. C. L. Stedman, the parents, left Montana several months ago for New Mexico in quest of health and planned to bring the children later. From their home at Miles City the boys were carried to Billings and here placed on a Burlington route thru sleeper. The train was piloted by Engineer G. A. Fouts. Two days later Fouts' engine and two other cars plunged thru a bridge into the Platte river. Fouts, whose quick work prevented a worse disaster, was much interested in the two Stedman boys.

how the boys' plight had captured Johnson's heart; he called them "about the best behaved children I have ever seen." But the article, which included a photograph of the two boys, also mentioned this poignant and telling fact: "the younger of the two brothers" (Ray), followed Johnson around and called him "papa." Although he was very young at the time, Ray never forgot this event, or how this kind train conductor took him home and cared for him.[3]

After living in New Mexico for a short time, Charles Stedman found a job in Denver, Colorado, working in a Burlington Railroad roundhouse. While the Stedmans were living in Denver, when Ray was about ten years old, his father vanished. To this day, no one knows why Charles Stedman deserted his family. Some speculate that it might have been the frustration of continually moving from one job to the next, or the effort of trying to support a chronically ill wife and three young sons. The family made many attempts to find Charles—all unsuccessful—and through the years Ray himself continued to search for traces of his father: "He looked for him diligently in every county we were in and never found him," Ray's daughter Susan remembers. "Somehow, the man disappeared off the face of the earth, and . . . that had a big impact on my dad."[4]

Soon after Charles abandoned his family, Ray's mother, Mabel, decided that she was unable to manage the strain of raising three boys. Ray was ornery, and his mother, suffering from asthma, would have to stop and rest in the middle of disciplining him to catch her breath.[5] She decided to place Ray and Alan in an orphanage in Denver, keeping her youngest son, Donald, at home with her. No one knows exactly how long Ray and Alan lived in the orphanage, but it wasn't long before Mabel's sister Beulah and her new husband, Fred Sheets, came to visit the boys while traveling through Denver. Fred was a schoolteacher in Ayr, North Dakota, and he and Beulah decided to take Ray back to Ayr with them. At this point, Alan returned to his mother while Ray spent the rest of his childhood and teenage years with his aunt and uncle.

The lonely train ride when he was three years old, his father's desertion and disappearance, and his mother's placing him in an orphanage—these events left indelible marks on Ray Stedman. He never forgot how it felt to be abandoned, and he understood the relief of being cared for in times of need. Through the years, God used these emotions and experiences redemptively in Ray's life. "His father deserted him," says Ray's wife, Elaine. "These days, if you have that kind of dysfunctional parenting, you are a victim and you have to live out your life as a victim. Ray turned it into something totally redemptive. He became a father to others,"[6] continually looking out for young men who were in need of fatherly nurturing.

God's sovereign care of Ray and His unwavering provision for his needs are evident in both the place where, and the people with whom, he spent the rest of his childhood. Fred and Beulah Sheets, churchgoing Methodists, were kind people with very high morals.[7] Although they, too, moved frequently and eventually had two sons of their own, Lowell and Wendell, they provided a stable childhood for Ray.

Being abandoned by his father also prepared Ray for a relationship with his heavenly Father. Not long after moving with his aunt and uncle to North Dakota, Ray attended an evangelistic tent meeting and heard the preacher speak about the "sins of the fathers" and how those sins affected later generations. He also heard of the wonderful promise of God to help and forgive. Ray decided that he did not want to live the kind of life his father had lived or was living. In response to the altar call, he went forward and knelt down to receive the Lord.

"This is the way I came to Christ," Ray said, when telling of his conversion. "I read the Bible and heard quoted from the Bible some wonderful promises. . . . As I heard these, hope flamed in my heart because this is what I longed to find . . . rest, fulfillment, supply, companionship, blessing, light in place of darkness. . . . And then I heard the story of . . . the cross in all its wonder and mystery. . . . I couldn't understand it fully—I was only a boy of about ten years of age when I heard this story and believed it. But I realized that here was a God who could do something about my problem, and I believed His Word. When I did so, the course of my life was altered—the direction of my life changed. . . . I found a new capacity to love. I had a new dimension in my life—new attitudes that I didn't have before."[8]

Ray often spoke of those first few months as a Christian with his characteristic warmth and humor: "I had a wonderful time of fellowship with the Lord that summer and the next winter, and there were occasions when I just would be overwhelmed with the sense of the nearness and dearness of God. I used to sing hymns until tears would come to my eyes as the meaning of those old words reflected on the relationship that I had with God. Then I used to preach to the cows when I would bring them home. Those cows were a very good audience too, by the way; they never went to sleep on me."[9]

The reality of God's presence in Ray's life did not keep him from occasionally drifting in his walk with Christ or, as he phrased it, experiencing some "stop-and-go progress along the way." Ray came to Christ in the summer, and the following fall his family moved from Ayr, where he had Christian fellowship, to a nearby town in the Red River valley of North Dakota that didn't even have a church. Gradually, because of that lack of fellowship, he drifted away from a relationship with God and "into all kinds of ugly and shameful things—habits of thought and activity that I am ashamed of."[10] This period of Ray's life, when he drifted spiritually, lasted through his four years in North Dakota, into his high school years, and even into college.

Winifred

IN THE SUMMER OF 1931, when Ray was almost fourteen, the Sheets family moved to Winifred, Montana, where Fred had been hired as the superintendent of schools. "Montana and the West was an exciting place to me. Though I missed my grade school friends back in the Red River Valley of North Dakota, I now looked forward eagerly to my first year of high school, and what life in Winifred would be like."

In those days the frontier seemed close at hand, for the town of Winifred served as a center for a vast, sparsely settled area. "It was still primitive in many ways, having no electricity, no phones except one line from Turner's haberdashery to Lewistown. There was no modern plumbing and every house had its outside privy, even the high school, which sat at the top of the hill at the west end of Main Street. The nearest doctor was in Lewistown and though there once had been a drugstore, it had closed its doors during the Depression."[11]

Ray spent his four years of high school in Winifred, living with the Sheets family in a small house in the center of town. During the summers he worked on various ranches in the area, often staying on those ranches for long stretches of time. Many of these family friends played an important role in Ray's life as they provided surrogate parenting for him. Throughout his ministry he peppered his sermons with warm, homespun illustrations from those years, revealing the great fondness and respect he had for Montana, the life he lived there, and the people he knew during those years.

One of the families who made a deep impression on Ray was the Dahl family. Ray's first job was on the Dahl ranch making hay and branding calves for fifty cents a day. He describes the Dahls as "a rancher and his wife, who bore no relationship to me, but virtually adopted me as a son when I was in high school. I spent many happy hours there doing the usual work of a ranch. But I was especially drawn to the rancher, who was like a father to me. He taught me and modeled for me patience, fortitude, manliness, and humor. We spent so many happy times together."[12]

Ray also spent a great deal of time on the Murphy family's ranch, about five miles west of Winifred. (Today all that is left of this ranch is a few rotted fence posts and a crumbling foundation.) Bill and Cecilia Murphy attracted many young "strays" like Ray to their ranch, providing work, companionship, and excellent home-cooked meals. On one occasion, Ray and a friend sat down to eat a piece of Cecilia Murphy's chocolate cake when a fly lit on Ray's piece. Whereupon he proceeded to put the entire piece of cake in his mouth, fly and all!

Ranch work brought Ray into contact with the western cowboy culture, which would become another significant part of his identity. Not the romanticized cowboy life seen on the silver screen or in dime-store novels, but the real cowboy life of hard work and colorful characters. A gravestone in Winifred's cemetery marks the death of Bill Murphy in 1934 when Ray would have been a junior in high school and active on the Murphy ranch. (Dramatic local accounts say that Bill Murphy was attacked and eaten by one of his own pigs!)

Ray also spent several summers working twenty miles north of Winifred in a remote area called the Missouri Breaks, through which the Missouri River flows. During the Lewis and Clark Expedition, William Clark called this "the Deserts of America" and declared, "I do not think it can ever be settled." Meriwether Lewis described it as a "dry, barren country." The area is dominated by rugged, brown bluffs set off by the deep blue sky and blazing sun. It is still considered one of the most isolated parts of the United States, and Congress has designated it a Wild and Scenic River. Here, Ray worked on a small farm run by the Stanton family right on the river, driving a truck loaded with fruits and vegetables to Stanton's General Store in Winifred. It would have been a slow, hot, and torturous ride from the river through the Missouri Breaks and into Winifred.

Yet even in the midst of such grueling work, Ray managed to have fun. Wendell Sheets, one of the younger cousins Ray grew up with, likened him to a wild Montana mustang that couldn't be tamed. Wendell recalls that just for fun Ray would ride a two-year-old steer and let it buck him off. He also tells of one Fourth of July when Ray and his friends, at eleven o'clock at night, raced their pickup trucks into Fort Shaw, an old Indian fort with a circular track, whooping and hollering like Indians.[13]

This rough cowboy culture often clashed with Ray's Christian faith, and at times he gave in to the temptations of cowboy life.[14] And yet, despite his periods of rebellion, Ray never lost a sense of God's presence in his life. "All through those seven years there was a relationship with God I could not deny. Somehow I knew, deep down inside, that I still belonged to Him; and there were things I could not do, even though I was tempted. I could not do them because I felt that I had a tie with God."[15]

———

THOSE EARLY YEARS IN THE climate and culture of Montana influenced Ray in several ways. First, Montana nurtured in him an independent, adventuresome spirit. Part of this was the cowboy influence, but part of it was also a result of being raised by his aunt and uncle. Although Ray was included as part of the Sheets family, he always felt independent from them.[16] One indication of this is that Ray never forgot that when his aunt introduced the family, she first identified each of her boys as "my sons," and then would refer to Ray as "my sister Mabel's son Raymond."[17] This "distance" gave him a sense of independence that he never lost—an independence that also shaped his view of ministry. I recall Ray telling a group of interns that Peninsula Bible Church (PBC) was not his employer and did not pay his salary. Instead, he was a "servant of Christ Jesus" and the Lord was the one who saw to it that he was paid. This sense of independence also prompted Ray to expand his ministry beyond the local church, traveling extensively throughout the nation and the world as PBC's "apostle at large."

Second, the Montana in which Ray grew up was a man's world. As mentioned earlier, both of Ray's siblings were brothers, and both of his Sheets cousins were boys. Ray's summers as a cowboy were spent primarily with men. Through the years Ray took many young men under his wing and became their spiritual father. In a society sadly lacking models of godly maleness, Ray left a valuable heritage.

He was a "man's man" whose most significant impact was in the lives of other men.

Finally, the long, cold winter months in Montana nurtured in Ray a love for learning. Growing up during the Depression and living in a home without electricity, he never enjoyed the luxury of radio or telephone, much less television. As a result, Ray read everything he could lay his hands on: stories of the Wild West, books on Montana history, and even the Sears and Roebuck catalog. He would take books to bed with him and read under the covers with the aid of a flashlight, violating his bedtime deadline.[18] It was also in this environment that Ray received what he considered a first-class education, and he dreamed of one day becoming a surgeon.

"Though the school I attended was in an isolated town far from the fine amenities of civilization," he recollected of his high school years in Winifred, "the education I received was first-class. The knowledge I was given of classical literature was far beyond anything now taught in the high schools of California. Though we only had a primitive chemistry laboratory I went on from there to become so proficient in chemistry that my professor in college asked me to take over the class if he could not show up someday. The typing and shorthand that I learned at Winifred High School kept me employed through most of the Depression, and led to my serving as a Court Reporter in the Navy."[19]

Although Ray had lost his father at a young age, he had been blessed with surrogate earthly fathers. He had also begun his committed life journey with his heavenly Father. But the Wild Mustang from Montana was still a long way from being tamed.

TWO

Learning the Ground Rules

IN 1935, AT THE AGE of seventeen, Ray Stedman graduated from high school. That fall, he and seventy-two other freshman began their college studies at Intermountain Union College in Helena, Montana.[1] College records reveal that Ray did not live in the men's dormitory, but rather at the Hotel Stevens, 213 1/2 Central Avenue, Room 12.

"That was a critical period in my life," Ray reflected years later. "Like so many young men facing college, I was not at all sure about what I was getting into. I had an outward appearance of confidence and the ability to handle anything that came, but within I had a deep sense of uncertainty. I was aware that I really did not know the ground rules of life. I pretended I did but I didn't, and inside I knew it. It was like trying to play a game when you didn't know the rules, but were trying to guess them as you went along. It was rough. I was baffled, as all young people are baffled, by the great questions of life."[2]

Earthquake at Intermountain

ON OCTOBER 17, 1935, soon after Ray entered college, a devastating earthquake struck Helena. The earthquake destroyed the buildings of Intermountain Union College, forcing the school to close for several weeks before relocating ninety miles north in Great

Falls, where the Methodist church, the Presbyterian church, and the Deaconess Hospital all opened their doors to the institution. In those Depression years, college was a luxury. So although many students returned home until the school reopened, Ray decided to stay in Helena and work to earn some much-needed money.

The day after the earthquake Ray wrote to his aunt, describing the event and assuring his family that he was safe and sound. Although it is a long letter in which he marvels that no one at his school was hurt, Ray doesn't mention anything about God. Clearly his personal relationship with the Lord, though real, was not foremost on his mind at this period of his life. The letter closes with Ray asking his aunt to send the letter on to his mother.[3]

The letter also reveals Ray's reckless, cowboy spirit. In one section he describes how, in the hours prior to the earthquake, a fight broke out after a football game. Ray and his six-foot-seven roommate (nicknamed "Tiny") stood in the door of Mills Hall with shovels to keep out the rioters. They even knocked down a couple of guys who threatened to wreck the hall.[4]

That same evening, as he and his classmates were celebrating at a school dance in the gymnasium, the earthquake struck. Ray tells how he and another fellow prevented panicked students from stampeding through the small doorway and organized others to lead students two-by-two down the stairs by matchlight. Although the school newspaper does not mention Ray by name, it does attest to what Ray would later describe to his aunt: "The dance was well underway when a slight quiver caused everyone to stand still. As if it was gathering momentum the shake became harder and harder. Then the lights went out, and the west wall began to fall, leaving a big gaping hole and the students saw the dream of many years fall before their eyes. Under the sudden emotional stress the minds of the students were easily handled. Some cool person called, 'Take your time and go out one at a time.' In a few minutes everyone was outside and safe from the falling bricks."[5] Whether this "cool person" was Ray Stedman we do not know, but he was certainly one of those students who kept his head and helped the others to safety. Later, he revealed more of his leadership qualities when he and five other students organized an emergency squad to deliver blankets to those without shelter, and for two hours, in the middle of the night, patrolled the damaged dorm area to keep people out.[6]

After the school was devastated with two aftershocks in the next few days, Intermountain Union College was forced to move its classes to nearby Great Falls. As a result, in January 1936, Ray evidenced his natural boldness and initiative when he wrote the following letter to Henry Ford at the Ford Motor Company in Michigan.

Mr. Henry Ford
Dearborn, Michigan

Dear Sir:
On October 18 and 31, two major earthquakes struck the little city of Helena, Montana, and left it a mess of ruined buildings, its population with nerves shattered, already overtaxed by previous shocks. Among those buildings which were ruined beyond use were those of Intermountain Union College, a little college built at the foot of beautiful Mount Ascension and within two blocks of the imposing Montana State Capitol Building.

Due to this disaster, the college was forced to move to the neighboring city of Great Falls. They located in the different churches about the city. Classes were carried on but under severe handicaps. This year is destined to be the last in the history of Intermountain unless by some means or other over five hundred thousand dollars can be raised in order to establish new buildings and create a starting budget.

This college, started by the West's most beloved missionary, Brother Van, has faced and overcome many obstacles before. It had never reached anything near financial freedom until the year 1935. Everything was going fine, the budget was balanced, the buildings had been redecorated and the college was "on its feet." And then came the earthquake!

Now, unless the necessary money can be raised this college, the only Christian College in the West from Denver, Colorado to Spokane, Washington, and Jamestown, No. Dakota, must close its doors. Its standards have always been high; its students among the finest. In order to perpetuate the standards of this college we are calling on you, as a man interested in the future welfare of American youth, for any contribution which you would like to make a worthy cause.

Respectfully Yours,
Raymond Stedman

It does not seem that a response was ever received from Mr. Ford. Nevertheless, the Intermountain Union College did survive and eventually relocated on the Billings Polytechnic Institute where the two institutions coexisted as affiliates. In 1947 the two institutions merged into a single college, which continues today on the same campus as Rocky Mountain College in Billings.

Ray finished out his freshman year at Intermountain Union College. The following summer, he worked at the Deaconess Hospital in Great Falls, still interested in pursuing his dream of becoming a doctor. During his entire time in Great Falls he lived with the Talcott family, who were active members of the Methodist church where the school had temporarily moved after the earthquake. This began his lifelong friendship with Burt Talcott, who later became a United States congressman from California.[7]

Whitworth

IN THE FALL, WITH Intermountain Union College still devastated by the earthquake, Ray transferred to Whitworth College, a Presbyterian-sponsored school in Spokane, Washington, for his sophomore year. During his year there, Ray gained a reputation for being wild. Years later, when he was speaking at The Firs conference center near Bellingham, Washington, Ray encountered the former Dean of Women at Whitworth. When she saw Ray and learned that he was the speaker for the conference, she announced to all, "Ray Stedman! We need to stand and sing, 'Amazing Grace!'" Another woman from Whitworth, when Ray met up with her several years later at Dallas Theological Seminary, told him that her prayer group at Whitworth had prayed for him because he was such a rebel on campus.[8]

In reflecting on these years, Ray described his spiritual condition: "I drifted away from that relationship with God, drifted into all kinds of ugly and shameful things—habits of thought and activity that I am ashamed of. I even developed some liberal attitudes toward the Scriptures. I didn't believe in the inspiration of the Bible. I argued against it, and . . . was known as a skeptic."[9]

Despite his drifting ways, however, Ray continued to be involved in a variety of worthwhile activities during his year at Whitworth, some of which were Christian in orientation. Ray and about fifteen of his Montana classmates formed a social group called the "Montana Club," which, as he told his family, "has the spirit of all Montanans."[10] He was involved with a volunteer fellowship group that held church services in small towns around Spokane, as well as a Christian Endeavor group. Ray also demonstrated an interest in writing and speaking; he had a column in the school newspaper and was a member of the debate team.[11]

Ray was a serious student at Whitworth. In keeping with his desire to become a doctor, he took courses in chemistry and biology. He also took courses in education and wrote to his uncle Fred about what was required to get a certificate for teaching in Montana.[12]

As was so common with many in the Depression era, however, Ray struggled to make ends meet. He was forced to quit the football team and was prevented from playing basketball because of work. Initially he took a job as a janitor, but later worked about sixteen hours a week as both a stenographer and a general assistant in the business office of the school. By the middle of his sophomore year, Ray had decided to leave Whitworth at the end of the school year. On January 23, 1937, he wrote home and declared, "I don't have the slightest intention of coming here for another year. It cost more to go out here than it would have cost for me to attend the University of Montana. If I ever get this bill paid up out here, I'm going to attend college on a strictly cash basis. No more worrying all the time as to whether I will get my bill paid up or not. When I next go to school I will have the money to plunk right down on the desk for the whole year or else I won't go until I get it."[13]

From Disappointment to Appointment

IN THE SUMMER OF 1937, Ray returned to Montana to work in construction in a small town near Great Falls, where he met a young man named Hardy Thompson. Hardy had recently become a Christian and was excited about his newfound faith. As the two spent time together, Ray sensed his own need to turn his life over to the Lord, which began a period of sustained spiritual renewal when Ray's entire focus and direction changed.

Hardy Thompson was a member of the Assemblies of God church in Great Falls, and he insisted that Ray come to services with him. Although Ray would later reject most Pentecostal theology and practice, it was in this context that God brought reality and life to his Christian experience. It was also at this church that Ray met a girl named Elaine Smith. Elaine was several years younger than Ray, but this did not keep him from noticing her as she sang a solo.

"I visited a church in Montana and sat on a balcony one fateful Sunday evening, and from the Olympian heights from which I was seated, I saw a beautiful young girl with long, blonde hair, singing a solo. She had the most angelic voice I had ever heard. I said to myself, in the impetuosity of youth, 'There is the girl I want to marry.' But I felt a terrible sense of frustration, for I knew the next morning I was scheduled to leave for Chicago to make my residence there."[14]

Ray had to leave for Chicago in the fall of 1937 because he had obtained a job there through the intervention of a friend from Whitworth College and through his correspondence with the office of the Board of Christian Education of the Presbyterian Church (USA). This position, which was temporary and would end in May of the following year, would allow Ray to pay off some debt and further develop his clerical skills—skills that would later serve him well.

It was the midst of the Great Depression and Ray was happy to have a job, even though at the age of twenty he was apprehensive about leaving family and friends for the big city. But it was on that bus ride that Ray felt God speak to him in his uncertainty and say, "I will be a Father to you."[15]

"I had never before visited a city as large as Chicago," Ray said years later as he described his cross-country bus ride from Montana to Illinois. "I knew only one person in Chicago, my uncle. I didn't want to show it, but I was scared. I was leaving all my friends. The town I came from was so small you could locate it right between the second and third Burma Shave signs! It was a thousand-mile journey by bus to Chicago, but all through that long trip I was strengthened and comforted by the sense that Jesus was with me. Although I was heading into the unknown, I look back on that as one of the most joyful bus rides of my life."

The uncle Ray refers to was his mother's brother, a very successful businessman and a professed atheist, who was neither kind nor generous to Ray during his stay in Chicago. Immediately after Ray arrived in Chicago, the city was blanketed by a blizzard that shut down transportation and businesses. "I had to sit alone in a hotel room for the duration of the storm," Ray said. "Looking back, however, my memory of that period is one of fragrant companionship with One who was with me, strengthening me, and helping me throughout."[16]

In fact, Ray's entire stay in Chicago, living in a spartan room at the YMCA, was a time of spiritual renewal. There, the Lord both assured him of His grace and began the process of revealing His call to ministry. Ray also taught a Sunday school class of high school boys, and he grew very close to several of the boys as they studied the Word and prayed together.[17]

"I shall never forget the day... when that truth burst upon me in all its fullness.... How vividly it all comes back to me—the joy, the untrammeled joy, that filled my heart as, lying on my bed in my room, it dawned upon me that if anything happened to me I had nothing to fear in the future. I was forgiven. God had already judged me in Christ and I was forgiven—set free. The joy of... this great fundamental truth of Christian faith—that in Jesus Christ, and in His work for us, God took away my sins.[18]

On Easter Sunday Ray arose before dawn to attend a sunrise service at Soldier Field. "As I was dressing in the darkness of that early morning, my mind went back to the account of the resurrection of our Lord and the women who visited the tomb in the early hours.... I remember feeling for the first time something of the tremendous reality of this event. It really occurred! It actually happened! Those women did make their way to the tomb that morning, and they were amazed to find the stone rolled away, and with beating hearts and incredulous minds they went to tell the disciples. All the marvelous events of that wonderful, unforgettable day actually occurred! Immediately my mind took in... the meaning of this in my life at that moment, and there came flooding into my heart a great consciousness of the presence of a living Lord. I shall never forget that morning. I stood by my bed weeping tears of joy as the thought flooded my heart that Jesus Christ was alive. It was a fact, an eternal fact."[19]

This "great consciousness of the presence of a living Lord" also began to change the way Ray thought about his future, for at some point during that time in Chicago he surrendered to what he believed was the call of God to be a minister.

"When I was still a young, growing Christian, I wanted to be a surgeon.... Then quietly... I began to realize that God was moving in a different direction and that He was suggesting to me that I consider entering the ministry. At first I resented this and fought against it, resisting the insistent plea of the Spirit. But when the Spirit is after someone, He never gives up. Finally, in a moment of surrender and dedication, overwhelmed with the joy of what Christ meant to me, in my own room alone, I said to Him, 'All right, Lord, I'll be a minister, if that is what you want.'"[20]

In a letter dated April 4, 1939, Ray wrote to his family, announcing his new direction in life.

"I am glad of this chance to come to Chicago away from all my friends and family for it has given me an opportunity to work some things out in my mind which have been bothering me for some time. In the first place I've decided to be a *minister*. This may seem like a rather sudden about-face from the study of medicine, but in reality it isn't, for it is something which I have been weighing and thinking about for a period of some years.... You will perhaps be surprised at the suddenness of all this—but it is sudden only because you have not known of it before, for I like to keep my thoughts to myself until such a time as I feel sure that they are what I want others to see in me and now that that time has come I am glad to let others know of my decision. The approaching crisis in world affairs demands men who have the courage of their convictions. Religion and morality are on the decline while paganism and immorality are on the upgrade. At such a time, those who would cleave to the time-tested truths of the gospel of Jesus Christ must make certain that their position is made unmistakably clear to all around them. Such is my desire, and so I have no hesitancy in making my decision known to, not only you, but to my other friends. . . . The world has yet to see what God can do with a man who is wholly consecrated to Him. By God's grace, I shall be that man."

In his candidness, Ray mentioned what he knew others might be thinking: "There are, undoubtedly, going to be those who will ridicule my position and point to things in my past life which are not commensurate with my present stand. To such I have no answer, other than that of Paul, who said 'putting all things behind me, I press on to the mark of the high calling of Jesus Christ.' It will be comforting to know that when folks make light of my decision, that you folks will be willing to 'take the stand in my defense,' as I feel sure you will do, but whether you do or not I can not retract for 'he that puts his hand to the plow, and looking back, is not fit for the kingdom of God.'

". . . This decision is no commendation to me, and God forbid that I boast in having taken such a stand, but rather it is 'my reasonable service,' to a Master who has done more for me than I could ever tell, and whose service, though it be hard, is yet the only thing left for me to do."[21]

The Young Preacher

RAY'S JOB IN CHICAGO came to its appointed end, and in the summer of 1940, after spending some time in Montana, he moved to Denver to help support his mother and brothers. Ray's older brother, Alan, was living with his mother and studying engineering in Denver, and Ray's income would help his brother finish his degree.[22] Despite Ray's efforts, his communication with Alan always remained awkward. Donald, five years younger than Ray, was presumably still at home. Ray and Donald maintained good rapport until 1945 when Donald was killed in battle in Germany.[23]

The continuous financial pressure under which he lived during these years made Ray doubly conscientious. While still in

Chicago, he had sent his family a detailed accounting of his budget, including comments on the dollar or so he could afford to send home each week. Once he was in Denver, he wrote to his aunt and uncle about his eagerness to pay off a debt he owed to Whitworth College. "I owe a small amount of money to Whitworth College in Spokane (about $150) and it may be the Lord would have me work here this winter and start out next spring with a clean slate in full-time evangelistic work. I know I could never go back to business permanently as I am spoiled for that. My heart is in the Lord's work."[24]

In Denver, Ray found full-time employment in the office of the Rio Grande Railroad, but his real passion was his volunteer work at the Denver Revival Tabernacle, where his primary job was publishing the tabernacle paper. On occasion he also preached in evangelistic rallies, hoping for a revival among the young people who attended these meetings.

"I have an office now, in the Denver Revival Tabernacle," he wrote to a friend. "It looks as if the Lord will have me work here this winter. I'm quite enthusiastic about it as there is a tremendous work to be done.... This work here is in a new stage and the time is about ripe for a real revival.... We hope to hold a youth rally of all the Pentecostal youths in the city. Then among the young people here in the Tabernacle there is a tremendous work to be done. There is a great need for a deeper consecration and a more yielded life among them. I wish I had a few young folks from Great Falls to show them what real consecration is."[25]

These rallies were not Ray's only opportunities to preach. Some of his first experiences in preaching were in a nearby prison. "Our meetings at the prison are coming along grand," he wrote in December. "There are several young men out there who have given every indication of having received genuine salvation. In our last meeting over 25 raised their hands for prayer. I preached on 'light out of darkness' and the Lord really blessed."[26]

Ray's messages were steeped in the Pentecostalism that had marked him since his days at the Assemblies of God church in Great Falls, and the Denver Revival Tabernacle had the same Pentecostal roots. This resulted in certain pressures being placed upon Ray to amend what he called his "Full Gospel" message, especially by prison authorities. As he expressed in one letter, "Certain pressures are at work to get me to compromise my message in favor of a little more of the world and a little less of God but as God enables me I have sworn to do my very best in preaching the entire Full Gospel message."[27]

A Kindred Spirit

NOW THAT RAY HAD settled into a job and a ministry, he began to correspond with Elaine Smith, the young woman who had caught his eye at the Assemblies of God church in Great Falls in the summer of 1937. Ray had returned to Great Falls for a visit in the summer of 1940, and while he was there he met Elaine and asked her if she would allow him to write to her. Ray began writing to Elaine shortly after he returned to Denver in August 1940, finding in her a kindred spirit with whom he could share the details of his growing walk with God and his burgeoning ministry. In his first letter he explained why he had asked to write her:

"You are probably wondering why it was that I asked to write to you. I'll admit it did seem awfully peculiar. I hesitate to try to explain myself for fear you might think me girl-crazy, which I'm not at all. However, from the first time I saw you from before I went to Chicago I wanted to know you better and while I was in Chicago I often wished that I had known you long enough to write to you, so when I saw you again this summer I decided I wouldn't let this chance slip by even at the risk of making a fool of myself. I never felt that way about anyone before but I sure am glad I did it. I hope you'll forgive me for being presumptuous and if you don't care to continue this correspondence any longer I won't feel hurt tho I will be disappointed."[28]

Over the next six months, Ray wrote Elaine four long letters to which she also responded. Despite their relative unfamiliarity with one another, they were often bluntly honest in their correspondence. For example, Elaine rebuked Ray for being too dependent on a mutual friend's estimation of him. "My head is bowed in meekness and shame over your rebuke about my dependency on Hardy's attitude towards me," he responded—and then proceeded to lecture Elaine for her similar dependency on another mutual friend![29] Three months later, Ray was once again candid: "Elaine, when you write to me why don't you break down a bit and be a little more friendly—not so cold and distant. I'd like to hear more about you, where you go, what you do, etc. Don't think I don't appreciate your letters but they are a little formal."[30]

Ray was smitten with Elaine, but she was four years younger and not quite prepared to respond with similar affection. "I sure would like to see you again, Elaine," he wrote in December. "I wish I could have had more time this summer to get to know you better. I think you're well worth knowing."[31] The following month he wrote, "Last night I borrowed my friend's car and went up on Lookout Mountain where Buffalo Bill is buried and watched the lights of Denver. It really was a relaxation but I wish you could have been with me. Now, that's a funny thing to say, isn't it because you never have been here with me but really, that's what I thought."[32]

More than anything else, however, these letters reveal that Ray sensed a kindred spirit in Elaine when it came to the things of God. In one of his letters he shared lines from a favorite hymn which he kept in his scrapbook:

Oh, for a faith that will not shrink
Though pressed by every foe!
That will not totter at the brink

Of any earthly woe!
Lord, give me such a faith as this
And then, what e'er may come,
I'll taste e'en now, the blissful joys
Of an eternal home![33]

Despite his growing affection for Elaine, Ray's letter of January 10, 1941, was the last he would write to her for almost two years. Having been swept off his feet by romance, in the summer of 1942 he would be swept into life-altering events that involved the entire world. Later that year, the United States entered World War II and young men eagerly joined the war efforts. Ray was no exception.

But the Ray Stedman who entered the war efforts was a very different person than the one who had entered college. The Wild Mustang from Montana was being tamed by the living God, and his immense energies were being harnessed and directed for the work of God's kingdom.

THREE

A Soldier in Active Service

In September 1940, Congress approved the Selective Training and Service Act, authorizing the first peacetime draft in United States history, and requiring all men between the ages of twenty-one and thirty-five to register. Ray Stedman originally received a deferred draft classification because of his intention to enter full-time Christian service, but with the Japanese invasion of Pearl Harbor on December 7, 1941, the twenty-four-year-old requested that his classification be changed so that he might join the war effort. Ray wanted to enlist in the Navy, but one of the requirements was correctable vision, and after a physical examination he was declared ineligible because of astigmatism.

At that time it was not unusual for young men to be rejected from Selective Service. In fact, prior to the attack on Pearl Harbor more than five million men were rejected for physical, emotional, or educational deficiencies. The rejection rate was so high that in 1941 President Franklin Delano Roosevelt convened a national conference to investigate the matter. The conference concluded that the main reasons men were being rejected from service were bad teeth and bad eyes, both of which could be traced to the lack of basic medical care and adequate nutrition during the recent Depression. After the attack on Pearl Harbor, far fewer men received deferments or rejections.[1]

After being rejected by the Navy, Ray decided to serve his country as part of the civilian labor force. World War II affected every aspect of life in the United States. Industry, education, agriculture, transportation, and even the entertainment business enlisted for "the duration." U.S. industrial war production was a major factor in deciding the outcome of the war, and the War Manpower Commission, organized in April 1942, was in charge of recruiting workers for defense industries.[2] Ray Stedman was hired to work on the paint crew of a company responsible for building facilities for the armed forces in the Hawaiian Islands.

In the summer of 1942, "after a long, wearisome trip by bus across the great deserts of Utah and Nevada," Ray arrived in Oakland, California.[3] While he waited for his ship to be ready to sail for Hawaii, he and a friend traveled across the bay to San Francisco and saw the sights. Meanwhile, Ray's hotel bill at the Hotel San Pablo was paid by the military. They also paid him seventy cents an hour plus two dollars a day for spending money. "This is the softest job I've ever had," Ray told his aunt Beulah.[4]

Not long after arriving in Hawaii and beginning his work as a painter, Ray once again immersed himself in ministry whenever he could, and by December he was preaching at a church in downtown Honolulu.

"Tomorrow [Sunday] I have to preach downtown," he wrote to Elaine on December 26. "Sometime, if you're kind to me and answer my letters, I'll tell you my dreams for a real gospel work here in Honolulu. And they're in the making now."[5] Just a few months later, Ray and some friends began producing a radio broadcast called "Hymn Time," which aired from 9:30 to 9:45 each Sunday morning. It featured a hymn, the story behind the hymn, a short message, and an invitation to accept Jesus as Savior.

"I have been much gratified with the success of the program thus far," Ray glowed in his report to Elaine. "The station manager told us it was by far the best gospel program on the air, of local origin, which was encouraging, though only so many words if the program fails in its efforts to reach souls for Christ. Pray for it, will you?"[6]

A Dream Come True

DESPITE HIS FRUITFUL MINISTRY, Ray still longed to be in full-time work, and in the spring of 1944 it seemed that God was finally opening the door. By this time, Ray's study of the Scriptures resulted in his moving away from Pentecostalism, and he made Olivet Baptist Church his home church and place of ministry. One of the leaders of Olivet Baptist Church indicated to Ray that they would like to ordain him and find him a pastorate in Texas where he could also attend the Southern Baptist seminary in Fort Worth. Ray was ecstatic and immediately sought to have his draft classification changed to allow for the move. His letter to Elaine about the matter reflects both his excitement over the opportunity and his concern that his patriotism not be in question: "Personally, I cannot help but feel that it is the Lord's moving. There was only one reason, it seemed to me, for hesitating. I am not a slacker and I recognize my duty to my country.... there are still several obstacles to overcome, but I sincerely hope and pray that the moment for which I've waited 5 years might be at hand. I honestly feel that he who preaches the gospel from a pulpit in America is fighting full force for the same ideals and liberties for which sailors and soldiers are dying abroad."[7]

Within a few days, however, Ray once again had to surrender his future to the Lord as the church decided to license him rather than ordain him. "This is a disappointment to me," he confessed, "but I fancy the Lord will see the matter through."[8] On the positive side, the entire incident served to ignite a renewed hope that he would indeed one day enter full-time ministry.

During the following weeks, another opportunity was presented to Ray: an office job with Libby, McNeil, & Libby. He accepted, and his new employer quickly recognized his abilities and offered him a position as a junior executive. This was a tempting offer for Ray, who had lived with financial pressure for so long, but he turned it down for another opportunity closer to his heart. Ray had developed a close friendship with a Navy officer named Ed Phillips. Ed was involved with the work of the Navigators, an interdenominational organization active with military personnel, and he was eager for Ray to join him in leading the thriving Navigator ministry. For Ray, this was a dream come true.

"This is the work I would love most to do in all the world," he told Elaine. "It is close to the servicemen, with a definite Navy atmosphere; is extremely important from the standpoint of both Christian service and patriotic endeavor; and is a work in which I could labor without reserve."[9] Years later, Ray would reflect on this period as being the most carefree time of his life.

The Navigators had been active in Hawaii for years, but when Dawson Trotman, founder of the organization, visited the island in April 1940, he found the work in a sad state. Then came the attack on Pearl Harbor, which created a tremendous spiritual hunger among servicemen, and attendance at Bible studies soon swelled. When Trotman returned to Pearl Harbor in January 1945, he found the largest Navigator work anywhere in the world, and Ed Phillips and Ray Stedman were two of the "faithful men." Ray and Ed even arranged a meeting for Dawson with the chief of Navy chaplains, who was passing through Honolulu on his way to the war area.[10]

"It was my privilege and delight to be a close friend of Dawson Trotman, to have spent a good deal of time with him and to come under the influence of his teaching and his methods," Ray said years later, describing his involvement with the work of the Navigators and his friendship with Daws. "The Navigators in those days did a great work in the Navy throughout the whole of the Pacific and Atlantic oceans, and hundreds of young men were led to Christ through their efforts during the war years. I used to attend a Navigator group which met in Honolulu on Sunday afternoons. Sometimes two or three hundred sailors, all of them Christians, would be there. We had some great meetings and great times together. It was a glorious work."[11]

But after spending time in Hawaii in 1945, Dawson Trotman became convinced that too much emphasis was being placed on group meetings and not enough on "man-to-man" time, when men could be taught to teach others according to the pattern of 2 Timothy 2:2. "All key hands have been made to see that for the most part meetings, meetings, meetings have practically robbed all of them of time alone with men. Remedies are being made gladly."[12] Ray took this counsel to heart, and the Navigators' emphasis on personal Bible study and one-on-one discipleship influenced him tremendously. He would later apply this method in his years of ministry at Peninsula Bible Church.

RAY'S INVOLVEMENT WITH THE Navigators and with Ed Phillips soon brought more changes in his life and even in his theology. Ed strongly urged Ray to enlist in the Navy so that he could reach fellow servicemen who were facing the very real possibility of losing their lives in the war. As an officer, Ed was able to help Ray enlist in June 1944 as a Second Class Petty Officer without having to go through boot camp. Both men had a passion to disciple servicemen in their walk with Christ. Recognizing the gulf that existed between officers and enlisted men, they agreed that Ed would focus his work on officers and Ray on enlisted men. Many of these enlisted men would naturally look up to Ray who, at age twenty-seven, commanded their respect.

During his next two years in the Navy, the clerical skills Ray had developed during his year in Chicago served him well as he worked in the Ships Service Department and in the legal office of the Navy as a court reporter.[13] Yet Ray always viewed his enlistment as an open door for ministry.

"Although I was unsure whether I was doing the right thing or not, I felt I ought to join," Ray would later say about his enlistment. "What I did not understand or realize was that the action I took would open a door which gave me what was perhaps the greatest opportunity I have ever had to teach the Scriptures to those who were in desperate need of such teaching. I was stationed at Pearl Harbor, and through that great port there passed from time to time all the sailors of the Pacific Fleet, many of them Christian young men who had won others to Christ aboard their ships. Along with others, I had the opportunity to have great Bible classes, with hundreds of sailors involved. All this was opened up to me because I was a member of the United States Navy myself."[14]

But along with the light of God's leading came some challenging moments of conflict in his ministry. In the summer of 1945, Ray became involved with a group of men who brought serious allegations of intimidation, pride, financial misdealing, lying, and gossip against Dawson Trotman. Although many of the allegations were true, one does detect in Ray's letters a strong note of spiritual pride as well.

Many painful letters were exchanged between Ray, Ed Phillips, and others and Dawson.[15] Even though Dawson wrote a letter to these men in Hawaii saying, "I am guilty," Ray and several others believed that his actions revealed that he had not truly repented. Finally, a mimeographed open letter addressed to "The Church," presenting proof of Dawson's guilt and calling on him to repent, was sent to hundreds of people. In time, Dawson would come to see this as God's needed chastening in his life, and Ray would come to deeply appreciate Dawson's ministry, but it would take two years for the air to be cleared between Ray and Dawson.[16]

Changing Theology

ANOTHER SIGNIFICANT CHANGE FOR Ray during this time was in the area of theology. As he studied the Scriptures, he began to question much of the teaching and practice of the Pentecostal church, and the teaching he received at Olivet Baptist Church only bolstered his developing convictions. To put it another way: "He studied himself out of the Pentecostal perspective."[17]

When Ray described his opportunity with the Baptist church and his hope of eventually attending seminary in Texas, Elaine expressed her concern: "I feel that affiliation with this denomination would permit you to minister a glorious salvation message, but would it not prove a 'bushel' to the light on the baptism of the Spirit?"[18] Ray responded with a lengthy letter describing his shift in thinking, as well as his concern that somehow this issue would prove to be an obstacle in their relationship.

"I made a change from the Pentecostal to the Baptist church after much, much deliberation and prayer," Ray wrote to Elaine. "That change was made because I found myself increasingly at variance with Pentecostal methods. I have many sincere and valued friends in Full Gospel churches and I have never regretted the time I spent in such churches. It has given me a depth of understanding and tolerance I could have gained in no other way. I hope to share a lifelong fellowship with Pentecostal people, but I personally cannot work under their banner. I detest denominationalism thoroughly and irrevocably and have little patience with men who constantly blow a denominational trumpet. Nevertheless, I recognize the fact of denominations and recognize that for the sake of harmony and fellowship a man should associate himself with a denomination that will allow him to preach as he understands the Bible and does not interpose obstacles in the form of church behavior to which he cannot agree. For that reason, I have chosen the Baptist church and since I have made that choice I have been much happier and have found a greatly broadened field for my preaching message."[19]

Although the day would come when Ray would challenge the very core of the Pentecostal understanding of the ministry of the Holy Spirit, at this point his issues had more to do with practical matters:

"Let me make it clear that I do not differ as much in doctrine as I do in practice. I most definitely recognize that the Bible teaches a Baptism of the Holy Spirit as a second work of grace. I recognize the Spirit's power and His presence and the Lord's command that each believer should be filled with the Spirit, but I often feel that Full Gospel churches are often guilty of quenching and grieving the Spirit by their insistence on only one form of His manifestations. As a pastor of a Baptist church or any other church, I shall definitely stand forth with regard to the necessity of the Spirit-filled life but I will place emphasis upon receiving the Spirit Himself and leave to Him the manner in which He makes Himself manifest."[20]

Another important change in Ray's theological development at this time grew out of the influence of the Navigators. Ray's description of a "typical Navigator" offers a telling clue: "You could always tell a Navigator because... he had a Scofield Reference Bible tucked under his arm. This Bible was pushed by the Navigators, and everybody had to have one. Since I was working at that time in the ship's service department in Pearl Harbor, we ordered great quantities of these Bibles. They were hard to get in those war years, and every shipment that came in went out like hotcakes. Every Navigator had to have a Scofield Reference Bible; that was the only 'Authorized Version.'"[21]

The Scofield Reference Bible played a significant role in Ray's developing dispensational theology. Cyrus Ingerson Scofield (1843–1921) pastored a small Congregational church in Dallas, Texas, and in 1907 he began to lecture at the Correspondence Bible School in Dallas (later to become Dallas Theological Seminary). Scofield was an avid proponent of dispensationalism. Although dispensationalists would later influence Pentecostals, especially in the area of prophecy, they stood against the traditional Pentecostal teaching on the baptism in the Holy Spirit and the normalcy of what they called "sign gifts" (tongues, healing, miracles) for the church. Scofield and other dispensationalists taught that the baptism of the Holy Spirit took place in a believer's life upon conversion and that the sign gifts had ceased after the first generation of Christians died. The Scofield Reference Bible, first published in 1909, consisted of Scofield's annotations and explanations, which incorporated this doctrine.[22]

Ray's dispensationalist theology would become more refined later when he trained at Dallas Theological Seminary. But his initial shift away from Pentecostal theology and practice took place in Hawaii through his study of Scripture, as well as through the influence of the Navigators and the Baptist church.

A Man in Love

SOMETHING ELSE OF SIGNIFICANCE occurred during Ray's time in Hawaii—a rekindling of his relationship with Elaine Smith. Soon after arriving in Hawaii, he wrote to her for the first time in two years.

"Do you mind if I write to you?" he said. "I know that the last time I saw you or heard from you was over two years ago, but, if I remember correctly, I owed you a letter then—so here it is. Besides, out here sometimes I get lonesome and would like someone to talk to.... I hope you don't mind."[23]

This began a correspondence that continued for the next two years, and their letters are marked by an increasing affection, warmth, and intimacy. In April 1944, Ray proposed marriage, but Elaine wanted to wait until he returned from Hawaii to determine her response. Ray was a man in love and used all his long-distance persuasive powers:

"You're a perfectly wonderful person and you don't know how greatly I long to see you. Time drags with leaden feet when I allow myself to dream of what the future may bring.... I hope to tell you someday how the very thought of you has been a steadying influence on me. Please know, dear, that I love you sincerely, honestly, wholly and only you. I feel that between you and me there is a sense of mutual understanding deeper than can be accounted for by our short personal acquaintance and our correspondence. I'm not going to put you on the spot again by asking a direct question, because I know and fully understand and agree with your attitude about it, but I want you to know, nevertheless, that if you should change your mind and not want to wait till I return and we see each other again, that engagement ring is still waiting and will be sent posthaste at your request."[24]

Interestingly enough, Dawson Trotman played a role in moving Elaine one step closer to accepting Ray's proposal. In January 1945, when Dawson arrived in Hawaii, he noticed a photograph of Elaine on Ray's desk and inquired about it. Ray explained that Elaine was not only his sweetheart but also a secretary for the Montana Branch Manager of the Standard Oil Company of New York. Daws asked Ray if she might be willing to come work for him in Los Angeles as a secretary on the Navigator staff. This request proved to be providential, as Elaine had by now begun her own journey out of the Pentecostal church.

"There were questions raised in my mind about the doctrine of the Holy Spirit," Elaine recalls, "because I had been listening to *The Old Fashioned Revival Hour,* and Dr. Fuller was doing this wonderful series on the Holy Spirit. I had never heard anything like it! I was intrigued by it. But, of course, we'd always been told that we had the ultimate experience; so I really felt very guilty about it, and I told myself . . . that I was just listening to it for the music, because the music was so wonderful."[25]

The Old Fashioned Revival Hour was a nondenominational, fundamentalist radio broadcast begun in 1923 by evangelist Dr. Charles E. Fuller.[26] Although it had broad appeal, it was considered heretical by the Pentecostal movement because Fuller did not align with their teaching on the baptism of the Holy Spirit. As a result,

Elaine's pastor put her on trial for heresy. "He didn't want me listening to anyone but him," Elaine recalls, "and was highly offended when a friend told him I was listening to *The Old Fashioned Revival Hour.* When he called me before the church elders, he presented a list of mostly made-up accusations. I had been virtually a volunteer assistant pastor, and he said I could continue to attend the church but could have no more ministry. He was later found to have embezzled money from the church, and soon after he resigned died of a heart attack."[27]

Elaine's own growing uneasiness with Pentecostal theology coincided with Ray's prodding her to join Dawson Trotman and the Navigators in Los Angeles. When she finally accepted the position and began working for the Navigators in February 1945, she lived with the rest of the staff and the Trotmans at a large home in South Pasadena provided by, of all things, *The Old Fashioned Revival Hour!* Elaine's new office was at the old Willard Hotel, which served as both an office for the Navigator staff and a meeting place for the Church of the Open Door, soon to be pastored by Dr. J. Vernon McGee. Elaine also immediately benefited from a visiting teacher, Dr. Jack Mitchell, who was teaching the Navigator staff on the doctrine of the Holy Spirit.

Elaine's work with the Navigators proved to be the catalyst she needed to further her relationship with Ray. In September 1945, after finally accepting Ray's marriage proposal, she moved to Hawaii to continue working for the Navigators and to get to know the man with whom she had been corresponding for five years and with whom she now planned to spend the rest of her life. Upon her arrival in Hawaii and prior to their wedding, Elaine stayed in the home of Pastor Victor Koon of the Olivet Baptist Church where Ray served as a deacon. Elaine also worked as a secretary for Harold DeGroff, who was in charge of the Navigator Home in Hawaii.

Meanwhile, the leadership of Ray's church had been urging him to attend the Southern Baptist seminary in Fort Worth, Texas, and even offered to finance his education. But Ray was beginning to have doubts about Southern Baptist polity, and an incident involving Elaine brought it to a head. Before Elaine could become a member of the church, she was required to be rebaptized. Although Ray himself had been allowed to become a member without being rebaptized, the church had since transitioned from a mission church to a denominational church and they now required all members to be baptized in a Southern Baptist church. Ray stood on principle against this.

"Ray would come to pick me up for a date," Elaine remembers, "and he'd be downstairs having some long debate with the pastor over this issue, while I'm upstairs in my room wondering, 'What in the world is going on?' because I wasn't invited into the debate. And I remember kneeling on my bed and saying, 'Lord, is this the man you want me to marry?' and as clear as though it were an audible voice, He said, 'Yes, and this is the way it's going to be.'"[28]

Ray and Elaine were married on October 22, 1945, in a beautiful garden wedding at the campus of the Olivet Baptist Bible Training School. When they left Hawaii in May of 1946, they left as soldiers who had been in active service for Christ. Now, as they made plans for the future, they were looking for their Master's orders as to where they could best serve Him next.

FOUR

~⸺⸺⸺

Equipped for Every Good Work

God's calling to preach the gospel was clear to Ray, but the specific arena of ministry he was to be involved in was not. The Navigators offered a Personnel Classification and Allocation Program through their publication, *The Log,* to counsel men on schooling and possible fields of service, and Ray took advantage of this offer.[1] The Navigators enthusiastically recommended a ministry called the China Inland Mission, founded in 1865 by Hudson Taylor as the first truly interdenominational foreign mission,[2] and for some time Ray felt led to serve in China. He had even begun to study Chinese at the University of Hawaii while he was still a civilian there. And in the spring of 1946, as Ray and Elaine sailed from Hawaii to San Francisco on the USS *Arthur Middleton,* they studied Chinese language flashcards to prepare for future service in China.[3]

Closed Doors

UPON ARRIVING IN SAN FRANCISCO, Ray and Elaine immediately made plans to visit the Los Angeles headquarters of the China Inland Mission to apply as candidates. But two obstacles closed this door for the young couple. First, since Ray still had not received an undergraduate degree, the mission required that he get more education before being accepted as a candidate. The second obstacle was even greater: Ray and Elaine began to doubt that CIM was the right mission under which to serve. Their major concern was the mission's requirement that children be separated from their parents and sent to mission schools. Ray and Elaine felt that they simply could not comply with this regulation and thus began to investigate other avenues of service.

But no matter what direction they explored, Ray's lack of a college degree was a major concern, so they began to examine educational alternatives. The GI Bill made it possible for servicemen like Ray to attend college, but which school should he attend? Many of his fellow-servicemen from the Navigators were attending undergraduate schools like Moody Bible Institute and the Bible Institute of Los Angeles (Biola), but for some time, Ray's Navy friend, Ed Phillips, had encouraged him to consider Dallas Theological Seminary, located in Ed's hometown. Ray's own inclinations also drew him to DTS, and he applied to the seminary. Then he and Elaine returned to Great Falls, Montana, to wait for an answer. Meanwhile, Ray worked for the railroad, as he had in Denver, and Elaine worked for the Socony-Vacuum Oil Company, which later became Mobil Oil.

Ray became increasingly convinced that Dallas Seminary was the school he should attend. But as the summer of 1946 drew to a close and he still had no word about his application, Ray made a characteristic decision. Throughout his ministry when Ray was convinced he should do something, he threw caution to the wind and just did it. Ray was so confident that Dallas was where they belonged that he and Elaine quit their jobs, packed their bags, and headed for Texas. It was a decision they would never regret.

Dallas Theological Seminary

DALLAS THEOLOGICAL SEMINARY HAD opened in the fall of 1924 under the leadership of the founder, noted Bible teacher Lewis Sperry Chafer, who would be president of the seminary until 1952.

The first class of thirteen students was the result of Chafer's passion to train men in expository preaching of the Scriptures from a dispensational perspective. In 1935 the seminary pioneered the four-year Master of Theology (Th.M.) degree, which required a year longer than most seminary programs. This additional year of study provided time for emphasis in systematic theology, Hebrew and Greek exegesis, and Bible exposition.[4]

Lewis Sperry Chafer was an ardent dispensationalist, as were all teachers at the seminary, and Chafer was the first theologian to organize a complete dispensational theology in his eight-volume *Systematic Theology*, published in 1948. Dispensationalism shares much in common with conservative Protestant theology; however, it is unique in the way it divides sacred history. A dispensation is defined as "an epoch in history characterized by a covenant or agreement made between God and humankind, or some segment of humankind." This agreement defines what is required of humans to receive salvation during that particular era. Most dispensationalists adhere to seven eras, but the number can vary from three to seven.

At the forefront of dispensationalist thinking is the verbal and plenary inspiration of the Bible and the need to interpret it in the most literal way possible. Dispensationalists also teach premillennialism, believing that this present age will end in judgment and the historical kingdom of Christ will be established on earth for a thousand years. However, many dispensationalists have added other distinctive elements to historic premillennialism, especially concerning the role of the church.

Dispensationalists teach that the church age is a unique dispensation that began at Pentecost and will end at Christ's second coming. This second coming will take place in two stages. In the first stage, called the Rapture, true believers will be caught up in the air to be with Christ. Thus begins seven years of tribulation, culminating in Christ's return to earth with His raptured saints. Then He will restore the nation of Israel as His chosen people and set up His earthly kingdom in Jerusalem for a thousand years. Dispensationalists teach that the true church is a spiritual entity that crosses denominational lines and consists of true believers.[5] Dallas Seminary, in the forefront of this teaching, was the school to which Ray thought God was calling him.

When he and Elaine arrived in Dallas, they promptly sought out the school's registrar, Dr. Nash, and were delighted to learn that Ray had been accepted to the school. Dr. Nash then explained why they had not heard from him. During a recent trip to Denver, Dr. Nash's briefcase had been stolen. Ray's application form, along with his address, had been inside the case, leaving Dr. Nash with no way to contact him. Ray and Elaine could plainly see that in the providence of God He had led them to make the long trip to Dallas without knowing if they were accepted.

Because Ray did not have an undergraduate degree, he was accepted as a non-degree student. As such, he would take every course required of a regular Th.M student. The only difference was that four years later when Ray graduated, he would receive a Certificate of Graduation rather than a Th.M degree.

Before long, however, Ray distinguished himself as an honor student and an outstanding thinker. He was a natural student of the original languages, especially Hebrew, and he loved to engage in dialogue with professors, questioning them to get to the heart of an issue.

Howard Hendricks, a fellow student who became a close friend of Ray's, recalls, "We always highly respected Ray because he had an incredible mind... I used to kid him and say, 'Ray, I think you've got a photographic mind. I had one once, but I ran out of film.' Ray would be the first guy out in every single test he ever took. If it was an hour test, he'd be out in thirty minutes, maximum. And he always aced it. I used to think, 'How in the world could a guy get all this stuff in his head?'"[6]

Life was not financially easy for most students at Dallas Seminary in those days. Ray was fortunate to receive a Navy pension of

$90.00 a month, but their monthly rent alone was $92.50. To make ends meet, Elaine worked in the seminary office and typed doctoral dissertations while Ray worked at a variety of jobs, including counseling at a camp for needy boys and selling programs at local football games.

"We lived very frugally, very frugally," Elaine recalls. "Our big treat on the weekend was to drive to a Seven-Eleven-type store and have a Milknickel—it cost a nickel—if we could afford it. And I wore clothes out of the missionary barrel from Scofield Church. I had a nice wardrobe when I left my job and went to Hawaii, but after the war they changed the fashions. Skirts, which had been knee-length, were now mid-ankle length. I had nothing left to wear!"[7]

In this setting, Ray and Elaine learned some powerful lessons about God's provision—lessons that would remain with them for the rest of their lives. Years later, Ray reflected on one incident that proved to be a great encouragement to the young couple.

"I'll never forget the day, in our extreme poverty, when there was a letter in my mailbox from a man whom I had never met, but whose name I knew. When I opened it there fell out a ten-dollar bill and a note from him that said he had heard about our ministry among the servicemen during the war, teaching the Bible. He said he wanted to help us financially and was praying for us. To this day I can recall the immense feeling of gratitude that I felt because some man, unknown to me, had thought of us, and was praying for us, and wanted to help us."[8]

Ray and Elaine lived on campus, along with seventeen other families, in a place affectionately nicknamed "Trailerville." This "village" was simply a group of seventeen trailers under a grove of pecan trees, located at the place where Chafer Chapel stands today. Life at Trailerville was anything but glamorous. There were no washing machines or dryers, so all laundry had to be hand-washed. Wooden boards served as walkways, but were often lost beneath the accumulated mud after heavy rains. These seventeen families also shared two toilet-and-shower facilities. With characteristic humor, Ray would often sing out the old hymn as he waited in line: "Why do you wait, dear brother? Why do you tarry so long?"[9]

But during their four years at Trailerville, Ray and Elaine's life was enriched by the deep friendships they made there, such as Don and Bea Campbell, who lived in a trailer directly behind the Stedman's. (Don would later serve as the president of Dallas Seminary from 1986–1994.) Howard and Jeanne Hendricks lived in the adjoining row of trailers, and Howard and Ray became the best of friends—a friendship that would remain rock-solid through the years.

"I have no brothers or sisters," says Howard Hendricks, "and Ray became my brother. For some reason we were just instinctively drawn to each other, and we spent hours and hours and hours of time together. Many of those hours were spent sitting under a pecan tree developing what Ray called 'nutty theology.' We would go over and over the stuff. We'd change sides—he'd be Premill, I'd be Amill—and then we'd switch sides just to test our thinking. It was there that we hammered out our philosophy of ministry."[10]

One of the other qualities that drew Ray and Howard together was their shared sense of humor. Howard affectionately named Ray "the Mayor of Trailerville" when Ray failed to show up at a Trailerville board meeting. From then on, whenever anything went wrong within the Trailerville facilities, Howard would stick his head out of his trailer and yell, "Stedman! Where's the mayor?"[11] Howard and Ray also dubbed Trailerville "Conception City" because of the number of babies born to the young couples who lived there.

Along with the great friendships he made at Dallas, Ray was also strongly influenced by several professors at the seminary. Dr. Charles Feinberg, his Hebrew professor, had a great affinity for Ray because he was so adept at learning the language. Years later, after Dr. Feinberg moved to Talbot Seminary, he would have a part in bestowing on Ray the degree of Doctor of Divinity in 1971. Ray also admired the keen mind of Dr. John Walvoord, who would succeed Dr. Chafer as Dallas Seminary president in 1952.

But the professor who had the most profound impact on Ray Stedman was Lewis Sperry Chafer.

"We were one of the last classes that Dr. Chafer taught," remembers Howard Hendricks. "He was in his eighties and was teaching a course on the spiritual life. The guy would teach the thing, come to an end, get up, and nobody would move. He'd go over and flip the light off, and walk out, and we'd be sitting there, absolutely stunned."[12] Chafer's teaching on the doctrines of the Holy Spirit, eternal security, and the grace of God marked Ray forever. Chafer believed so deeply in God's grace that he gave all his students an "A" so they could see the principle of unearned favor in action. Chafer's teaching on grace also impacted Elaine, who credits Chafer's book, *Grace,* published in 1922, as the catalyst that set her free from the legalism under which she had been raised.[13]

But it was not just Chafer's teaching that had a profound effect on Ray. Having no children of his own, Chafer would often select certain students as his "favorite sons." Ray Stedman was blessed to be one of these sons. Chafer's affection for Ray was such that he crossed the normal boundaries existing between students and professors. After Ray's second daughter was born, Chafer could not bear to see her return to the stark conditions of the trailer in Trailerville, so he and his wife took the Stedmans into their home.[14]

These expressions of fatherly care and concern had a profound effect on the fatherless boy from Montana. But the incident that marked him most took place while Ray was an intern at the Emmanuel Baptist Church in California during the summer after his third year of seminary.

"I will never forget an incident in my own ministry when I was a young man," Ray remarked. "I was still a student at Dallas Seminary, but was spending my summers in Pasadena. I was working one summer as a youth minister in a church there, when

Dr. Lewis Sperry Chafer . . . came into town and was gracious enough to spend an afternoon with my wife and me."

Ray showed Dr. Chafer around the church where he was working, an impressive and beautiful building. When Ray told Dr. Chafer that the congregation was without a pastor and was seeking one, Dr. Chafer said to him, "Do you think you might end up here in this church?"

"I don't know," said Ray. "Who knows what God will do? I don't have any particular plans for that."

"I don't know either," Dr. Chafer said, "but it would be a good place for you because I believe God is going to give you a great ministry."

Ray later said, "I do not know what he had in mind by that. . . . But his words have been a great encouragement to my heart. Many times as a young man I remembered that Dr. Lewis Sperry Chafer had seen something in me that was an encouragement."[15]

Years later, in his own ministry, Ray would become known as a man who showed the same kind of affection for his own sons in the faith. Just prior to his death, I wrote to him in much the same vein as Ray had spoken of Chafer: "You have been a wonderful model of a pastor to me. But, more importantly you have given me something that I desperately needed—your blessing. In various ways you have shown me that you believed in me, or at least in God's presence in me. You have blessed me by seeing something of God's call upon my life even when I wasn't sure it was really there. I'd like to say that I'm beyond all that now—that I know who I am and don't need that blessing. But I know that I do and nobody reminds me of this like you."[16]

Opportunities for Growth and Learning

SUMMER BREAKS FROM SEMINARY provided opportunities for Ray to learn from experienced men and to grow in the practical aspects of ministry. After his first year at Dallas, in the summer of 1947, Ray served an internship with Dr. J. Vernon McGee at the Lincoln Avenue Presbyterian Church in Pasadena, California.

During that time, Elaine's father became quite ill, and she spent the summer in Great Falls while Ray worked in Pasadena. This was a difficult separation for the young couple, particularly as Elaine was expecting their first child. On May 20, he wrote to her from Fort Sumner, New Mexico, as he was driving to Pasadena: "Honey, I miss you an awful lot and would sure give an awful lot to have you with me right now. Bachelors are awfully unhappy people!"[17] Throughout his correspondence with Elaine during this time, Ray affectionately referred to their unborn baby as "Bruce."

Ray was eager to have children, and the minute it seemed a pregnancy was likely he went around Trailerville proudly announcing it. He wrote to Elaine, "I can't wait to get my hands on that little tyke, Bruce, so please hurry him along if at all possible. Does he still upset your stomach considerably or are things leveling out somewhat?"[18] It would be six months before the "little tyke" was born on January 3, 1948, and much to Ray's surprise, "Bruce" would be Sheila!

"Though I think he was surprised to have a girl baby," Elaine recalls, "she quickly won his heart, and mine, too, of course."

When Ray arrived in Pasadena, he discovered that his ministry was to be primarily with the young people and that he would have the opportunity to speak at two youth camps.[19] As the days passed Ray began to see himself as a catalyst for change in the youth ministry at Lincoln Avenue, moving them more in the direction of outreach to unchurched kids.

"Just now had a long talk with the sponsor of the C.E. for High School and Jr. High who has a real problem," he wrote to Elaine in mid-June. "I believe Young Life tactics are the answer and they are willing to try them. We are very near a Jr. College and a Jr. High School and I believe they can be reached. That project calls for your prayers."[20] Less than two weeks later, he told her that the transition to an outreach-centered Young Life model was progressing well.[21]

Being in Pasadena also placed Ray in close proximity to Dawson Trotman and allowed for some much-needed healing between the two men. Daws lived in the Los Angeles area, and Ray and Daws met together several times. They "had good fellowship together"[22] and began to experience some healing in their relationship. One of the valuable lessons Ray learned from these painful encounters was how to work through disagreement without compromising the standards set forth in God's Word.

"I had dinner at 509 again and afterward Daws and I thrashed out our difficulty. I had told you I was willing to admit there were questionable features about that mimeographed letter [the letter sent in 1945 regarding Dawson's misconduct] if and when Daws was ready to admit his backbiting and lordly attitude. Well, last night he did so, saying that the Lord had dealt with him a great deal and from our talk I was convinced that it was genuine. Accordingly, I promised to give him a statement he could print in the Log if he cared about the letter. We still differ somewhat about his treatment of H– and some Navigator practices but those are pretty much differences of opinion and hardly call for discipline. I am glad the hatchet is buried and peace reigns again."[23]

After his second year at Dallas, Ray returned to Pasadena, this time accompanied by his wife and daughter. One of the struggles Ray had to contend with each summer was how to finance the trip and make ends meet during their first few weeks before receiving a paycheck in Pasadena. They had very little cash to work with and it took all their savings to buy gasoline to make the trip. As Ray said, "We always arrived absolutely flat broke." Through this experience, however, he gained a powerful illustration of redemption.

"Usually we had spent the last of our money four or five hundred miles back and had gone without a couple of meals and slept in the car. There would be a week, or sometimes two, until my first check arrived. And so I always had to pawn something. The only thing of value I had, beside my wife, was my typewriter. So the first thing I did in Pasadena was to take my typewriter down and pawn it. (The pawnbroker and I became good friends as the summers went by.) We would live on that money until my first check came. Then I'd redeem the typewriter. Now, for that two-week period the typewriter was absolutely useless to anyone. No one could use it. I had no right to use it; the pawnbroker had no right to use it. He couldn't sell it to anyone else. It was in hock, in pawn. It was useless, absolutely useless.... When I bought the typewriter back, redeemed it, it was restored to usefulness."[24]

During Ray's second summer at Lincoln Avenue, he completely immersed himself in ministry with the youth. He also continued to observe Dr. J. Vernon McGee, whose faithful exposition of God's Word would influence Ray's preaching in years to come. Like McGee, Ray preferred preaching through the books of the Bible; and like McGee, his preaching was marked by simplicity, a conversational tone, and homespun stories and humor. Yet with a powerful model like McGee came a powerful temptation, as Ray confessed years later.

"When I graduated from seminary, I thought that the power needed for a ministry lay in the man of God—so I studied men. I followed them. I saw men that were being used of God, and I said, 'What is it that is the secret of their power?' When I thought I found it, I tried to imitate it, and to adapt it to myself. I caught myself aping men—talking like them.... coming fresh from the influence of the ministry of Dr. J. Vernon McGee, I used to talk like him. I wore bright red shirts, because I thought that was the hiding [the secret] of his power. I finally realized that the power did not lie in the man."[25]

The following year, Dr. McGee left Lincoln Avenue Presbyterian Church to become pastor of Church of the Open Door in downtown Los Angeles. So Ray spent his third seminary summer once again doing youth ministry at Emmanuel Baptist Church in Pasadena.

By this time, Ray and Elaine were expecting their second child, and their daughter Susan was born during Ray's fourth and final year of seminary on January 25, 1950.

The man who expected to have four sons was now well on his way to having four daughters. Elaine confesses that she didn't know Ray's true feelings about this: "There was one overall deficit in our marriage, and that was communication. I think I could write a book about that. For instance, if Ray felt any disappointment about having all girls rather than the four boys he planned, he never expressed it to me, and certainly not to them.... I truly do not know whether he just stuffed any disappointment he may have felt or whether he genuinely received it as God's gift—perplexing maybe, but good nevertheless. I still marvel at the irony, that God should assign a house full of females to a man who had so much perplexity about women. But I never heard a complaint after any of our daughters' births. And when he announced the last to the congregation at PBC he said, 'I guess I'm just destined to live my life surrounded by beautiful women.'"[26]

—————

FOR RAY, THE HIGHLIGHTS of those Dallas years "were the visits of special expositors who came for two weeks at a time and lectured to the students. One of them was ... Dr. H. A. Ironside, the long-term pastor of the Moody Church in Chicago ... a great Bible teacher."[27] Ray loved Dr. Ironside's teaching, and he quickly took the initiative to try and develop a relationship in a very practical way. Noting the older man's deteriorating eyesight, Ray offered to assist with writing out Dr. Ironside's notes, putting to good use the typing and shorthand skills he had learned in Chicago and Hawaii. As a result, Ironside developed an affinity for his eager student and asked if Ray would travel with him as his chauffeur and assistant during the summer after Ray's graduation from Dallas. Although this would mean separation from his wife and two young daughters, Ray could not resist the opportunity to spend time with a man of Ironside's stature. So while Elaine and the children spent the summer of 1950 with her parents in Great Falls, Montana, Ray accompanied Dr. Ironside in his travels and speaking engagements. Dr. Ironside's widow wrote of Ray's contribution to the publication of her husband's book on Isaiah:

> In December 1949, Dr. Ironside gave lectures on the Book of Isaiah at Dallas Theological Seminary. One of the students, Ray C. Stedman, made wire recordings of the classroom lecture.
>
> Mr. Stedman also did a great deal of secretarial work for Dr. Ironside during his stay at the seminary. He was so efficient and helpful that Dr. Ironside asked him if he would be willing to travel with us during the summer, and help with the writing of his exposition of the Book of Isaiah, which had long been delayed on account of his failing eyesight.
>
> Mr. Stedman joined us in June 1950, after his graduation from the seminary, and for two months served not only as chauffeur, secretary, and companion, but as a "brother beloved" was so helpful in all the varied activities of the itenerant ministry that we came to love him as a son. Without his help and cooperation the publication of Dr. Ironside's "Isaiah" would have been impossible.
>
> Traveling constantly, Dr. Ironside's reference library consisted of M. A. Vine's *Isaish—Prophecies, Promises, and Warnings*; F. C. Jennings' *Isaiah*; a one-volume Bible encyclopedia; and J. N. Darby's New Translation of the Holy Scriptures.
>
> As Dr. Ironside was unable to read at all during this time, except with the aid of a powerful magnifying glass, his

method of working under this handicap may be of interest. Mr. Stedman writes:

"In general our procedure was as follows: I would read to him the portion chosen for comment, out of the Authorized Version—a portion which had previously been read to him and over which he had been meditating. He would take a moment or two to gather his thoughts and then would begin dictating, seldom pausing for rephrasing or changes. I would then read the next section and he would dictate on that until an entire chapter had been covered. After that I would read through the next chapter, usually from Darby's "New Translation" and also the corresponding portion from Jennings and Vine. This would form the basis for this meditation in preparation for the next day's dictation.

"Occasionally we would discuss interesting sections of the chapters together and he would ask me to look up certain words in a one-volume Bible encyclopedia he carried. I was always amazed at the way he kept his comments from simply being a "rehash" of Vine and Jennings, but always managed to bring out some interesting sidelight which the others had overlooked."

When Mr. Stedman left us to go to the pastorate of the Peninsula Bible Fellowship at Palo Alto, California, the first thirty-five chapters of Isaiah were completed and typed.

That summer proved to be another turning point for Ray as he carefully observed both the life and teaching of this seasoned pastor. One of the treasures he brought home with him three months later was a card file he had made of Dr. Ironside's illustrations.[28] (Providentially, this would be his last chance to glean from the great expositor, because Dr. Ironside died the following fall.)

"It was a great and choice privilege to be with Dr. Ironside for three months," Ray said years later, reflecting on that life-changing summer. "It was a fascinating time for me. Because he was almost blind with cataracts in both eyes, I was his constant companion. I was his chauffeur, his secretary, and his companion. We lived, ate, bled and died together for three months. Because I was young I listened to him with great interest, and watched everything he did. I saw his great strengths as a Bible teacher. I saw his warmth and compassion as a human being, and I saw some weaknesses. . . . He made an unforgettable impression upon me."[29]

What Ray did not know was the impression he had made on Dr. Ironside, Dr. Chafer, Dr. McGee, Dr. Mitchell, and Dr. Walvoord, nor could he imagine what that would mean for his future.

FIVE

Laying a Foundation

As Ray Stedman and Howard Hendricks hammered out their "nutty theology" under the pecan trees in Dallas, one of the things they often discussed was the church. Both men had a vision for what the church could be and how it should function, a vision that was very different from what they were seeing around them.

First and foremost, Ray believed that the blueprint for the proper functioning of the church was to be found in the New Testament. Based on this premise and his continued study of the Scriptures, Ray believed that the church was a living organism, not an organization or an institution. In keeping with this, he was convinced that the traditional division of clergy and laity, common in most churches, should be obliterated. Ministry should be carried out not by the so-called clergy, but by ordinary members of the body, because every member of the body of Christ was gifted by the Holy Spirit. The church's pastoral leadership was called and gifted to equip others to do the work of ministry. And at the very heart of this equipping ministry was the exposition of the Scriptures, which was necessary for the edification and maturing of the saints.[1]

A Vision Becomes Reality

IN 1948, WHILE RAY STEDMAN was at Dallas studying in seminary and hammering out his thinking on the church, a group of five businessmen from the San Francisco Peninsula began meeting together and sharing their vision for ministry on the peninsula, which encompasses the metropolitan area extending from San Francisco to San Jose. Most of these businessmen were from Palo Alto, home of the prestigious Stanford University. Gustaf Gustafen, Cecil Kettle, Harry Smith, Bob Smith, and Ed Stirm met weekly in the home of Pearl and Bob Smith to pray about the needs they saw around them in the peninsula area. Each of these men was already well-known for his commitment to national and overseas ministries, but now they were becoming particularly concerned about the local young people, many of whom attended nearby Stanford University. These men knew of no current gospel witness on the campus. Their 6:30 a.m. discussions soon led to prolonged times of Bible study, prayer, and fellowship. Before long these meetings proliferated into home Bible classes designed for outreach, and soon they needed a suitable Sunday night meeting place.

On September 12, 1948, the community calling itself "Peninsula Bible Fellowship" held its first meeting at the Palo Alto Community Center, with about thirty people present. Gustafen, Kettle, Stirm, and the Smiths defined the purpose of this group simply: "To know Christ and make Him known." It was not their intention to start a church, they said, but rather a cross-denominational movement in which people could experience warm fellowship and hear the Scriptures taught with accuracy and relevance. Friends of these five men were often invited to teach the group, and three of their favorite teachers were Drs. John Mitchell, J. Vernon McGee, and John Walvoord. As the fellowship grew, they obtained a post office box and incorporated the group in order to collect funds to pay for the rental of the community center.[2]

Then, in the spring of 1950, Peninsula Bible Fellowship, now known as PBF, received letters from Drs. Mitchell, McGee, and Walvoord. Each of these men wrote to PBF without the knowledge of the others, and each recommended a young man named Ray Stedman, soon to graduate from Dallas Seminary, for ministry with PBF. Amazingly, these three letters arrived at PBF's post office box on the same day.[3]

The five leaders at PBF were not blind to the providential nature of such an occurrence. And since Bob Smith needed to make a business trip to Dallas, the group suggested he meet with Ray Stedman while he was there. So in April, Bob met with Ray and Elaine in their little trailer under the pecan trees on the Dallas Seminary campus.

"That meeting with Bob was pivotal to all that followed," Elaine recalls. "He was a prince of a man with whom we had immediate rapport. As he unfolded the vision for Peninsula Bible Fellowship, it was clear he and the men he represented had the same ministry perspectives that Ray had."[4]

As a result of that meeting, it was decided that Ray and Elaine would drive to Palo Alto immediately after graduation in May for a closer look at PBF. There they met with the five founders, who made it clear that they were not seeking to start a church. Their vision for ministry resonated with Ray, and the feeling was mutual. They offered Ray the position of Executive Secretary of the Peninsula Bible Fellowship without ever having heard him preach. He was not offered a salary but was promised that "all your needs will be met."[5] This nontraditional agreement fit the "Wild Mustang from Montana" perfectly, and he agreed to return to Palo Alto after his summer work with Dr. Ironside.

Early Ministry at PBF

RAY, ELAINE, AND THEIR two daughters, Sheila and Susan, arrived in Palo Alto on September 2, 1950. The next evening Ray preached his first message at PBF to about ninety men, women, and children. The text he chose was Ephesians 4:11–16:

And He gave some as apostles, and some as prophets, and some as evangelists, and some as pastors and teachers, for the equipping of the saints for the work of service, to the building up of the body of Christ; until we all attain to the unity of the faith, and of the knowledge of the Son of God, to a mature man, to the measure of the stature which belongs to the fulness of Christ. As a result, we are no longer to be children, tossed here and there by waves, and carried about by every wind of doctrine, by the trickery of men, by craftiness in deceitful scheming; but speaking the truth in love, we are to grow up in all aspects into Him, who is the head, even Christ, from whom the whole body, being fitted and held together by that which every joint supplies, according to the proper working of each individual part, causes the growth of the body for the building up of itself in love (NASB).

In his opening message Ray laid the foundation for what would someday become known as "Body Life." The bedrock conviction upon which Body Life was founded was that Christ is the living head of His church, which is His body, and that there is no room for superstars among God's people. Each member of the body is to employ the gifts he or she has received from the Lord and is to grow in spiritual maturity through the teaching of God's Word.

Ironically, Ray's vision of an every-member ministry did not keep him from almost ceaseless work. In addition to preaching, he was involved in teaching home Bible classes that were effective in reaching out to unbelievers. As more and more families joined the fellowship, he also worked with youth. Although no one called him "Pastor," Ray actually functioned as youth pastor, pulpit pastor, and outreach pastor at the same time. As a result, he saw very little of his family in those early days.

While the ministry flourished, Ray's relationship with Elaine suffered.

Family Life

NEITHER RAY NOR ELAINE had entered marriage with a solid understanding of what a marriage should be. Elaine's parents were not compatible, and she had learned from an early age to play the role of peacemaker. Ray had been abandoned by his father and emotionally neglected by his mother. He had grown up primarily with men and simply never had learned to understand and communicate with women. From the beginning of their marriage, therefore, he tended to bury himself in his work to the neglect of his wife.

"When I came out to the Islands, he was so busy, and I didn't have any friends," Elaine says, reflecting on their first months of married life in Hawaii. "I felt so lost... I remember crying all night long. It just wasn't what I thought it was going to be. It wasn't deliberate neglect on Ray's part; he just didn't know. He really didn't know what to do and how to be a friend."[6]

Ray and Elaine also had been taught that a biblical marriage was one in which the husband, as head of his wife, was superior to her and should control her in every way. Elaine recalls how early-on this thinking affected their ability to communicate.

"Ray had been trained that he was to tell me what to do—that is what he had been told was the biblical role of the head of the house. If I didn't do it, then it was a disobedience problem. So you really can't communicate in that situation because all the guilt is one-sided.... It doesn't make for good communication. It doesn't train you how to exchange ideas and hear one another.... He thought he was doing the right thing; I couldn't convince him otherwise. I tried a few times and it didn't work, so I gave up and sulked."[7]

Ray and Elaine's struggle to communicate affected their spiritual lives as well. Ray believed that a husband was responsible for his wife's spiritual condition. Early in their marriage, he tried to lead the two of them in Bible study.

"We tried to study together when we were first married," Elaine recalls. "He didn't expect me to make any contributions. I was just supposed to be taught. I was not submissive enough for that. I wanted to be a part of it, and I have always been a pretty good thinker.... So after a few tries, we didn't study together. That didn't help our communication either."[8]

At this point in their relationship, Elaine's understanding of what it meant to be a good wife was to simply care for the children and be supportive of her husband's ministry, which was what many ministry wives did in the 1950s. This was not something she did reluctantly, for she believed they were a team when it came to ministry. When she felt the Lord speaking to her on her knees in Hawaii, saying, "And this is the way it's going to be," she understood that to mean that Ray did not belong to her; he belonged to the ministry God had for him and to whatever the Lord was doing in his life.[9] In later years, Ray and Elaine's view of marriage would mature and ultimately become more biblical, and Ray learned to insist that the young pastors who came to work at PBC put their families first.

Elaine's family kept her busy. In 1953, her mother came to live with them. Then, while Sheila and Susan were in their preschool and elementary school years, another daughter, Linda, was born to Ray and Elaine on May 7, 1954.

The man who had planned to have four sons was now living with five females! And despite his busy schedule, Ray did manage to spend time with his precious girls and sometimes found special ways of doing this. For example, he told his daughters that when they turned eight, they could have an airplane trip with him—a promise he kept to each one. He also made up a song for each of the girls and would sing it to them: "Sheila Rita, life is sweeta...," "Susanvanduzen is the girl of my choosin'...," "Linda, did y' hear those mockin' birds sing last night; they was singin' so sweet in the moonlight..." And, later, after their daughter Laurie was born, "Little Annie Laurie is my sweetheart...."

Sheila, the firstborn, remembers her dad being a firm disciplinarian, but with a very tender and sweet side as well. Born with an adventurous spirit like her father, Sheila recalls the special times they had together when she was a child.

"Maybe during that time Dad saw in me the potential to be his companion in adventure, since I was always begging him to take me wherever he went. Soon I received my very first .22 rifle—a gift from Dad that I treasured like bags of gold! I was ten years old and felt very grown-up because my dad thought I was mature enough to handle a gun." Ray would take Sheila to the mud flats of the Bay for target practice on Saturdays, and before long he allowed her to hunt pheasant and rabbits with him.

"When I turned twelve," says Sheila, "Dad bestowed on me a .410 shotgun. Now I was really living! We would go duck hunting together now—hiding in the blinds—in our own adventure together! When I was fourteen, he took me on horseback up into the hills above Santa Rosa to hunt deer. I thought I had died and gone to heaven! Never once did Dad show any fear that I would mess up and shoot wrong. He was a very patient teacher and I felt so confident that I would always be safe beside my dad. To me, he was the great white hunter who could conquer any enemy of any size."[10]

A Flourishing Ministry

THE POSTWAR YEARS BROUGHT tremendous spiritual hunger, and the ministry of PBF flourished. The home Bible studies proved to be a perfect way to meet this need. In his book, *Body Life*, Ray reflected on the effectiveness of these small groups.

"Typical of our early small groups were the Home Bible Classes. The primary goal of Home Bible Classes was not to teach Christians, but to attract non-Christians and interest them in the themes of the Bible and in spiritual truth. These groups were deliberately low-key and non-threatening in approach. There was a total absence of activities with a 'churchy' flavor, such as hymn-singing, opening prayer, chairs lined up in rows, or a speaker standing behind a lectern. Each group had a host and hostess who opened their home to friends and guests, giving the class the welcoming feel of a purely social occasion. A lay teacher taught from the Bible, seeking to capture the biblical concepts and express them in contemporary terms. Discussion was invited—freewheeling and no-holds-barred. Anyone was free to challenge what was presented if they cared to, and their challenges were listened to carefully and courteously. An answer was sought from the Scriptures themselves.

"These meetings were an instant success and became so popular that the discussion would sometimes involve scores and even hundreds of people (we had some very large homes available!) and would often continue until the wee hours of the morning. No mention was ever made of PBC at these home meetings, for they were regarded as the personal ministry of the Christians involved. There were soon many new converts coming from these classes, who were then urged to become active in a local church, preferably one close to them. Thus the whole body of Christ in our area began to profit from these classes, and many of the new converts naturally ended up at PBC."[11]

These Home Bible Classes, coupled with Ray's hard work, soon resulted in a fellowship bursting at the seams, and PBF hired a staff member to minister to the youth. The small room they rented at the Community Center was no longer adequate. First they moved to Palo Alto's social hall and then to the city's theater. Finally, in February 1952, the group purchased a three-and-one-half acre lot in what seemed at the time to be the far fringes of Palo Alto.

On November 7, 1954, PBF had a groundbreaking ceremony, and on June 15, 1955, they held their first meeting in the new building. Four days later, Dr. J. Vernon McGee preached at the first Sunday service, held in the evening. Suddenly the fellowship that "didn't want to be a church" looked more and more like a church, and there was no question who the pastor was.

Fresh Thinking About the Church

SOME OF RAY'S EARLY preaching at PBF sounded typical of what he was—a young man fresh from seminary. His earliest sermon in print is an exposition of Hebrews 6:1–12, "The Supreme Need for Fruit Bearing." The sermon contains virtually no illustrations, little application, and dense exegesis replete with Greek verb tenses. In the latter half of the 1950s, however, Ray's style began to change. On April 29, 1956, he preached on "The Christian and Worldliness," a sermon full of practical applications, illustrations, and personal transparency. It also had a radical edge as Ray challenged the traditional understanding of worldliness: "The truth is that worldliness is not a matter of things, of doing this, or doing that. But worldliness is a matter of the attitude of the heart, the attitude of life in thinking and dealing with things."

Ray then went on to offer a radical challenge to the church to be distinct from the world but not separate from it. "We're not to be thinking like the world, you see; our attitude is different. Our thoughts are different. And yet we're to be with them.

"We're to be out-and-out Christians. Distinct but not distasteful. We're to be sheep among wolves, as our Lord says. That is, we're not to stay in the sheepfold. We're disobedient if we stay in the sheepfold.... He wants us out among the wolves, boldly out there.

"Well, you say, isn't that dangerous for sheep to go out in the midst of wolves? Yes, it is. Of course it is. But that's the thing that makes it gripping, vital, interesting, challenging, stimulating. It's this danger!

"The Lord wants us to live on a frontier where we're constantly under danger, and we'll be safe just as long as we're loyal to the Shepherd and never begin to think or act like a wolf. When we do that, we're really in trouble. But as long as we think and act like a sheep, we're safe among the wolves."[12]

In 1957, this sermon became an article published in *The King's Business*, the monthly magazine of Biola Bible College. When this appeared in print, one group at a well-known evangelical church in Los Angeles gathered all the copies they could find and held a book-burning ceremony! These Christians insisted on total separation and simply did not agree with Ray's emphasis on being "in the world but not of the world."

PBF was developing into a church, and as it did, Ray also needed to address issues such as church government in his preaching. Yet even in doing this, he continued to exhibit a fresh approach to church doctrine. In the late 1950s, Ray preached a sermon explaining and defending his conviction that Christ was the only head of the church and that the church should not be governed by the people as a democracy, or even by the clergy. Instead, the Lord "chooses to make His will known through men whom He designates and equips to carry on the spiritual oversight of His work." He went on to explain how these men were sometimes called "elders" in the New Testament, and at other times were called "bishops" or "overseers." Ray was convinced, even at this early stage of his ministry, that together these men were to shepherd the flock of God, seeking the mind of the Lord for the church through unanimous agreement. Although Ray was not the first man to uphold such a model, what made his position unique was his absolute conviction that Christ was the living Head of the body.

"How comforting it is to know that we are not left to run things ourselves.... When problems come before the church, we do not need to stew and fret and attempt to solve them ourselves. We are, of course, to investigate and discuss and plan. The Lord wants us to know what is happening. We are to look into matters to see what the underlying principles affecting them may be. The Lord does not work apart from us, but through us. But in the final analysis, we are not to listen to the voice of the people; we are to listen only to the voice of the Lord. We can be sure that when He is in the midst of His church, direction will be given.

"This church is not ours, it is His church. It was bought with His blood. He cleansed it and purified it by His Word. He appointed its ordinances. He is the one who has chosen those to guide in spiritual matters and has equipped them with the necessary qualifications to do the work. It is the Lord who has distributed the talents of gifts and ministry among the whole congregation so that each one has a special talent, a special gift to be exercised in the ministry of the church."[13]

The New Covenant

IN THE LATE 1950S RAY also began to develop his thinking about what he later called "The New Covenant." The basic premise of the New Covenant is that the believer is indwelt with the living presence of Jesus Christ and that the ability to live the Christian life comes not through self-effort but through the sufficiency of Christ. Bob Roe, a long-time associate of Ray's, summed up the New Covenant this way: "Christ died that I might live. I must die that Christ might live in me."

Actually, Ray had begun thinking about this subject during his years in Hawaii. "I will never forget how, as a young man in the service during World War II, I was on a watch one night, reading the book of Romans," he said, in commenting on Paul's statement in Romans 6:14: "Sin shall not have dominion over you, for you are not under law but under grace" (NKJV). This verse leaped out at him, and the Spirit made it come alive. "And I saw the great promise that all the things I was struggling with as a young man would ultimately be mastered—not because I was so smart, but because God was teaching me and leading me into victory. I remember walking the floor, my heart just boiling over with praise and thanksgiving to God. I walked in a cloud of glory, rejoicing in this great promise: 'Sin shall not have dominion over you, for you are not under law but under grace.'"[14]

At Dallas Seminary, Ray had the opportunity to refine his understanding of the New Covenant under the tutelage of men like Lewis Sperry Chafer, who wrote in his book *Grace*: "They [the fruit of the Spirit] are never gained by struggle, long or short; they are the immediate experience of every believer who comes into right adjustment with the Spirit. Therefore the way to a victorious life is not by self-development; it is through a 'walk in the Spirit.'"[15]

During his first decade at PBF, Ray's understanding of the New Covenant was also sharpened by others. In 1957, he began a correspondence with Miles Stanford on the subject of what Stanford called "the Deeper Life." Stanford was a well-known dispensationalist teacher and author, his best-known book being *The Green Letters*, published in 1963. The correspondence between Ray and Miles Stanford reveals that there were many things about the Deeper Life movement with which Ray agreed. He concurred with the need to deal with the roots of sin and not just the symptoms, the need to appropriate the indwelling life of Christ, and the inability of the human will to obey the Word of God by itself. He confessed to Stanford, "I learned the truth of these realities years ago and have lived in the light and blessing of them for a long time. I do not say I have yet attained, but I press on to the mark."[16]

But Ray also took issue with some aspects of the Deeper Life movement and was straightforward regarding these matters, though remaining warm and cordial. For one thing, he did not like the designation "Deeper Life" because it implied a superior sanctity, and he disagreed with the notion that the believer was passive in the process of sanctification.

"For years that kind of definition kept me from realizing the values of Christ's work for me because it implies that the will is to be somehow disconnected and God is going to come in and work apart from the believer's own desire or will," he wrote to Stanford. "However, when I learned that faith is not getting out of the way but getting right into the very purpose of God and willing to do the thing He says to do because He says it, then I achieved the victory I long sought."[17]

Ray also took issue with Stanford's emphasis on the need for a human teacher in learning the truths of the Deeper Life, believing that the Word of God was sufficient means for the Spirit to use in leading a person in understanding these truths.

"I am also surprised to see that you seem to feel that these truths which you call deeper truths cannot be known apart from personal teaching (by writings or otherwise) by someone who had already learned these," he wrote to Stanford. ". . . My own experience has been that after years of nominal Christianity it was when I first began to honestly face the word of God and walk in its light that I began to experience victory in the things of the flesh. When you quote believers as asking, 'Why have I had to struggle and fail against sin and self all these years?' I would say the simple answer is because they have not read nor heeded their Bibles. . . . I am confident that an honest hunger for the Word of God will result in giving the Holy Spirit all He needs to be able to lead that person into a full and complete experience of a life of victory."[18]

Despite these convictions, Ray's understanding of the New Covenant was still a work-in-progress. Then, after a four-year hiatus in their correspondence, Ray wrote Stanford in August of 1961, telling him that through his own study of Paul in the Corinthian letters he had come to see "the very truths which you labored to acquaint me with." Although he still did not like the term Deeper Life, Ray admitted that he "could not help but rejoice at the very way God has taught me the very truths which you graciously set before me. . . . I do know what you mean now."[19]

Ray's thinking in this area developed further as the result of an Overseas Crusades missionary conference in Taiwan at which he spoke in the summer of 1960. Arranged by Dick Hillis, whom Ray had met through the Navigators while in Hawaii, this was Ray's first major speaking engagement outside the United States. Major

W. Ian Thomas, founder of the Torchbearers, was scheduled to speak with Ray, and the two men developed a close relationship. Ray found in Thomas's teaching on "The Saving Life of Christ" the right balance of biblical and experiential truth.

"It was the way Ian Thomas framed it; it just fell in place for Ray," Elaine recalls. "When he came back, I could hear the difference in his preaching right away."[20]

Ray later invited Thomas to come to PBF as a visiting speaker and often quoted him in reference to his New Covenant teaching. "Major Ian Thomas has written some excellent summaries of the Christian's relationship to Jesus Christ," Ray said in a sermon in November of 1963. "He wrote this about Christ: 'He had to be what he was to do what he did... And he had to do what he did that we might have what he is.' There is the glory—the good news—of the gospel. It is not particularly good news to be told our sins were forgiven by the shed blood of Jesus Christ if we must then struggle on through this life doing the best we can, falling and failing, struggling and slipping, going through periods of doubt, despair, discouragement, and defeat, until at last we get over on the other side and find the releases we crave. That is not very good news, is it? But that was never intended to be the gospel. The good news is that not only does final fulfillment await us over there, but that right now we may have what he is."[21]

While in Taiwan, Ray had an opportunity to learn from experience the truths he was hearing. He was to teach six hundred Chinese pastors through two interpreters, and he took comfort in the fact that a veteran missionary like Dick Hillis would be there to help him along. But the Lord had other plans. Dick was forced to return to the States when his mother became ill, and Ray was left alone to handle the conference.

"I have never forgotten the depression and loneliness that came over me," Ray later reflected. "I am sure that is how Paul must have felt as he was left alone in Corinth."[22] And like Paul, Ray learned through experiences like this one that his adequacy did not come from himself or from any man, but from God.

With the foundations of the New Covenant in place, Ray took some time to reflect on his first ten years of ministry at PBF. He had every reason to believe that the people he shepherded were learning that they "might have what He is." In a 1960 sermon entitled "Ten Remarkable Years," Ray commented on two signs of health in the body. The first sign was unity: "Ten happy, healthy years. Mutual concern, quick response to needs, frank discussion, forgiving attitudes." The second sign was influence, which he attributed to a Bible-centered ministry, adherence to the ministry of the saints, and seeking the mind of the Lord with unanimity.

He also issued a statement of vision for the next ten years. Instead of growing to over a thousand people, he wanted PBF to reproduce new church bodies and train young men for missions and pastorates.[23]

What Ray could not have anticipated is the way God would use the tumultuous sixties to change PBF and to deepen his own understanding and experience of the New Covenant.

SIX

A Steward of the
Mysteries of God

On Ray Stedman's tombstone in Grants Pass, Oregon, are engraved these words, placed there at his request: "He was a faithful steward." Ray received many accolades during his lifetime, but he wanted to be remembered as simply a servant who faithfully dispensed God's glorious truth to God's people. His sense of calling and self-identity came directly from 1 Corinthians 4:1: "Let a man regard us in this manner, as servants of Christ, and stewards of the mysteries of God" (NASB). Thus, Ray's stewardship was defined by his exposition of God's Word. From the very beginning of his ministry, this was his purpose.

"By the time I graduated from seminary," he explained, "I was already deeply immersed in the world of biblical exposition; I believed in it and I was anxious to get my teeth into it. Then I came to Palo Alto to a church that had just begun. In fact, it was not even a church when I arrived. I didn't actually come as a pastor but as a director of activities. During this time I eagerly began to go through books of the Bible and preach from them, using much material from others, but about four months after I arrived I found my barrel was totally dry. I had to dig in and begin to learn for myself what the text of Scripture actually said and how it related to contemporary life."[1]

The Hard Work of Exposition

THIS PROCESS OF DIGGING into and teaching the Scripture would require the best of his time and energies, but Ray saw this work as essential to the building of a healthy church: "The only thing clear to me at the time of my arrival was a deep conviction *derived from Ephesians 4,* that the work of the ministry belonged to the people and not to the pastor. I was rather vague as to what that ministry was, but felt from the first that my task as pastor was to unfold the Word of God in its fullness, as best I could understand it, and leave to laymen the major responsibility for visitation of the sick, presiding at and leading church services and evangelizing the world [emphasis added]."[2]

Ray's convictions about biblical exposition came from many sources. Certainly, as mentioned in previous chapters, Ray was influenced greatly during his time in seminary by Drs. Chafer, McGee, and Ironside. But even prior to his years at Dallas, Ray was becoming convinced about the primacy and power of exposition. "I first came to understand and value expository preaching from the writings of G. Campbell Morgan, the prince of English expositors in the early decades of the 20th century. I ran across his books while trying to teach an evening Bible study class of sailors at Pearl Harbor during World War II. I learned from him not only how to discover the patterns of thought-development in a biblical passage, but how to organize those patterns into contemporary presentations that would touch directly upon the issues of life today. In forty years of preaching and teaching I have never been able to match Morgan's beauty of language and richness of literary allusions, but I have had him continually before me as a model to follow."[3]

Biblical exposition means different things to different people. Ray defined exposition as "preaching that derives its content from Scripture directly, seeking to discover its divinely intended meaning, to observe its effect upon those who first received it, and to apply it to those who seek its guidance in the present."[4]

Ray also understood the dangers of a mechanical view of exposition. Expositional preaching "is definitely not a dreary, rambling, shallow verse-by-verse commentary, as many imagine," he said. "Nor is it a dry-as-dust presentation of academic biblical truth, but a vigorous, captivating analysis of reality, flowing from the mind of Christ by means of the Spirit and the preacher into the daily lives and circumstances of twentieth-century people."[5]

From the onset of his ministry, Ray's method was to preach through entire books of the Bible. He would often alternate between the Old and New Testaments so that his congregation would receive a "balanced diet" of God's Word. "This has great advantages over textual preaching in that it forces one to handle the difficult themes of Scripture as well as the more popular ones. Further it keeps truth in balance since it follows the pattern of Scripture itself in mingling several themes in one passage, and thus makes possible the apostolic goal of 'declaring the whole counsel of God.'"[6]

But Ray also understood that the congregation could become weary if a series grew too long. So he would sometimes break off one series in favor of another, and then later return to finish the first series.[7] Often during these interludes he would address some current issue or theological question that was relevant to his congregation.

Expositional preaching of this kind requires a great deal from the preacher, and Ray was willing to pay the price. After choosing a book of the Bible based on the needs of the congregation and the current cultural climate, Ray would read through the book several times in different translations. From these readings he derived a general outline of the book to guide his preaching. He would then plan to preach through each major division of the book, choosing passages that established a single main theme and were short enough to adequately interpret in a thirty-to-forty minute sermon. Finally, after studying the historical background of the passage, together with any lexical or grammatical issues, Ray created a detailed exegetical outline of the passage so he could put the truth of the text into his own words and reveal the logical development of the writer's thought. Ray called this outline "the backbone" of his message. He also consulted commentaries to reexamine his own exegesis and gain added insight.

At this point, with eight to ten hours of work already invested, Ray felt strongly that his preparation was only half done. He had his content, but he did not yet know how he was going to present it. Therefore, his next step was to decide what to include and what to omit from his sermon, then to add illustrations, an introduction, and a conclusion to his sermon notes. Although Ray took these notes to the platform when he preached, he tried to know his material so well that he needed only the briefest glimpse to stay on course. Ray believed that eye contact was crucial to any message, and through the years many have commented on his warm, but piercing eyes.[8]

Ray would complete a sermon by Friday afternoon or Saturday morning so that he could leave his notes alone for at least half a day before preaching. This was the time when he prepared his heart and body through rest, prayer, and other work that took his mind away from the sermon.

"Following this approach, through the years I have gained a growing sense of the grandeur of preaching," Ray reflected in later years. "I have seen many examples of its power to transform both individual lives and whole communities. I have increasingly felt a divine compulsion to preach, so that I know something of Paul's words, "'Woe is me if I preach not the gospel!' But even more—I feel a deeply humbling conviction that I could never be given a greater honor than the privilege of declaring 'the unsearchable riches of Christ.' I often hear in my inner ear the words of the great apostle: 'This is how one should regard us; as servants of Christ and stewards of the mysteries of God!' A servant of Christ! A steward of the mysteries! I can think of no greater work than that."[9]

ALTHOUGH RAY WORKED HARD at his preaching, he was not a strict homiletician, as others will attest. David Roper, then a recent graduate of Dallas Theological Seminary, arrived at PBC in 1960 and played an important role there for the next twenty years, preaching when Ray needed to be absent. During those years, David says, he does not recall Ray ever explaining to him how to put a message together or even critiquing him. But he does remember Ray breaking many of the homiletic rules they had learned in seminary.[10] For example, Ray's preaching occasionally lacked organization and cohesion, and at times it seemed like just a running commentary on the text. Also, Ray's sermons often did not begin with a carefully crafted introduction or end with a memorable conclusion that emphasized the main theme of the message.

Howard Hendricks saw this as a weakness in Ray's preaching, but adds, "Weakness is a relative term. I'm well organized in preaching. Ray used to tell me, 'Man, I wish I could preach like you do—you're able to put it down....' But Ray was more of a storyteller type... he'd weave and maybe his outline didn't necessarily fit.... people had a hard time following him unless they got infected with his style and how he did it."[11]

Despite Ray's occasional lack of organization, Brian Morgan, who interned and later pastored alongside Ray at PBC, remembers him as a master at bringing needs to the surface, especially in his introductions. "The most powerful sermon I ever heard him give was to a group of pastors on the nature of discipleship." Ray began by writing five things on a napkin.

"First he created the need. Instead of saying we are going to talk about discipleship, he started talking about the present evil, especially in California... divorce, cults, etc." Then Ray asked, "How are we going to change lives?" He made an historical transition by referring back to Jesus' day and how evil was escalating, and then he went on to give the five steps of discipleship. "Five hundred preachers are listening... and he's preaching from a napkin!" says Morgan. "That sermon—not only the message but the form—shaped me, and I still basically use that kind of methodology. But I'll never forget the difference between Ray's approach and the other teachers who basically came in and just started teaching a topic without even really creating a need, asking a question or using language with questions people aren't asking today—a lot of seminary jargon."[12]

Simplicity and Sincerity

EVEN IF PEOPLE COULD not always follow Ray's train of thought, his warm conversational style drew people in. J. I. Packer described Ray's preaching style as "to chat it over with the congregation."[13] Ray's voice was soft, yet rich and commanding. His cadence was natural and his pace tended to be slow. As time went on, he seldom stood behind a pulpit.

"I always felt like he was talking to me," David Roper remembers. "He was in a conversation with me... a fireside chat or something. There was no artifice with Ray; there was no pretense; he was just old Ray with a gravy spot on his sweater. And he'd just stand up there and talk to you. And you knew that this guy understood life, he understood me, he understood the Word."[14]

Packer adds, "Right from the first sentence you knew this chap was a very attractive human being who had been where you were, who understood people like you.... Few preachers I know have had as much honest, unpretentious humanity to them."[15]

Ray's low-key style was a direct result of his conviction that preachers far too often rely upon the flesh. He believed that all ministry should be characterized by simplicity. "When I look at Christianity today," he said in one sermon, "I am sometimes appalled at the degree that we depend upon the flesh. I am amazed and intrigued as we look at the Scriptures to see that God always works in simplicity and with a low-keyed approach. God loves that. Our attempts, and the flesh's attempts, are almost always characterized by high gear, high promotion, and complexity. I learned long ago that when things start getting very complex, when you need finely tuned organizations to carry them out and hundreds of people—somehow you've missed it; for God's work is characterized by simplicity."[16]

Ray's simplicity and lack of pretense also communicated sincerity and concern. Dr. Bill Lawrence came to PBC as an intern in 1964 and immediately noticed this. "What you see is what you get. His sincerity is something everybody was attracted to."[17] It was this quality, along with Ray's genuine concern for others, that allowed him to communicate effectively to skeptics and to those whose lifestyles were at odds with the very truths he taught. "I think his great ability was his ability to accept people," says Howard Hendricks, "even people who didn't agree with him or didn't understand him."[18]

One outstanding example of this, says Dave Roper, was Ray's manner when given the microphone at a meeting of the Gay People's Union at Stanford University. "Ray could be so . . . sweet. I don't know how else to say it. He just had a gentle way of talking and he had very kind eyes. He would state truth—I mean truth that would really inflame the crowd, but he would state it in such a way . . . they sensed he loved them. When it was over they gave him an ovation and a number of people came to him. . . . Non-Christians were not the enemy. . . ."[19]

But the simplicity and sincerity of Ray's style should not be confused with shallowness of content. He had an uncanny ability to relate truth to life. When David Roper joined the staff of PBC, he was no stranger to good preaching. He had recently graduated from Dallas Seminary and had grown up listening to his father preach at Scofield Memorial Church in Dallas. Nevertheless, when

David heard Ray preach, he sensed something different. "He was able to relate truth to life. That's what first impressed me about Ray.... I'd never heard anyone preach quite like that—to clearly show how the Scripture relates to life."[20]

A Master Illustrator

PART OF RAY'S ABILITY to relate truth to life lay in his skill at using illustrations. Most of Ray's illustrative references came out of everyday life—often his own life. He was an acute student of life and people, and he also drew heavily from his experience growing up in Montana. In a sermon from Hebrews, for example, he used the following illustration in comparing Moses, the servant, with Jesus, the Son:

> When I was a boy in Montana I was invited to visit a well-known, wealthy ranch, by one of the hired men. As we came up to an imposing ranch house, he did not take me into the house: instead, he took me to the bunkhouse out in back. I asked him what it was like in the ranch house, and he said, "Well, I can't take you in there; that belongs to the family."
>
> I saw a beautiful palomino horse in the pasture, and I told him how I would love to ride on that horse. And he said, "I'm sorry, you can't; that belongs to the family." All day long, I was frustrated, because everything I wanted to do, he could not let me do, because he was only a hired man.
>
> But later on, I got to know the son of that family, a boy of my own age, and do you know what we did? We rode that palomino horse all over the place, and we went into the house, and we even went into the kitchen and helped ourselves to food in the refrigerator—anything we wanted—and we made ourselves perfectly at home. A son has greater liberty than a servant. Moses was just a servant, but Jesus was the master.[21]

Ray also was an avid reader, and many of his illustrations came from the books he enjoyed. Ray loved history, and he would mine these books for sermon material. In a sermon on a passage from 1 Timothy, Ray used the life of Abraham Lincoln as an illustration of how personal suffering shapes a person.

You never really get to know anybody until you know what he has been through. Recently I read the book by Elton Trueblood, *Abraham Lincoln, Theologian of American Anguish*. The book traces the years of Lincoln's presidency, a time when he was growing by leaps and bounds in Christian stature as a mature believer in Christ. The key to his growth was the personal anguish he suffered. Not only was there the terrible pressure of the War between the States—he took very personally and felt very keenly the awful bloodbath the nation was passing through as thousands of boys from both North and South were dying on the fields of battle—but his . . . son, his beloved 12-year-old Willie, died while he was president. There were also the daily vituperative attacks of the press upon him. He was lampooned, ridiculed, mocked, and insulted in most of the papers. There was widespread opposition against him.

Rather than crushing him, rather than making him react with anger, bitterness, and vituperation in return, however, all of this humbled Lincoln. As he himself put it, "I was often driven to my knees with the overwhelming conviction that I had nowhere else to go." If you . . . visit the Lincoln Memorial and read there the words of the Second Inaugural Address . . . you will see that through all the agony, the pressure, and the anguish that he underwent, Lincoln came to understand and to see more clearly, perhaps, than many of his successors the sovereignty of God in national affairs; how the hand of God was governing the conduct of the war and bringing about judgment on a people that would result in righteousness, justice, and truth in the land again.[22]

Sometimes Ray's illustrations involved taking a simple metaphor and expanding upon it. In a sermon he preached in 1962, Ray likened life to a funnel.

> Somebody has said that life is like a funnel: There are two ends to a funnel; you can enter it at either end. The non-Christian . . . is constantly seeking to fling back the bars and to enjoy life at its fullest. So he enters the broad end of the funnel, and as he proceeds, he finds that, inexorably, it grows narrower and narrower and more limited and restricted, until, at last, it is nothing but a tiny narrow aperture where there is hardly room to live, and it is not worth the effort. This is why so many finally blow their brains out—take their own life—because life is no longer worth living, it has become so restricted and narrow and limited. But the Christian life is like entering the other end of the funnel. At first it seems narrow. At first it seems like you are being denied some things. But as you go on, it begins to broaden out, becoming wider and wider, until, at last, as the apostle says, "all things are yours"—the universe and all that is in it. . . . That is the effect of faith.[23]

Ray not only excelled at using augmented stories and metaphors, he also mastered brief, concrete images that stuck in the minds of his listeners. When he preached on the parable of the unrighteous judge, he said, "Who can be more hard-boiled and unyielding than a judge, and an unrighteous judge, especially? Here is a tough, hard-bitten, self-centered old skinflint with a heart as cold as a bathroom floor at two o'clock in the morning!"[24] In the conclusion of another sermon, he cautioned against taking the call of God to live a Christian life in a godless world as "something to do on weekends, a low-calorie dessert to add to life to make it more agreeable."[25]

Ray also loved to use poetry in his sermons. He possessed what others believed was a photographic memory, so these poems were almost always offered without notes. One of his favorites illustrates the love of God:

> *Isn't it odd,*
> *that a being like God,*
> *Who sees the facade,*
> *still loves the clod*
> *He made out of sod:*
> *Now isn't that odd?*[26]

On another occasion he used a poem to illustrate self-centered life controlled by the flesh:

> *I had a little tea party this afternoon at three.*
> *'Twas very small, three guests in all,*
> *Just I, myself, and me.*
> *'Twas I who ate the sandwiches*
> *And I drank up the tea.*
> *'Twas also I who ate the pie*
> *And passed the cake to me.*[27]

The Authority of Obedience

ULTIMATELY, THOUGH, RAY'S effectiveness as a preacher was not a matter of his conversational style or his ability to illustrate, but his character. First and foremost, Ray was a man of integrity. When he spoke, people had a sense that he lived out the truths he was preaching. On one occasion he said, "I have never dealt with a book of the Bible without having to stop in the preparation of the message to kneel in prayer and confess to God and deal with something in my own heart."[28]

David Roper, who had ample opportunity to observe Ray in the pulpit, believes Ray possessed "the authority of obedience": "He was a man who was obedient to the truth, and that gave him a... weightiness; what the Old Testament called 'glory' in the sense of weight. You had to listen to what he said because you knew that if he wasn't already obedient, he was moving toward obedience in those areas."[29]

Because of his integrity, people trusted Ray. "I think his character affected his preaching in the sense that it was the underlay of the whole ministry that he had," says Howard Hendricks. "I saw it in his leadership. I saw it in his preaching. I saw it in the boards that we served under.... he was trusted by people. Ray wouldn't promise something that he wouldn't produce, if it was humanly possible."[30]

Ray's integrity as a preacher is illustrated by an event that took place early in his ministry when he was invited to speak at his first Bible conference.

> You know what that does to a preacher? He wants so much to succeed, to do a great and wonderful thing, to preach a great and powerful message that will never be forgotten. I had prepared and worked very hard on a message about the revelation of God in the world of nature. I thought I could preach a powerful message that would sway the people, but everything came apart. I could not say anything right, the message ground on and on, and when I finally finished, I stumbled out of that place into the dark. I walked around the corner of the lake, dejected, feeling lower than the proverbial snake's belly.
>
> Standing on the other side of the lake in a swampy kind of place, with croaking frogs all around me, I heard the voice

of God—a still small voice that said to me, in the words of Scripture, "He that thinks he knows something, knows nothing yet as he ought to know it." And then the Lord gave me three things that have guided my ministry ever since.

Those three things were: First, never be concerned with how many people you're preaching to, whether it's two or three, or two or three hundred, preach the message God gives you. Second, never be concerned with how much they're going to give you when you get through. Third, never be concerned with how well you think you've done.

"I can't say that I've always followed those," Ray admitted, "but when I've departed from them I've felt the Spirit of God depart from me as well. When I've been faithful to them, I've left it up to God and He's done His usual wonders with some very feeble work on my part."[31]

Ray's integrity was balanced by his humility. "His humility stands out for me," Roper remembers. "Jesus says, come to me because I am meek and lowly in heart. To me the best communicators are humble. Ray was never threatened by anyone else's success. He was always happy when somebody else got recognition."[32] Charles Swindoll puts it even more succinctly: "Ray never pulled rank, never polished his own trophies."[33] Ray's humility was often seen in his ability to laugh at himself. On one occasion, after a fan was installed in the ceiling above the pulpit, Ray stood in front of his congregation, looked up at the fan and said, "Well, now when they talk about the 'Big Blower,' I'll know they aren't talking about me."[34]

At times, however, his sense of self-deprecation took a more serious note, as it does at one point in his book *Body Life*:

Again, the ministry of shepherding and teaching must be done without desiring personal glory. How well pastors know that right here is where the full force of temptation to pride can strike! There is something very pleasing to the ego to stand in front of others and have every eye fastened on you and every ear open to what you have to say. It is terribly easy to begin to crave that feeling and to find subtle ways of nurturing and encouraging it.

As a pastor I must confess that I had to stop the practice of going to the door after a service and greeting people as they went out. I found that when I did it regularly, it fed my ego in such a way that I had a terrible battle with pride. People were saying nice things to me and I found myself loving to hear them. It is very easy for a pastor or teacher to perform his ministry for hidden reasons of personal prestige or glory.[35]

The Floating Decimal Point

THE STRENGTH OF RAY'S character was matched by his tremendous intellect. Ray read widely from theological books and journals and maintained a working knowledge of the original biblical languages. He quoted from theologians such as Barth, Thielicke, and Bultmann, and he often exhibited unique insights into the text.

Unfortunately, those unique insights could also be one of his weaknesses. Ray's exegesis of the Old Testament was typological and at times even followed allegorical lines. For example, a sermon on the book of Esther, later recorded in his book *The Queen and I*, was thoroughly allegorical:

> Each of us is a king dwelling in a capital city (the body), and reigning over an empire which touches everyone we know. At the moment of your conversion, if you are a Christian, you gained a queen—a spirit made alive in Jesus Christ to serve as a place of communion between you and the Holy Spirit of the living God who dwells in your heart, symbolized in this story in the person of Mordecai.

In Chapter 3 we watch the consummate ease with which the flesh, that is, this Haman within each of us, deceives the human will into making a decision that threatens to destroy the entire kingdom. This whole story is a picture of a Christian who sincerely sins.[36]

"I'd say that is probably the one area that we disagreed on," says Howard Hendricks, commenting on Ray's hermeneutic. "I'm pretty literalistic . . . I stick pretty close to the text and I don't do much of what I'd call spiritualization. But he got into some of the books like Esther and he lost me and I used to give him gas about it."[37] Bill Lawrence calls this Ray's "floating decimal point" and attributes it to Ray's keen intellect. He also remembers a controversy that arose over Ray's interpretation of Hebrews 6.

In a notoriously difficult passage, Ray came up with a novel explanation for how it might appear that one described as a Christian could lose his or her salvation:

> If the spiritual life follows the same pattern as the physical life, we all know that physical life does not begin with birth. It begins with conception. Have we not, perhaps, mistaken conception for birth, and, therefore, have been very confused when certain ones, who seemingly started well, have ended up stillborn? Is there in the spiritual life, as in the natural life, a gestation period before birth when true Spirit-imparted life can fail and result in a stillbirth? . . . If this be the case, then the critical moment is not when the Word first meets with faith, that is conception. . . . But the critical moment is when the individual is asked to obey the Lord at cost to himself, contrary to his own will and desire. When, in other words, the Lordship of Christ makes demand upon him and it comes into conflict with his own desire and purposes, his own plans and program. . . . That is

the true moment of birth.... In grace, the Lord may make this appeal over the course of a number of years. But if it is ultimately refused, this is a stillbirth. The months, and even years, that may be spent in the enjoyment of conversion joy was simply Christian life in embryo....[38]

When Ray preached this sermon at Dallas Seminary, his unorthodox interpretation struck some of the professors as heretical. As a result, for a brief period of time Ray was not welcome at the school.[39] But it was extremely rare for Ray to venture outside the bounds of Christian orthodoxy. David Roper attributes many of Ray's unusual interpretations to Ray's breadth of understanding of the Word, what theologians call "the analogy of Scripture," which allowed him to pull things together from various parts of Scripture. The results, according to Roper, were that, "You weren't always sure how he got what he got, but what he got was biblical. It was never outside the parameters of Scripture."[40]

The Grand Themes

THROUGHOUT RAY'S FORTY YEARS of preaching at PBC and around the world, he kept returning to two grand themes: the mysteries of God and the New Covenant.

The first of those themes grew out of his own self-identity as a "steward of the mysteries of God." Ray saw the proclamation of God's Word as the unveiling of these mysteries, and he often talked about the believer's privileged position to know these mysteries. In a sermon entitled "The Secrets of God," Ray defined what he meant by God's mysteries:

Mysteries, in Scripture, are not "Who Done Its." They are not insoluble problems, strange and mysterious riddles nobody can grasp. They are secrets hidden from the general public, but available to those who are in the inner circle because they are willing to be taught by the Spirit. And they are essential to life.... they are not unfamiliar themes. They have been preached here many times. They are set before you constantly, so they won't be new and startling. But what you should think of as we go through them is: How much do I know these? How much can I handle this kind of truth? How much can I impart it? How much is it showing up in my practical daily existence? That is where these secrets become available to the world around.[41]

Ray often spoke of the mystery of the kingdom of God, the mystery of lawlessness, the mystery of godliness, the mystery of the future, and the mystery of God. He believed that to understand these mysteries was to understand reality, and when people began to understand reality they would begin to live accordingly. This is the reason Ray never browbeat people with endless exhortations about being obedient, but rather focused on getting them to see what was real. "Nothing has ever commended itself more powerfully to me than to remind myself that when I step into the pulpit to open the Word of God, what I'm giving people is basic, utter, fundamental reality," he said. "When they begin to think like the Bible, they are thinking realistically. When they depart from it, they wander off into fantasies. And when you get a congregation understanding that fact, you will have some tremendous changes in congregational behavior."[42]

One of these mysteries, the mystery of godliness, constituted the second great theme of Ray's preaching. Most often Ray called this "The New Covenant," which he said "is the very heart and soul of the Word of God. It is that 'secret and hidden wisdom of God' (1 Corinthians 2:7) which Paul sets in sharp contrast with the wisdom of the world. It supplies the lost secrets of human behavior which are necessary to live as man was intended to live. Since it is grounded in the crucifixion, burial, and resurrection of Jesus, and the presence in the believer of the Holy Spirit, all other truths flow out of it, as water flows from a central spring. It exhorts us to the daily practice of our union with Christ and reminds us of the availability of his power and comfort at any moment. It should, therefore, be the chief subject in the curriculum in every church, and the central theme of most pulpit preaching. Though it is illustrated frequently in the Old Testament, it is not explained there. It is pictured by type and symbol, but the process is never made clear for it is 'the mystery... kept secret since the world began' (Romans 16:25), but now is to be made known to the nations."[43]

Because Ray viewed the New Covenant as central to the Christian life, he would often remind people of this truth even when the particular text he was preaching said nothing about it. He believed merely to exhort church members to practice godly living without an understanding of the New Covenant was to throw them back upon the flesh, "that tainted source of self-serving motivation that can produce nothing but a cheap imitation of the real thing."[44] But with an understanding of the New Covenant, individual believers, and ultimately the church, would realize their full potential as children of God.

"When individuals in a church are taught to grasp and practice this New Covenant dynamic, they become noticeably different," Ray wrote. "They are no longer spiritual cripples, needing to be coddled and catered to by the pastoral staff, but become, instead, the beautiful imagery of Jesus, 'rivers of living water,' capable of ministering to others and manifesting the refreshing qualities of love, joy, and peace to all who touch their lives. They learn to revel in the daily adventure of expecting the Lord to use them in the most ordinary activities, but producing often extraordinary results."[45]

ABOVE ALL ELSE, Ray Stedman was a preacher. There were many who were more homiletically polished, but Ray never seemed to care. His passion was to be a faithful steward of the mysteries of God, and in that regard he had few peers.

Luis Palau, who met Ray in 1960 and considered him a spiritual father, sums it up well: "He had a great mind and a transparent life, so to him what appeared obvious was not obvious to the rest of us. . . . As an expository preacher, I can't think of any weakness. I couldn't wait to hear him. I cannot think of one moral flaw in Ray Stedman. He was utterly consistent in his life and his preaching."[46]

SEVEN

The Winds of Change

Ray Stedman's commitment to expository preaching of the Scriptures remained unchanged throughout one of the most turbulent periods of American history—the sixties. The 1960s dramatically changed American society. The Civil Rights movement and the Vietnam War coincided with, or perhaps even caused, a widespread reexamination of traditional morality, and the church in America was profoundly influenced by these changes. While mainline denominations declined, many evangelical and non-denominational churches flourished.[1]

In the 1950s, these evangelicals, who were outspokenly conservative in doctrine, had rejected the sectarianism, anti-intellectualism, and cultural isolation of the fundamentalists. Evangelicals were also beginning to reflect the material prosperity being enjoyed in America, as suburban churches like Peninsula Bible Church were planted and vast resources were channeled to support parachurch ministries, mission organizations, and pilgrimages to the Holy Land.[2]

With an emphasis on eastern mysticism and self-actualization, much of the new spirituality that emerged in the culture during the 1960s was unorthodox if not heretical. There was also a reaction against this new spirituality in that a significant segment of the youth culture was attracted to a conservative form of Christianity that still allowed for countercultural expressions. These young people were part of what came to be known as the Jesus Movement in the late sixties and early seventies, a movement especially prevalent in California. "From the cradle of the counterculture in San Francisco's Haight-Ashbury to the suntanned set of California's beach scene, thousands of young people were 'turning on to Jesus,'"[3] says sociologist Ronald Enroth. Those evangelical churches and leaders pliant enough to make room for this counterculturalism were in a perfect position to benefit from these winds of change.

Ray Stedman was forty-two years old when the sixties began. With his receding hairline, Montana roots, and fundamentalist education, the man could not have seemed more ill-suited to lead a church through these turbulent times. But even in middle age, Ray always had a maverick side to him, and his fearless, creative independence served him well when it came to leading a church through this turbulent era. Thus, the 1960s were a time of growth and expansion both at PBC and in Ray's ministry.

Body Life

IN 1960 PBC WAS comprised of approximately six hundred people. By the end of the decade almost three times as many called PBC their church home, and it was known throughout the nation as a place where young people who were part of the Jesus Movement flocked. In 1972 Ray published his most popular and influential book, *Body Life*, in which he defined his vision for the church according to the pattern of Ephesians 4.

Several chapters in *Body Life* were developed from messages Ray had preached to his congregation in 1966. The final chapter, "Impact," was designed to give the reader a practical example of the outworking of the *Body Life* principles. Therefore, it serves as a retrospective look at Ray's leadership and what happened at PBC in the sixties and early seventies.

Ray wrote about what God had done at PBC with characteristic humility:

With considerable reluctance, I now turn to the experience of a single church in order to demonstrate from real life how these principles work in the modern world. The church I have in mind is the one in which I have been privileged to be a pastor-teacher for over twenty-one years (since 1950). It is the Peninsula Bible Church, located on the San Francisco peninsula, at Palo Alto, California. I am fully aware that there are many churches that could serve as illustrations of the principles we have studied, and doubtless some of them would be much clearer and better examples than the Peninsula Bible Church. But my limited experience forces me to write only about the church I know best, known familiarly to its members as PBC.

I must also make clear at the outset that by no means is PBC a perfect church. We've made many mistakes through the years and some of them have been grievous indeed. We are still very much learners, being led along by the Holy Spirit into continually unfolding vistas and clearer understanding of the principles we seek to follow. We have learned much from

Ray on the cover of the October 1971 issue of *The Wittenburg Door*, which featured a lengthy interview with him.

the experience and teaching of others, and feel most keenly our debt to members of the body elsewhere for their deeply needed ministry to us. Compared to many other churches around we have found what many regard as an enviable plateau of success; but compared to the New Testament standard, we often fall very short, and can perhaps be best described by the word of Jesus to the church at Philadelphia in Asia Minor: "Behold, I have set before you an open door, which no one is able to shut; I know that you have but little power, and yet you have kept my word and have not denied my name" (Revelation 3:8 RSV).[4]

Ray went on to describe the beginnings of PBC and the success of the Home Bible Studies in reaching unbelievers, and the subsequent development of the PBC staff. In the late 1950s PBC expanded by hiring numerous men and women to work with youth. They also called one of the five founding businessmen, Robert (Bob) Smith, to be Associate Pastor. The fact that Bob had no seminary training reflected Ray's growing conviction that men were better trained in the context of the local church than in a seminary where they were so often divorced from the practical realities of ministry. Nevertheless, a few years later, in 1961, PBC turned once again to Dallas Seminary to hire David Roper to work first with high school students, then in Christian Education, then with college students, and eventually as leader of the pastoral training ministry called Scribe School. In 1968 PBC added William Dempster to work with children, and in 1969 Ronald Ritchie, another Dallas Seminary graduate, was hired to oversee the expanding high school ministry.

This addition of staff was a relief and an encouragement to Ray, but it also added new challenges for a man who was never a strong administrator. When selecting staff, PBC operated on the principle of unanimity. Prior to hiring David Roper, for example, several men interviewed for the job, and each time the same elder opposed the hire. Ray refused to try to override the board's decision to wait. "I never saw Ray use raw power," remembers Roper. "He would never do that. He used the power of persuasion. And he was persuasive simply because he brought us back to biblical principles."[5]

Although the elders eventually agreed on hiring Roper, he recalls the unusual way he was interviewed: "I went out there and they picked me up and took me to Bob Roe's house. We sat in a circle with the elders. We introduced ourselves, and we chatted a little while, and then they asked me a question, which I began to answer. And then they got into an argument among themselves, and they never got back to me. They just ignored me. They just went on, arguing away, and I sat there thinking, *What in the world is going on?*"[6]

Ray's involvement with staff was normally "hands-off," and he did not see it as his job to disciple or manage the staff. His influence on them was mostly through staff meetings at which he would discuss the text he was to preach on the following Sunday. The outstanding thing about Ray's leadership, believes Roper, was that "he gave us such freedom; he never would coerce or second-guess us."[7] At the same time, his wisdom and character were such that his influence was unrivaled.

Ray never took the title of Senior Pastor and refused to operate on such a basis. "But, in fact, he was the senior pastor," says Roper. "And nobody would question that, simply because of his authority.... It wasn't a forced authority; it was just there. It was inherent in the man.... We'd be sitting in a board meeting, and we'd all be muddling around, and Ray had this uncanny ability to see through all the guff and just get right to the heart of an issue, because he had this breadth of biblical knowledge that he brought to bear on the problem....We'd sit there and kick something around for hours and then Ray would say, 'This is what we need to do, guys. This is where we need to go.' And we'd all say, 'You bet!'"[8]

Ray rarely critiqued sermons preached by others on the PBC staff. He encouraged them not to try to imitate him, but just to be themselves. Nevertheless, his model was a powerful influence on the young pastors. Roper remembers an important lesson he learned from Ray shortly after he came to PBC. Having been presented with a high school ministry that was bursting at the seams, David realized he was in over his head. He walked into Ray's office and complained, "Ray, I feel inadequate."

"You are," said Ray, and then went on to quote one of his favorite New Covenant verses: "Not that we are adequate in ourselves to consider anything as coming from ourselves, but our adequacy is from God" (2 Corinthians 3:5 NASB).[9]

Roper also recalls Ray's transparency and humor. On one occasion he confessed to the congregation that while speaking at a Christian conference center, he was sorely tempted to steal a coffee carafe from one of the rooms. The next day someone went out and bought Ray a beautiful carafe and placed it on his desk. The following Sunday when Ray got up the pulpit he said, "You remember last week I told you about the coffee carafe? I just want to tell you, this week I've been coveting a color television set!"[10]

A Heart to Raise Up Leaders

ONE OF THE FRUSTRATIONS fellow staff members did have with Ray, however, resulted from one of his most endearing qualities. Because of his care and concern for young men in need of spiritual fathering, Ray would often keep on staff at PBC men who in one way or another were probably not a good match for the church. Others could see the problem, but Ray just kept giving these men another chance. No doubt his own experience of having been abandoned and then adopted came into play in these circumstances. Bill Lawrence, who interned at PBC in 1964, called this phenomenon "Ray's kennel," and commented, "Like stray dogs to a kennel, he kept bringing people in, and the people in the church who had to figure out how to fund this would get real unhappy."[11]

Of course, not all of these young men were misfits in their positions. In 1958 Ray traveled to Argentina with Dick Hillis of Overseas Crusades, where he met Luis Palau, a young man who came to hear Ray speak at a theater in Buenos Aires. Palau had never heard of Ray Stedman; he came to hear him because he was under the impression that Palo Alto was somewhere near Hollywood. Luis, a native of Argentina, who was twenty-four years old at the time, was part of a separatist church, and the combination of Hollywood and the gospel sounded intriguing.

After hearing Ray speak on the believer's call to be "salt and light" in the world, Palau recognized something different about this man's teaching, and he introduced himself after the meeting. As the two men got acquainted, Ray discerned a unique giftedness in this young man and encouraged him to come to the United States to study for the ministry. When Luis said good-bye at the airport a few days later, he thought he had seen the last of Ray Stedman. But within a few days he received a letter from Ray with further encouragement to come to the States, and even an offer of financial help.

In the summer of 1960, Luis Palau came to Palo Alto and stayed for two months in the Stedman home before spending a year at Multnomah School of the Bible. The following summer, he interned at PBC and developed a relationship with Ray that was so close that Ray subsequently referred to Luis as his son and even offered to legally adopt him. As his spiritual father, Ray was ruthlessly honest with Luis. "He really worked me over and tried to get me to crucify the flesh," Luis remembers. At the same time, he always felt Ray's fatherly support. "He opened many doors and gave me credibility. I always felt he was really proud of me. My dad had died when I was ten years old, so to me he was my dad." Besides Ray's loving support, Luis learned lessons from Ray that summer about expository preaching and the New Covenant that have remained with him throughout his worldwide evangelistic ministry.[12]

Luis Palau participated early-on in the summer internship program at PBC that had begun to grow out of Ray's desire to provide practical ministry experience for seminary students, much like he'd had with Dr. McGee. As Ray and the staff quickly discovered, most of these young men and women were deficient in three major areas: an experience of walking according to the principles of the New Covenant; an understanding of spiritual gifts and how the body of Christ should operate; and the manner in which the church should relate to and impact the world around it. This program, which started with two or three interns each summer, became so popular that at one time PBC had twelve summer interns, and eventually the demand forced them to expand the internship to involve more than just one summer. By 1971, PBC had twenty-five interns who stayed at PBC for one to two years at a time. And within a few years, under the leadership of David Roper, the focus of the program, eventually called Scribe School, shifted to allow for a full two years of training, which included seminary-type instruction and mentored ministry experience with a pastor.

Scribe School was a reflection of Ray's growing conviction that not only did seminary students need practical experience, but also that pastoral training should take place exclusively in the local church. Howard Hendricks remembers well how Ray persistently tried to convince him to leave Dallas Seminary and come to PBC to train pastors. "This was not just an ancillary idea that he pulled out of a hat someplace," says Hendricks. "Every time we got together he talked about this.... This was his point: that the seminary followed the university model rather than the pastoral model. If you see it in terms of medicine, it would be ridiculous to train a guy in medicine without a hospital."[13] When it came to training pastors, Ray was way ahead of his time, because today almost all major seminaries require extensive practical ministry experience for Master of Divinity students.

Another of the internship participants was a young Dallas seminarian named Charles Swindoll, who arrived at PBC in 1961 for a summer internship. Years later, after hearing of Ray's death, Swindoll reflected on the impact that internship and thirty years of friendship with Ray had had on him. "I remember my trip with Cynthia to Palo Alto, California, and the beginning of a brief but life-changing internship with Ray. I remember those eyes that just had a way of looking right back into the rear of my cranium, as he probed me with questions about character and commitment to ministry and love for wife and family, as he challenged me to be the man that I so wanted to be and that he was.

"I thought about the laughter we had had together over three decades of time. Such a touch he had on my life.

"I thought about the times that he charged me to think theologically. I don't know of anyone I've ever known who thought theologically more than Ray Stedman. He had incredible insight into the biblical text and practical wisdom, but never an attitude of arrogance or needless dogmatism. He was a man of strong character and firm convictions, but I never knew him to be insulting or intolerant. He was comfortable being alone and often would spend hours in the books as a real student of the Scriptures. But I never found him inaccessible or aloof. He was a man's man."[14]

In 1965, Bill Lawrence, another student at Dallas Seminary, did his summer internship at PBC. Bill later went on to pastor one of the first churches that PBC planted in the Bay Area, South Hills Community Church in San Jose, and has served on the faculty of Dallas Seminary since 1981. He, too, remembers the impact of his internship and Ray's leadership. "I remember sitting in board meetings where men prayed and acted in concert together or they didn't act at all. I saw men who had been developed by a pastor who loved them and whom they respected in profound ways. I saw a staff that studied and worked together. I learned the ministry of the New Covenant, meeting with the staff for study each week under Ray's leadership. I went on the Stanford campus and saw five people come to Christ that summer—two of them later came to DTS for a time. I taught the college class and was amazed at what God did in the lives of several people in the group. All of this was life-changing in virtually every way I could think of."[15]

The influence of Scribe School also penetrated the nearby secular campus of Stanford University. In the late 1960s, several Stanford students spent their college years being mentored by David Roper and sitting under the ministry of Ray Stedman. Later, after they, too, attended Scribe School, some of these young men— including Jack Crabtree, Brian Morgan, and Steve Zeisler—went on to join the staff of PBC.

Brian Morgan, who still serves on the staff of Peninsula Bible Church, Cupertino, says, "I came to Stanford in the fall of 1968 when the campus was in the midst of revolt. But brooding over the visible chaos, which came like a whirlwind and vanished with the dawn, was an invisible revolution of a deeper kind that seized me unawares and touched me. At the center of that revolution stood Ray: Hearing his sermons on Leviticus, Romans, and Genesis. His prophetic voice, wild imagination, ringing clarity, and piercing application. Traveling with him to pastors' conferences, and conventions where you went to hear him teach, but in the process he birthed your soul into full sonship, and then lifted you up to the equality of brotherhood."[16]

Ray and His Words Travel

ALTHOUGH RAY HAD BEEN writing for small publications for some time, it was during the mid-sixties that PBC began printing his sermons, which eventually led to the publication of his books. In 1965, Peter Irish, a graduate student at Stanford, heard Ray preach from Ephesians 6 on spiritual warfare. Peter was so enlightened by what he heard that he determined to make these messages available in printed form. He organized a group of volunteers to transcribe and edit the messages, type them on stencils, and run off mimeograph copies for distribution. These printed sermons became so popular that he was encouraged to do the same with other messages, and soon Ray's sermons were traveling all over the world. As this ministry expanded, PBC purchased an offset press, Peter was brought onto staff full-time, and Discovery Publishing was born.

Ray's first book, an exposition of the Olivet Discourse called *What on Earth's Going to Happen?* was published by Regal Books. His second book, and arguably his most well-known, *Body Life*, was published in 1972 and became an influential force in evangelical church renewal during the late twentieth century. Later, many of Ray's printed sermons were edited to become books such as *Folk Psalms of Faith* (1973), *What More Can God Say? A Fresh Look at Hebrews* (1974), *Understanding Man* (1975), *Secrets of the Spirit* (1975), and *Authentic Christianity* (1975).

In the latter part of 1970, Ray and several colleagues began to talk with Paul Winslow, a successful businessman who was a part of PBC, about the administration of both Scribe School and the publishing ministry. The group met for several months as Paul gathered information, and their decision-making resulted in the birth of Discovery Foundation, Inc. Eventually, Discovery Foundation became the umbrella under which several ministries flourished. Besides Discovery Publishing and Scribe School, Discovery Art Guild, led by well-known songwriter and musician John Fischer, became a clearinghouse for Christian artists creating everything from songs to ceramic pots. Discovery Foundation also sponsored two pastors' conferences each year. Conferees came for two weeks at a time from all over the world; they were hosted by the PBC body and taught by the staff. Often Ray had met and invited these pastors while on one of his speaking trips, or sometimes they had just been lured by reading one of Ray's many printed sermons that continued to fly around the globe.

Ray's sermons were not the only things flying around the world. Ray himself traveled extensively in the sixties, often accompanied by Dick Hillis of Overseas Crusades. Often Ray would also bring along one of the PBC interns. And everywhere he traveled, speaking for various churches and Bible colleges, Ray preached on familiar themes such as the New Covenant and the proper functioning of the church as the body of Christ.

A significant amount of Ray's travel was also the result of his serving on numerous boards, including Overseas Crusades, Mount Hermon Conference Center, and Bible Study Fellowship. Ray's speaking engagements for the first half of 1968 took him to Costa Rica and Mount Hermon in January; Wheaton College, Moody Bible Institute, Forest Home Conference Center, and Simpson Bible College in February; a Mennonite conference in Dallas in March; Evangel College in April; and Mount Hermon and Forest Home in May. Later that year he traveled to South America, Europe, the Middle East, the Far East, and Southeast Asia—all in one trip!

Ray's travel did, however, create some frustrations for the staff at PBC. David Roper remembers decisions being made while Ray was gone, only to be met with his disapproval and subsequent change when he came home.[17] Nevertheless, Ray still managed to carry most of the preaching load. During the sixties, he preached through the books of Romans, Esther, Hebrews, 1 John, Ephesians, Acts, Daniel, and Genesis 1–25. He also preached expositional series on prayer, parables, spiritual warfare, Psalms, the Olivet Discourse, the Christian and possessions, and the Christian and moral conditions. In addition to his Sunday morning sermon, Ray often preached on Sunday nights, including one sermon on each of the sixty-six books of the Bible.

Stretching the Faithful

AS IS ALWAYS THE CASE, growth necessitated change, and in 1969 the church was forced to begin holding two services each Sunday morning to accommodate the growing congregation. But these changes had another wrinkle. Many of these people were not typical churchgoers, and the Jesus Movement stretched the faithful at PBC.

"When Ray and I arrived in Palo Alto in 1950, we found a city of quiet dignity, perfect climate, and quality education amid enchantingly green hills and flowering orchards," remembers Elaine Stedman. "The population was about thirty-five thousand. What a privileged environment for our two babies, eight-months and two-years, and the young couple we were. But during the children's' elementary school years this seemingly idyllic scene was invaded by air-raid alerts.... Frightened children were dismissed to their homes, fearing a bomb attack. Some people were building bomb shelters, and there was talk of erecting public facilities as well.

"Then there was Vietnam. And beatniks became hippies, the 'flower children.' The drug culture emerged, and Cubberly High School in Palo Alto became center stage for revolutionary upheaval.

"PBC, that quiet, well-ordered congregation, was caught in the middle of these baffling, frightening phenomena. Jesus Himself was asking admittance for barefoot, bearded escapees from the kingdom of darkness. With fear and trembling we opened our doors. They tinkered with our self-righteousness, infected us with their contagious excitement, and shattered our complacency. And I finally had to give up my hat and gloves."[18]

One of those "Jesus People" was Ted Wise. Ted and his wife, Elizabeth, had come to San Francisco in 1960 with "beatnik sentiments," but were soon disappointed with their lifestyle and drawn to Jesus through the reading of the New Testament and the witness of a small Baptist church in Marin County. "While on my way to my own Damascus...," says Ted, "I found it necessary to cry out to God to save my life in every sense of the word.... I could choose Him or literally suffer a fate worse than death." Soon, as many Jesus People did, Ted and Elizabeth tried to follow the lifestyle pattern of New Testament Christians. They sold all their possessions and lived communally with other Christians in Marin County. Eventually they rented a storefront in Haight-Ashbury to feed people and preach Christ.

Traditional churches did not take kindly to their living arrangement. "We naively thought they would see that we were simply doing it right," Ted remembers, "living out the New Testament in 3-D. Slim chance. Fat attitude." The one church that welcomed Ted's ministry was PBC, which invited Ted to join their staff and start a drug rehabilitation program, which he eventually did together with a counseling outreach. The beatnik from Marin County was subsequently seen frequently following hard on the heels of the Montana cowboy. "Ray Stedman became my mentor and teacher. I learned that in the beginning I had indeed read the New Testament rightly. What the Bible taught me on that first reading was that Christianity was something that was supposed to happen to me, not something I did to myself."[19]

Ray's penchant for embracing the disenfranchised drew in many who normally would not enter a church. But Ray was never one to passively wait for people to show up in the pews. Thus, in the spring of 1975 he and an intern attended a meeting of gay students at Stanford University, which featured two speakers: one a gay woman who was a professor at San Francisco State University, and the other a gay man who was ordained in the United Church of Christ. Ray listened to them speak for over an hour. The woman was vitriolic and denounced the church in almost every form. The young man was milder and told of his experience of rejection in the church.

When opportunity was given for audience participation, Ray stepped up to the microphone. "I'm Ray Stedman, the pastor of

Peninsula Bible Church here in Palo Alto," he said. "On behalf of the church, I want to apologize for much of what I've heard here today. You are right . . . the church has failed you in many ways. We oftentimes have not shown the love of Jesus." He then went on to tell about freedom from a lifestyle that ultimately is destructive. When he finished, the crowd gave him a standing ovation and many approached him for further discussion.[20]

The following Sunday Ray told the church about what had happened and described his feelings for the participants: "As I looked at that roomful of young people, I did not see a room full of lesbians and faggots, though they were calling themselves those names. I saw some hungry, mixed-up, stunted, fragmented, and hurting young people—wanting somehow to find the secret of life, thinking they had found it—but on a wrong track, and destroying themselves in the process. Over and over, Paul's words in Romans about homosexuals kept coming into my mind: 'They receive in their own persons the due penalty of their error' [cf. Romans 1:27b RSV]. The stance of the church toward those who are involved in wrongful and evil things is never to be one of denunciation. It is never to be one of stigmatizing and of rejecting. It is to be one of open-armed acceptance, but with an honest evaluation of what is going on, and the offer of the way of release."[21]

━◦◦━

PEOPLE OF EVERY WALK and experience were drawn to Ray because they could tell he genuinely cared about them, and the growing presence of these disenfranchised culminated in the Sunday evening Body Life service. Prior to this time, the Sunday evening services were typically dry, recalls David Roper, following a conventional pattern of song service, announcements, Scripture, special music, and preaching. Attendance was rather sparse, running about 150–250 with only a handful of youth present. Then in late 1969 Ray returned home from a conference and started to encourage

121

people to stand up and share honestly about how they were strug-gling in their Christian walk. It took time for the practice to take root, but the dam really broke when one prominent leader stood and shared about his battle with sexual temptation while traveling for business.[22] This practice of open sharing fit perfectly with the then-prevalent encounter group movement and the cultural empha-sis on personal transparency. It also fit well with Ray's idea of how the body of Christ should function. He took literally the principle in James 5:16, "Confess your sins to one another," and he often quoted Galatians 6:2 as a proof text for Body Life, "Bear one another's burdens, and thus fulfill the law of Christ"(NASB).

"The biblical principle of the Spirit's gifting of Christ's body for ministry created a welcoming environment for this 'invasion,'" recalls Elaine. "In the Sunday evening meetings, where we learned to iden-tify various scents, including the aroma of pot, barefoot, straggle-haired youth crammed our turf and our hearts. That astounding opportunity to combine the teaching of the Word with the sharing of life experiences marked the inception of 'body life,' a term now endemic in the evangelical vocabulary. Ray eventually wrote under that title to spread the news of God at work in His people."[23]

News of Body Life spread throughout the nation. In May 1971, *Christianity Today* reported in great detail what happened at a typ-ical Body Life service:

> It happens every Sunday night. Eight hundred or more people pack into a church auditorium designed to seat com-fortably only 750. Seventy per cent are under twenty-five, but adults of all ages, even into the eighties, are mingled with the youth, and people of widely varying cultural back-grounds all sit, sing, and pray together.
>
> A leader stands at the center front, a microphone around his neck. "This is the family," he says. "This is the body of Christ. We need each other.... Let's share with

each other." When a hand goes up toward the back of the center section, a red-haired youth runs down the center aisle with a wireless microphone. It is passed down the pew to the young man, who stands waiting to speak. "Man, I don't know how to start," he says, his shoulder-length hair shining as he turns from side to side. "All I know is that I've tried the sex trip and the drug trip and all the rest but it was strictly nowhere. But last week I made the Jesus trip—or I guess I should say that He found me —and man, what love! I can't get over it. I'm just a new Christian, but man, this is where it's at!" A wave of delight sweeps the auditorium, and everyone claps and smiles as the leader says, "Welcome to the family. What's your name?"

Other hands are waving for recognition. The leader points to a well-groomed, attractive woman in her mid-thirties. "I just wanted to tell you of the Lord's supply to me this week," she says into the mike. She is a divorcée with small children. Her income had dwindled to the point that she'd had only forty-two cents to eat on that week. But unsolicited food had come. The family had eaten plenty, and she wants to share her thanksgiving. Another enthusiastic round of applause. . . .

Other needs are shared. One youth asks for prayer that he might be able to buy a car cheaply so he won't have to depend on hitchhiking to get to his college classes on time. When the prayer is finished, a middle-aged housewife stands at the back and says, "I don't know how this happened, but just this week the Lord gave me a car I don't need. If Ernie wants it, here are the keys." She holds up a ring of keys, and the crowd applauds joyously as the boy runs to pick up the keys.

Then an offering is announced. The leader explains that all may give as they are able, but if anyone has immediate need he is welcome to take from the plate as much as ten dollars to meet that need. If he needs more than ten, he is warmly invited to come to the church office the next morning and explain the need; more money would be available there. While ushers pass the plate, a young man with a guitar sings a folk song. . . .

After the song, someone calls out a hymn number, and everyone stands to sing it together. Then the teacher for the evening takes over. There is a rustle of turning pages as hundreds of Bibles are opened. For perhaps twenty-five minutes the teacher speaks, pacing the platform, Bible in hand. He illustrates with simple human incidents, some humorous, some sobering. The crowd is with him all the way, looking up references, underlining words, writing in the margins. . . .

When the meeting is dismissed, few leave. They break up into spontaneous groups, some praying, some rapping about a Bible passage, some singing quietly with a guitar, some just visiting and sharing with one another. Gradually the crowd thins down, but it is a good hour or more before everyone is gone and the lights are turned out.[24]

Ray's independent and creative spirit made him the right man to lead the church through this turbulent era. But within his family, the sixties took a damaging toll. Indeed, in many ways, especially as husband and father, Ray was not prepared for the challenges of the sixties, and he and his family would not emerge from this decade unscathed.

EIGHT

Treasure in a Clay Pot

Ray Stedman was not just a pastor; he was also a husband and a father. And during the sixties, the two-story Stedman home on Wellsbury Way in Palo Alto bustled with the busy lives of his four daughters: Sheila, born in 1948; Susan in 1950; Linda in 1954; and Laurie in 1962.

Because of his own experiences as a child—abandoned by his father, emotionally distanced from his troubled mother, and adopted by his loving aunt and uncle—Ray was devoted to his wife and daughters. Yet these childhood experiences and their resulting emotional effect on his life also ill-equipped him to deal with many of the demands of being a husband and father. Ray tended to be emotionally disconnected with the women in his home. Consequently, it was in the family arena, more than anywhere else, where Ray experienced the truth of the New Covenant—that God's strength could be perfected only in his own weakness.

In many ways, the Stedmans were a typical suburban family of their day. They lived in a comfortable home, their daughters attended decent schools, they enjoyed family vacations, and they endured the normal squabbles associated with seven people and three generations living under the same roof. (Elaine's mother lived with them until her death in 1983.) But it was the underlying foundation of God's love and truth that held the family together.

Good Times as a Family

RAY'S DAUGHTERS HAVE ESPECIALLY fond memories of camping trips with their father. Because of her weak back, Elaine usually did not participate in these adventures, and with good reason. It was never enough for Ray to simply find a convenient campsite with all the usual amenities. Instead, he drove a borrowed Jeep or Land Rover off-road to the highest lake or remotest river in the area. Ray loved to scare the girls by making his own roads up the side of a mountain or driving as close as possible to the edge of a cliff. During the night, as the girls snuggled in their sleeping bags, Ray would playfully scratch on the outside of the tent and growl like a bear.[1]

Ray's sense of humor took various forms. On one camping trip, he stood shaving with his electric razor plugged into a tree that looked as if it might have been struck by lightning. He convinced the girls that if they ever found a tree that had been hit by lightning, they could stick an electrical plug into it and get electricity. Ray collapsed with laughter when, on their next camping trip, Susan announced she was bringing her curling iron to plug into one of those trees![2]

Ray's love of adventure and risk was revealed clearly during these outings. His daughters remember him as fearless, possessing an unshakable faith that no matter how bad a situation became, everything would somehow work out. And Ray always seemed able to escape tough situations unscathed. On one occasion he took Elaine and Laurie out in a small boat on San Francisco Bay on a Sunday afternoon. In the middle of the bay, the motor hit bottom, severing the shear pin and leaving them powerless. The wind blew so hard that their small paddles proved useless. They wondered where they would end up, and if they would ever get back in time for the Sunday evening service. It was not uncommon for people adrift in the middle of the bay to spend the night on the mud flats! Finally, the direction of the wind changed and pushed them back close to the west shore, where Elaine's brother picked them up in time to make it to church. To the girls, this was just another example that their father could escape any situation.[3]

Ray's daughters also remember their father's love for music. Ray was not a musician, but he loved music and he taught his daughters to appreciate good music. Unfortunately, this did not keep Ray from singing Scottish songs and cowboy tunes in an off-key voice at the top of his lungs. Together the Stedman family sang everything from hymns to songs they learned on their favorite television program, *Sing Along with Mitch*. Ray's love for music deeply influenced Susan, and she was accepted into the Wheaton Conservatory of Music after high school.[4]

Ray's unpredictable ways carried over into his spending habits. While Elaine was very frugal, Ray was an impulsive buyer. When he wanted something, he rarely shopped around or waited for a bargain, but would race to a store and buy it. Ray was also extremely generous and enjoyed purchasing impractical gifts for his family. Valentine's Day was often an occasion for him to get red roses for Elaine and new dresses for the girls. Ray had exquisite taste, and they were never disappointed with the gifts he chose for them.[5]

Ray's generosity also translated into hospitality. "We would always have a big meal after church," remembers Laurie, "and my parents would always invite somebody home who looked like they didn't have anyplace to go. Usually it was my dad who invited someone. If it was getting close to the time to leave the church, I would remind my dad to invite somebody. I loved having people over. I looked forward to that. We would also have people over on Sunday evenings after church."[6]

As a result, a variety of characters came through their doors, and many stayed for more than a meal. When J. Vernon McGee preached at PBC, he stayed with the Stedmans, and the girls have never forgotten his bright colored pajamas. As mentioned earlier, Luis Palau stayed with the family for two months when he first came to the United States in 1960, and his Latin sense of humor brightened their home. When former Black Panther Eldridge Cleaver professed to becoming a Christian, Ray opened both his church and his home to him and his family, precipitating a media frenzy in the Stedman front yard.[7]

Ray and Elaine also created an atmosphere in which learning and thinking were highly valued. Ray prized reading so much that he paid his daughters to read books, including the Bible. When the girls were teenagers, he asked them to present him with a written outline of his sermon after they had listened to him preach. Although they resented it at the time, they say, it taught them to think logically—a skill they used in school and later in their careers. Ray also loved to play chess, and he rarely lost. When he was not beating a fellow staff member or the computer, he played with his daughters, often giving them a handicap so they had a chance to win.[8]

But one of the greatest legacies Ray left his daughters was the model of a strong marriage that lasted forty-seven years. Though Ray and Elaine were reserved in their outward expressions of love for each other, their commitment to each other was unquestioned. Every morning when Ray was home, he and Elaine began their day together at the breakfast nook, reading from a devotional book and praying for the family. Ray and Elaine were partners in every sense, freeing each other for the work God had for each of them and thus allowing the Lord to use them in a deeper way.[9] Ray's one-sided authoritarianism, which characterized their early years of marriage, eventually mellowed into servant leadership. As the years passed, their marriage became even more of a mutual partnership as Ray recognized Elaine's tremendous gifts. This truly came to the fore in 1975 when Elaine distinguished herself as an author with her book, *A Woman's Worth*. When Ray read the manuscript, he was stunned and delighted by Elaine's insight and encouraged her to use the gifts God had given her in both speaking and writing.

RAY C. STEDMAN

Ray Stedman at the age of 2

Ray Stedman at the age of 4

Background: The Missouri Breaks area of Montana

Newlyweds in Honolulu c.1945

Bible class in bomb shelter, Honolulu, 1945

*Ray (right) and Clark Harvey
Ray led Clark to Christ*

Ray (right) and Ed Phillips

*Elaine and Ray (center) with friends at the Olivet Baptist Bible
Training School in Hawaii*

Ray with staff in Israel

Ray and Elaine at Olivet Baptist Bible Training School

Ray in front of PBC

Ray with the PBC staff

Ray (third from right) with Dr. H. A. Ironside (second from right), 1950

Ray & Elaine Stedman

Winifred, Montana

Ray at Coliseum in Rome

Ray receives honorary doctorate degree from Talbot Seminary, 1971

The Four Musketeers: (from left) Ray, Charlie Luce, Bob Smith, Bob Roe

Ray (second from left) with Uncle Fred & Aunt Beulah, 1946

Ray with airplane

Ray's wife and daughters, 2002: (from left) Sheila, Susan, Elaine, Linda, and Laurie

Ray as a young man on the Montana range

*Ray reading Scripture to tour group in Israel on the site
of the Sermon on the Mount, April 1967*

The deep warmth and love between Ray and Elaine is reflected in many of Ray's letters to her when he was away from home, speaking or teaching. In October 1968, he wrote to her from an airplane en route to Saigon:

> All day my thoughts have been running back to twenty-three years ago in Honolulu. Sometimes it seems very close in time, and other times it seems worlds away. I'm grateful for this almost quarter-of-a-century the Lord has given us together, for our family and friends, and the ministry we have shared. By nature we both tend to be reticent about our feelings but I think it's appropriate on this day to tell you I love you very much and feel the Lord has fulfilled all His promise of marital happiness which lay unfolded on that wedding day so long ago. You have done well as a wife and mother and now that we see our first-born about to leave the family nest for good it is good to realize that the years ahead will be different but not empty.[10]

Troubled Waters

DESPITE THE FOUNDATION OF love in the Stedman home, through the years the family experienced some great heartache. At different periods of time, each of Ray and Elaine's daughters went through a significant season of rebellion; at times the relationship between Ray and his daughters was strained or even fractured. Because of Ray's visibility, and his and Elaine's deep mutual desire for their daughters to follow Christ, these periods of family discord caused them tremendous pain.

Several factors probably contributed to the difficulties in the Stedman home, and one major factor was Ray's devotion to his ministry. Like most evangelical leaders of his generation, Ray traveled extensively, seldom counting the cost to his family. "Billy Graham said that if there was one thing he would have done differently, it would have been to spend more time with his family," says Elaine, reflecting back to those times. "I think Ray really felt that way too. But that was the way that we were trained to think about ministry; that ministry was first and the family came in wherever they fit in. We both thought that way, so we did not object to it. It was tough though. The hardest things that happened with the girls happened when he was gone."[11]

Another factor was the spirit of the time and place in which Ray and Elaine raised their daughters. During the sixties, traditional Christian morality was not only questioned but mocked, and nowhere was this more evident than at Cubberly High School in Palo Alto, which was known as the local center of the hippie movement with all the attendant activities: antiwar protests, drugs, and sexual experimentation. Ray's three older daughters all attended Cubberly, and Linda remembers that the students basically took over the school. "During those days at Cubberly there were groups of people smoking pot in the parking lot with no intervention. Most teachers simply avoided the area. The bathrooms were filled with cigarette smoke during breaks. Many students had some sort of venereal disease. Students seemed to be protesting everything they could think of."[12] Being Ray Stedman's daughters, the girls felt pressure to conform to their parents' standards and the church culture of which they were a part. At the same time, they desperately wanted to fit in and "be normal" in a school environment that could not have been more different from their home and church.

It is ironic that a church that became a haven for the Jesus People was the very place Ray's daughters felt they could not be themselves and work through their struggles as normal teenagers. But in the sixties, the evangelical culture in general and PBC in particular were not always as accepting as they would later become in the Body Life services in the early seventies. Both PBC and Ray Stedman experienced a process of maturation in this regard. But for much of the sixties, PBC was a typical evangelical church and Ray was a strict pastor and father. "Dad would not allow me to date a non-Christian," recalls Sheila, "and so I was limited to the guys at church, which didn't appeal to me much. . . . I wasn't allowed to go to school dances, or any movie not created by Disney, and of course never a secular party."[13]

And without doubt, people in the church expected more from them than from other young people. "They got some pretty hard knocks," says Elaine. "Things that really derailed them. I don't think Laurie [the youngest] did, because after Body Life, things changed so much at PBC. It was a different atmosphere and a different way of looking at things. But before that it was very traditional and more was expected of them. People would say things like, 'How could you do that when you have such wonderful parents?' But the girls knew their parents! They knew we were just people."[14]

Another factor was that although Ray was always affectionate with his girls, one of his weaknesses as a father was his inability to relate to them on an emotional level. Elaine believes this was a handicap inherited from his upbringing. "He loved his kids. But because they were girls, he felt awkward with them at times. He didn't quite know how to handle their emotional outbursts. . . . He did not understand the female. He did not grow up with females. He had two brothers. He had two male cousins. He didn't relate well to his mother at all. He didn't have a close relationship with his aunt. . . . It was a good relationship, . . . But there was no closeness, no real intimate sharing. He never learned that kind of sharing and intimacy of communication."[15]

Susan, Ray's second daughter, agrees. "The one thing I felt was most lacking from my dad was an ability to relate to me emotionally. He was so mental, and so logical, that anything that operated on the emotional level would just throw him. He had a real hard time with that. . . . And I think part of that might have been from his childhood, and his mother being so overemotional."[16]

Ray's weakness in this area made it especially difficult for him to talk with his daughters about the temptations they were experiencing. Sheila remembers wanting to talk with her dad about her struggles, but feeling unable to do so. "I was always seeking approval from him, so I decided it wasn't safe to tell him of my dilemma. I wanted badly to tell him, but the few times I tried he would tell me it was wrong to think that way and that it hurt him to hear such things. I think that was the biggest 'wart' with Dad back then because he unknowingly blocked me from sharing my pain and kept me from being honest with him."[17]

Linda recalls that her father himself often would react emotionally and resort to bribes. "He tried to send me off to L'Abri in Switzerland in order to bribe me not to get married."[18] Ray once even threatened to leave the ministry. "Dad made the mistake of threatening to leave the ministry because of me," recalls Sheila, "so the guilt was piled on and I felt I had to escape even more."[19]

What Ray's daughters did not know was that the threat to leave the ministry was anything but a bluff. More than once Ray doubted his own fitness for the ministry enough that he actually approached the PBC elders about resigning. He felt he was no longer qualified to serve if his children were out of control. But the elders convinced him that since the daughter in question was already out of the house, he should not take responsibility for her actions. In one particularly moving meeting, all the elders shared communion and prayed for Ray. This event, and particularly Ray's transparency and integrity, left a deep impression on several of the elders.[20]

One can't help but wonder about the role of the Christian's adversary in all of this. Scripture says, "Our struggle is not against flesh and blood, but against the rulers, against the powers, against the world-forces of this darkness, against the spiritual forces of wickedness in the heavenly places" (Ephesians 6:12 NASB). Luis Palau believes that many of the difficulties in the Stedman home were the result of spiritual warfare.[21] Although Ray never publicly spoke about his daughters' experiences, his book *Spiritual Warfare* reflects many of the insights he must have first applied to his own battles.

> Remember this—the aim, the goal of Satan in all this clever stratagem, by which he has kept the human race in bondage through these hundreds of centuries, is to destroy, to ruin, to make waste. That is his purpose toward you and me. A young man I know, who had been raised in church, though he is only twenty-one years old, has already become a mental and physical wreck. Why? Because he has turned aside from the truth and followed the philosophy of Satan. Satan is accomplishing his aim, destroying this life which God loves. That is what he is attempting to do with us.[22]

But as with so many of Satan's tactics, they backfired when it came to Ray. "I really believe that Satan's favorite inroad to attacking Dad's ministry was through his daughters," says Linda. "However, I think our rebellion challenged and strengthened Dad's faith more than any other events in his life. It brought him to his knees time after time."[23]

Internalizing the New Covenant

IT WAS ON HIS knees, because of his sense of inadequacy as a father, that what Ray called the New Covenant became more than just a doctrine to him. In 1975 he wrote *Authentic Christianity* as a clear explanation of that covenant, the essence of which is that Christians are vessels designed to contain the life of Jesus.

> But the Christian is more than an empty vessel. He has something within—or, more accurately, Someone within. We have a treasure in our clay pot! And more than a treasure—a transcendent power! That is humanity as God intended it

to be. The clay pot is not much in itself, but it holds an ines-timable treasure, beyond price, and a transcendent power, greater than any other power known to humanity.[24]

Ray had come to learn that the life of Jesus dwelling in the believer would not exempt him from experiencing hardship and heartache. Indeed, it was these experiences that allowed for the experience and demonstration of the life of Christ within:

Undoubtedly, one of the greatest misconceptions held by many is that being a Christian means that life should sud-denly smooth out, mysterious bridges will appear over all chasms, the winds of fate will be tempered, and all difficul-ties will disappear. No, Christianity is not membership in some red-carpet club. All the problems and pressures of life remain, or are even intensified. Christians must face life in the raw, just as any pagan will. The purpose of the Christ-ian life is not to escape dangers and difficulties but to demonstrate a different way of handling them. There must be trouble, or there can be no demonstration.[25]

When Ray wrote, "There must be trouble, or there can be no demonstration," he wrote out of his own life experience. Out of his personal sense of inadequacy and failure as a father Ray learned that "the surpassing greatness of the power" was indeed from God and not from himself. Out of his own trouble at home came a demon-stration of the life of Christ within.

Because of his suffering, Ray became a softer and more empa-thetic and "human" pastor and father. When he spoke of believers simply being "cracked pots" who held a treasure inside, people knew that he spoke out of his own brokenness. He became more com-passionate, tender, and patient with those who strayed. People on his staff and in his church saw the change, as did his family.

Susan views her own rebellious years as a way of knocking Ray off the pedestal she and so many others had placed him on. "When I went through those rebellious years, I had to knock him down; and he was way up there, so the fall was pretty hard for him and for me.... It's taken me all these years to know my father as a human being, and accept him as a human being, and I don't ever want to put him on that pedestal again. Because it wasn't where he wanted to be, and it wasn't his place to be there, and I just love him so much more now that I know him as a human being and accept him for who he really is."[26]

And when his daughters began to experience the consequences of poor choices and needed help, they found their father—and their mother—waiting with open arms. "Over and over again . . . I pushed my parents to the limit," says Laurie. "But I always felt like they loved me. I never felt rejection. . . . There was always forgiveness."[27] Each daughter experienced this forgiveness and has her own story to tell of a special "homecoming" with her father, when he became the channel of God's grace to her.

"Dad and Mom were so supportive through the years," Linda remembers. "In 1981, in the midst of a very difficult marriage, I left my husband and took our sons back to Palo Alto to live with Dad and Mom. They welcomed us with open arms. By then, I was desperate to find my way back to the Lord. My view of God was so distorted by my own sin and the worldly philosophies I had embraced. Dad quickly got me connected with a Christian psychiatrist—a preacher's kid himself—who helped me get a clear perspective of God's grace, and assured me that God loved me right where I was, in spite of all my sin and rebellion. It was the beginning of spiritual healing in my life."[28]

Sheila's "homecoming" took place after her father had already retired and was battling cancer. "On a visit to see Mom and Dad in Grants Pass, Dad found out he had cancer. I was in shock! How could that be? We had grown closer over the years, he had grown softer and sweeter, had retired from PBC, and was finally able to relax and enjoy less pressures of the ministry. . . .

"My son, Jason, had been living the party life in high school, was dating lots of girls, but lately had been dating a particularly sweet girl, Jennifer, and had found out, just weeks before the terrible news about Dad, that he was going to be a father. He and Papa had formed a very close relationship since his birth, being the first grandson and the apple of Papa's eye. When Jason heard the news, he rushed down to Grants Pass with Jennifer and told Dad how sorry he was for messing up his own life and now his treasured Papa was dying. Dad, in his gracious, loving manner, reassured Jason that it was not bad news at all, but great news that he would be seeing his Lord soon, and that he, Jason, should realize that life is only temporary. That he should marry Jennifer and turn his life over to the Lord. And do you know, that was *the* turning point in Jason's *and* my life. . . .

"From that day forward, both me and my children have all come back to a real, personal, fulfilling relationship with our heavenly Father and it has a great deal to do with Dad's own example of who a father should be. He forgave us when we rebelled against him, and loved us in spite of our ingratitude and selfishness! When I look back on our life together I realize how incredibly blessed I was to be chosen to be my earthly *and* my heavenly Father's child!"[29]

During the sixties and early seventies, PBC became one of the most well-known and innovative churches in the nation, and Ray became a Bible teacher and author of international renown. But it was in the context of his family that God was refining and conforming Ray into the image of Christ.

In the end, Ray Stedman was a portrait of integrity not only in the church, but in his home as well.

NINE

Contending for the Faith

Ray Stedman was not combative by nature. For years he tried to create an atmosphere of freedom and diversity at PBC, encouraging those around him to study the Scriptures and develop their own convictions about faith and practice. At the same time, he was passionate about the truth; and, when necessary, he was willing to fight for what he believed to be doctrinal and moral purity. This sometimes placed him at odds with fellow workers and beloved sons in the faith.

Church Discipline

ONE OF THE INDICATORS of Ray's commitment to the truth was his commitment to church discipline. At least four times over the course of Stedman's ministry, he was forced to lead the body at PBC in the process of disciplining one of its members according to the pattern prescribed in Matthew 18:15–18. Ray was convinced that, as painful as it was, church discipline performed in a humble spirit of love and concern was necessary to maintain a healthy body of believers, as he clearly indicated in the following words from his sermon on September 30, 1984.

"Today we must do what we have had to do only three previous times in the thirty-six-year history of Peninsula Bible Church. That is to obey the word of our Lord Jesus given in Matthew 18 concerning the handling of a serious moral failure in a member of this church.... As we go through these words together, let us remember that these are the words of Jesus, and, as such, they cannot be ignored. He is the Lord of the church, the Head of the body, and, as such, is dealing here with the procedure for handling unjudged sin in our midst."[1]

Ray also believed that lack of church discipline was at least part of the cause of the downfall of many televangelists in the 1980s. When commenting on Paul's commending of the Ephesian elders to the "word of God's grace," Ray said: "Last week I received a manuscript of a new book that will be published soon by Moody Press. It is a collection of articles written by some of the outstanding evangelical leaders of our day examining the teaching of certain televangelists who are occupying much time and space on our television sets these days. It is a searching, but objective, examination of whether such teaching is in line with the Scriptures.... What is the ground of testing? It is whether a teaching agrees with the Scriptures, with the 'word of God's grace,' as he calls it there. If this were more widely practiced today we would probably have been spared much of the terrible, shameful scandals that have occupied the front pages of our papers and other media.... Our Lord... does not charge [the Ephesians] with being judgmental, or say, as many do today, that churches have no right to judge. He points out that this was part of the teaching they had received, and He commends them for it."[2]

One of the joys of Ray's ministry was seeing this painful disciplinary process work redemptively in the lives of those who had been disciplined. After one leader had been gone from the church for several years as a result of being disciplined, Ray and his colleagues had the joy of seeing the man repent. In March 1980 he wrote a letter to the elders, confessing the depths of his sin and the depths of despair to which he had sunk. He spoke of his repentance and his desire for restoration and concluded with the following words:

It is impossible for me to retrace my footsteps and right every wrong; however I welcome the opportunity to meet and pray with any individuals who have something against me that needs resolution. I am looking and waiting for the further grace and mercy of God in this matter. What you have bound on earth has been bound in heaven, and I now know your actions were done in love for my own good and that of the Body of Christ.[3]

Two weeks after the church received this letter, Ray read it to the congregation, with full permission from the writer. Ray then went on to describe the way in which he and his ministry colleagues had responded and welcomed the man back into the body.

"A few days ago a number of us who had been closely associated with him asked him to join us in a 'welcome home' dinner," Ray said. "We killed the fatted calf. (We had barbecued veal. This was the first time veal steaks have ever been barbecued, I think.) Then we asked him to stand up, and we welcomed him back, as one who had been dead but was alive again. We called out to bring a gold ring to put upon his finger. We bought him a new sport coat and put it on his back, and welcomed him home as the prodigal son.

"He felt so welcomed, and forgiven, that he sat down afterward to tell us what God had taken him through in these intervening years, how God had dealt with him in ways that were ruthless and yet loving, and what a hell he had gone through. He said, 'I've come to know the full meaning of the words, "It is a fearful thing to fall into the hands of the living God."' But it was a joyful time of restoration and of renewing our love and fellowship.

"We rejoice, as I am sure the angels in heaven are rejoicing, that God has effected this discipline not by human pressures, but by the power of God at work in an individual heart in obedience to the word of the living God."[4]

Battles Fought Close to Home

SOME CONFLICT THAT RAY was forced to manage came from within his own staff and was more directly centered on him and his teaching. In 1980, two members of the Scribe School staff began to express reservations about Ray's teaching on the New Covenant. Ray taught that the life of Christ dwelling in the believer provided all the resources one needed to overcome sin, and that it is the believer's responsibility to appropriate the power available to him in Christ in order to overcome sin.

Fundamental to Ray's teaching on sanctification was his view of man as a threefold being: body, soul, and spirit. Ray taught that upon conversion, God implants His Spirit within man's spirit and gives him a righteous standing, called justification, which is permanent and unchangeable. But salvation does not stop there. God's plan provides for the transformation of body and soul as well. The former will be transformed when believers are ushered into the presence of Christ, but the soul is transformed now as the believer learns to appropriate the life of Christ within.

As Ray stated in his comments on the book of Romans, "The soul of man, as he is born of Adam, is under the reign of sin. The flesh (if you want to use the biblical term for it) rules us. The life of Adam possesses us, with all its self-centered characteristics. Even though our spirit has been justified, it is quite possible to go on with the soul still under the bondage and reign of sin. So, though our destiny is settled in Christ, our experience is still as much under the control of evil as before we were Christians. That is the cause of the miserable experience of being up-and-down, sometimes reckoning on the promises of God for justification, then experiencing again the implacable bondage of sin ruling in the life, causing selfishness and self-centeredness.

"Well, what is God's program for this? To sum it up in one word: sanctification. God intends us to see that in Jesus Christ this whole thing has been taken care of, even as our destiny was, so that we can be as free from the reign of sin as we are from the penalty of sin. . . .

"When we finally learn that there is nothing we can do for God, but that He intends to do everything through us, then we come into deliverance. That is when we begin fully to realize the experience of mind, emotion, and will brought under the control of Jesus Christ and the fulfilling in glorious, triumphant power all that He has in mind for us. That is the sanctifying of the soul."[5]

Another way of stating this principle is to say that in conversion, righteousness is imputed to the believer's spirit, and in sanctification, righteousness is imparted to the believer's soul.

Those who were critical of Ray's view of sanctification had adopted what they believed to be a Reformed view of sanctification, in which sanctification was not dependent on the believer's appropriation of what was already provided for in Christ, but rather on the sovereign grace that God provides in gradual portions throughout one's lifetime. In short, Ray believed everything was already provided to live a life free from sin, while those who disagreed with him were teaching that freedom from sin came only in gradual allotments according to divine sovereignty. Furthermore, unlike Stedman, they taught that there are no means (i.e. faith, Bible study, prayer, or church attendance) by which a believer can promote the sanctification process. Although a believer should strive to live a righteous life, freedom from sin is impossible unless God chooses to dispense the grace to overcome it.

His critics were quick to point out that in Ray's ideological framework, so popular among evangelicals, a sinless life was at least a theoretical possibility. Although Ray did not teach perfectionism, at times his teaching did sound as if full deliverance from sin was available now by allowing the triumphant power of Christ to rule in the soul. His critics placed far more emphasis on the future hope of the gospel to bring complete sanctification upon the believer's death.

As time went on, it became increasingly apparent to all parties involved that these differences were significant enough to cause a parting of the ways, since they struck at the very core of Ray's New Covenant teaching. Eventually, those who disagreed with him left the PBC staff, and one of the effects of their departure was the demise of Scribe School. By this time, Ray was convinced that the program had become too academic and needed to return to its practical roots. Eventually, the internship program at PBC was reshaped to be more practical and less academic, but it no longer existed as a viable option to seminary for most young pastors in training.

On a personal level, however, Ray was deeply hurt by the disagreement, even experiencing a period of uncharacteristic depression. In the midst of the conflict he was accused of being a poor exegete and expositor, and he felt betrayed by young men into whom he had poured his life.[6] At the same time, some of Ray's own personal weaknesses were also exposed. It had always been difficult for him to admit when he was wrong, and he had a tendency to emotionally cut off those who disagreed with him and/or disappointed him. Because of this, it could be difficult for him to process and work through such disagreements in a way that was redemptive in the lives of those at odds with him, as well as his own life. This left some feeling that although PBC was a very accepting place on the surface, Ray himself had too easily written them off. For example, when one staff member was asked to leave the staff over the sanctification debate, the phone call was made not by Ray himself but by one of the elders. In an indirect way, however, Ray did address the issue from the pulpit as he taught from 1 Timothy 1:1–7: "It is essential that there be unity in the teaching of a church. There are differences of style that are quite permissible; there are different gifts (they are expected to vary) among teachers; there are different choices of subjects of the revelation of God. The heart of truth, however, must remain unsullied, because the Scripture is the most powerful weapon the church has to correct error and to deliver people from bondage into freedom. The teaching of the truth, therefore, must be central in the ministry.... We must be careful to return to the biblical and apostolic witness of the truth as it is in Jesus. Anything that takes away from our understanding of the totality of the end of the old life—or from the fullness of supply of a totally new life available to us now—is a weakening of the apostolic witness and promotes speculations and vain discussions which go nowhere in a church."[7]

Several years later, shortly before Ray's retirement, another difficult doctrinal disagreement arose with another young staff member. This particular young man was one of Ray's most cherished sons in the faith; but when he began to reveal a tendency toward non-dispensational eschatology, Ray became very upset. When it came to eschatology, Ray was an ardent premillennialist. He believed in a clear distinction between Israel and the church, the Rapture of the church prior to the Great Tribulation, and the second coming of Christ to establish His millennial kingdom on earth. When this staff member preached a sermon in which he used what Ray believed to be amillennial terminology, Ray responded by writing him a letter from his summer home in Grants, Pass Oregon:

> There is another matter which I feel increasingly concerned about and wish to bring up to you with this letter. I have been reading through your recent messages... and have been troubled by the increasing allusions to amillennial concepts which I see in them....
>
> You may recall that last year I talked with you about this same matter and pointed out that nowhere does the New Testament ever refer to the Church as Israel, let alone "the new Israel" or "spiritual Israel." To use such terms is to

substitute theological interpretation for biblical terms. Furthermore, it is a direct challenge to the doctrinal statement of PBC which espouses a premillennial view and which was recently reviewed by the elders and unanimously reapproved. This means that whether you intend to do so or not, you are teaching what is contrary to the beliefs of the elders, and using the platform of PBC to do so. This is highly unethical, not to say, naive! . . .

It grieves me greatly to have to say all this to you . . . but I fear the enemy is using you . . . to lay the groundwork for division in PBC. . . . No one is saying you do not have the right to adopt a different doctrinal position from the elders if you think it is true. What you don't have the right to do is to use PBC as a platform to teach it. . . .[8]

Ray's own affinity for this young man no doubt deepened the sense of betrayal he felt as another young son in the faith departed from his own theological convictions. But Ray viewed this and other such battles as spiritual in nature, and ones in which the truth was at stake. As much as he disliked the conflict, he was willing to sacrifice relationships to defend what he believed was the truth.

Prior to this time, PBC never had a formal doctrinal statement beyond stating that the sixty-six books of the Bible were God's inspired Word. Now, Ray and the elders created a full doctrinal statement, partially in response to this particular crisis. A few months later, Ray asked the elders to insist that the young man either align himself with the PBC doctrinal statement or leave the pastoral staff. Ray also reinforced PBC's commitment to a literal millennium as he preached through the book of Revelation.

But the elders did not accede to Ray's wishes. Instead, they agreed to continue to study God's Word, dialogue with the staff member, and remain prayerful before the Lord. In essence, they were saying that despite their great love and admiration for Ray, they did not agree with him that this was an issue over which the pastoral staff and elders should divide.

The entire episode was just as much about Ray's sons in the faith growing up and thinking for themselves, as Ray had taught them to do, as it was about a doctrinal issue. But for one who saw these matters in such black-and-white terms, as Ray did, this must have been a difficult pill to swallow. Yet, in the end, he was willing to let go of his own desires and trust the Holy Spirit to direct the elders in leading the church he so dearly loved. And later, with encouragement from a trusted mediator, Ray sought the young man's forgiveness for some of the hurtful things he had said.

Throughout his ministry, Ray Stedman contended for the faith as he understood it. While at times his commitment to what he believed to be the truth placed him at odds with those he loved, he never stopped loving them and the church in which they served. In this manner, Ray remained a faithful steward of both the Word and the ministry entrusted to him for fifty years.

TEN

Passing the Torch

In the fall of 1975, Ray Stedman celebrated twenty-five years of pastoral ministry at PBC, an anniversary that might have passed unnoticed except that the elders remembered and brought Ray's longtime friend, Howard Hendricks, into town as a surprise. As Ray began his sermon on the morning of September 28, he didn't even notice his old friend striding down the center aisle. Finally, when Howard was standing right in front of the pulpit looking up at him, Ray noticed.

"Howie Hendricks!" he said. "What in the world are you doing here?"

"I'm taking over," Howard replied with his usual wit. "Sit down!" And he then proceeded to preach the sermon as a tribute to Ray.

Later in the service, after many words of appreciation had been expressed to Ray, he stood up and pointed to a banner prominently displayed on the wall. It was a quote from Zechariah 14:9: "And the LORD will be the king over all the earth; in that day the LORD will be the only one, and His name the only one" (NASB).

After twenty-five years of ministry at PBC, Ray's commitment to expository preaching had not changed, but the focus of his ministry now took a different direction. With the waning of the Jesus Movement, his ministry increasingly focused on discipling and teaching the next generation of leadership at PBC, encouraging and equipping young men to be pastor-teachers. Much of Ray's equipping ministry was focused on the staff that had been added to adequately disciple those who flocked to PBC during the sixties and early seventies. By 1975, twelve pastors were ministering at the church.

Bob Smith, who had been hired in 1960 to be an associate pastor, continued to serve in a variety of capacities; and more than anyone else, Bob was Ray's right-hand man in ministry. Bev Forsyth, who was Ray's administrative assistant from 1966 until 1990, sees Bob Smith's role as crucial to Ray's success: "The team of 'Bob and Ray' was a great team to work with, and I had that privilege for many years. Bob Smith was the man behind the preacher, the one who kept things running and balanced at home base so that Ray Stedman was free to do what God had called him to do—teach the Word in season and out, here and around the world. After Elaine, Bob was Ray's greatest supporter."[1]

Ron Ritchie, who had been hired in 1969 to oversee the growing high school ministry, was reassigned in 1974 to work with "Careers Alive," an innovative singles ministry that had been meeting in the second floor auditorium of a local restaurant for about five years. By 1974, over fifty people were attending these meetings. Under Ron's leadership, this ministry more than doubled in size within a year.[2]

David Roper continued to do most of the preaching when Ray traveled, but his main focus had shifted from college ministries to overseeing Scribe School. After a year or two of training, several Scribes were ready to move into pastoral roles at PBC. Steve Zeisler was hired to oversee the college ministry; Jack Crabtree and David Smith were hired to teach within Scribe School; and Brian Morgan was hired to pastor the junior high ministry. Although Roper left PBC in 1976 to pastor Cole Community Church in Boise, Idaho, he had developed the program to an extent that Ray's dream of training pastors in the church was coming to fruition. After Roper's departure, Scribe School continued under the leadership of

Crabtree, Smith, and Ray Ortlund Jr. Other members of the pastoral team included Bob Roe, Walt McCuiston, Paul Winslow, Doug Goins, and Gary Vanderet.

Despite the fact that Ray was well into his third decade at PBC and approaching the age when many men begin to think about retirement, his preaching and leadership were still the catalysts for continued growth. One of the challenges that this growth presented was inadequate facilities and parking, causing frustrated neighbors to sign petitions against the church. Ray and the elders began to think seriously about finding another facility, but they had reservations about becoming a megachurch. Ray preferred to start smaller churches throughout the Bay area to maintain smaller, more personal congregations. Already, PBC had played a significant role in starting Valley Bible Church in Cupertino, South Hills Community Church in San Jose, and Central Peninsula Church in Foster City. But PBC still continued to burst at the seams.

In 1984 PBC purchased an old church building located about twelve miles south of Palo Alto. Instead of trying to relocate the entire church on one new campus, the elders made the unorthodox decision to subdivide the current body and staff onto two campuses—the existing one at the original PBC site and the new property in Cupertino—while maintaining one elder board to oversee them both. In March 1985, after renovating the new property, PBC Cupertino (not to be mistaken with Valley Bible Church mentioned above) was dedicated, with Paul Winslow, Brian Morgan, Kim Anderson, and eventually Gary Vanderet serving as lead pastors. Ray's primary focus continued to be preaching at PBC and serving the larger body of Christ.[3]

On the Road Again

WITH THE CHURCH MINISTRIES well organized and under the care of such a strong pastoral team, Ray was freed to broaden his own

preaching ministry. By the mid-seventies and into the early eighties, he was preaching only about twenty-six times a year at PBC,
with the rest of the Sundays devoted to outside speaking engagements, nationally and internationally, at retreats, pastors' conferences, organizations, Bible colleges, and seminaries.[4] The variety of
his speaking engagements revealed his broad appeal across the evangelical spectrum. Ray's gracious style and commitment to biblical
exposition earned him a welcome hearing among those with whom
he might not agree on all theological matters, but with whom he
could fellowship around the person of Christ and the Scriptures.

Ray's travel also gave him opportunity to develop relationships
with many of the young interns, staff, and elders at PBC. Ray rarely
traveled alone, but would usually invite a young man to go with him
on his speaking engagements. Ray considered these young men his
"sons in the faith" and often commented that he wanted them to
have the opportunity to learn by watching, much as he as a young
seminarian had done with Dr. Ironside. I have a personal knowledge of this. In 1979, a week after I was first introduced to Ray as
a new intern at PBC, I was invited to travel with him to Brazil
where he was speaking at two pastors' conferences sponsored by
Overseas Crusade. My role was mostly to observe, but Ray also
found opportunities for me to share my testimony and teach a youth
Bible study. I quickly discovered that traveling with Ray was an
adventure—especially trying to keep up with him as he raced from
terminal to terminal in major city airports. Although he took his
teaching ministry seriously while on the road, Ray poured much of
his energy into developing relationships. Often he would not know
exactly what he would teach on until a few hours before he was
scheduled to speak! But he was always available to his fellow pastors, staying up late into the evening discussing and answering
questions, or just getting to know them over a meal or a game of
chess. There was always a great deal of laughter, and even some
tears.

Sometimes, however, Ray's fun-loving spirit offended more conservative Christians. Jim Heaton, an elder at PBC, remembers making one trip with Ray, Ron Ritchie, and fellow elder Ed Woodall where Ray spoke at a pastors conference, which Jim describes as "very conservative." By the time the weeklong conference was over, Jim was convinced they would never invite Ray back. Besides tipping over a boat and almost breaking his wrist, Ray refused to observe the prevailing etiquette of the staff dining room, resenting the idea that staff should be separated from the conferees. One morning while reluctantly eating breakfast with the rest of the conference staff, Ray took off his shoes and socks and allowed Ron to wash his feet after the manner of Jesus in John 13. It was a way of both making a point and poking fun at what they considered to be an elitist attitude among the staff. As Jim puts it, the staff "came unglued" and it was the last time Ray ever spoke there.[5]

Whether or not Ray and his friends took their freedom in Christ to an extreme is a matter for debate. But like it or not, Ray was always himself, without pretense, and he believed that he and his team were modeling as well as teaching a lifestyle based on the New Covenant.

Ray's ministry on the road also paved the way for a new PBC outreach. For eight years the church had hosted two pastors' conferences a year, including international pastoral teams from as far away as Nigeria. Then, in the mid-eighties, the PBC staff began to travel abroad, as well as to Christian colleges in the United States, to hold pastors' conferences. Under Paul Winslow's strong administrative leadership, Ray and the staff traveled to Indonesia, Australia, Singapore, Israel, and Africa.[6] These trips were an extension of Ray's conviction that ministry takes place best in the context of a team, where different people with different gifts can minister in different ways. This was true not only in the conducting of conferences, but in the everyday life of the people at PBC, who occasionally were left without pastors upon whom to depend. With the absence of the pastoral staff for as much as two weeks at a time, the ministry of the saints continued and sometimes even mushroomed. The people had already heard many times from the pulpit that the ministry belonged to them and not to the professionals; now they were called to act on it—and did.

But throughout those years, when Ray was at home he continued to faithfully exposit the Scriptures at PBC. From 1975 through 1990, he preached through the books of Mark, Romans, Job, 1 and 2 Corinthians, 1 and 2 Timothy, Ecclesiastes, John, Colossians, 1 and 2 Thessalonians, Nehemiah, and Revelation. In addition to the individual sermons being available in printed form, many of these studies, as well as earlier ones, eventually became books. From 1976 to 1990, Ray published seventeen books, including, *The Ruler Who Serves* (1976), *The Servant Who Rules* (1976), *Riches in Christ* (1976), and *From Guilt to Glory* (1978).

COBE

ONE OF THE GREATEST CONTRIBUTIONS Ray Stedman made to the church at large came in the last decade of his ministry at PBC. As he traveled around the country, he became convinced that there was a lack of sound preaching in America's pulpits. He viewed this as the reason the church in America was failing to have the impact it should. "There is a serious lack of biblical exposition from pulpits," he wrote in 1986, "and a failure of people to grasp the countercultural challenges inherent in biblical truth. Thus the local church falters, and the body designed by God to be a potent force in the world presents a sad commentary on its high calling."[7]

In response to this need, Ray became the catalyst for a national movement aimed at the recovery of biblical exposition in America. With strong encouragement from his associate Bob Smith, Ray gathered a group of similarly concerned evangelical leaders to discuss the importance of biblical exposition in the church, which eventually became the Committee on Biblical Exposition. Included in this group were some of America and England's finest and most devoted expositors: John Stott, Richard Halverson, James Boice, Stephen Olford, and Howard Hendricks. This committee staged two national conferences, called the Congress on Biblical Exposition (COBE), one in Anaheim, California, in March 1986, and the other in Houston, Texas, a year later. Several regional conferences were also held during this time and later.

The stated mission of COBE was "to motivate and encourage Christian leaders in the essential discipline of biblical exposition (which is) straightforward and powerful communication of truth from the Scriptures in such a way that speaks its message accurately and relevantly—without addition, subtraction, or falsification."[8] In March 1986, *Eternity* magazine gave COBE a strong endorsement:

> On its surface, the Congress on Biblical Exposition (COBE) meeting this month in Anaheim, California, represents just another in the list of seemingly endless conferences and conventions in which the leadership of America's churches may avail themselves at any given moment. But a quick look inside the pages of COBE's registration kit reveals that it is undoubtedly the conference to attend in 1986. Not since Amsterdam '84 or the Lausanne Conference on World Evangelization in the early 1970s has so much theological horsepower been assembled for one event.[9]

As the chairman for COBE, the last thing Ray wanted was just another conference on how to grow a church. He deplored church growth tactics. The whole purpose of COBE was to call churches back to what he believed was fundamental to their calling: the preaching of the Word of God, without which numerical growth was nothing but a fleeting and fleshly human endeavor. To accomplish this goal, Ray and the committee gathered men and women from numerous evangelical backgrounds. Dispensationalist preachers such as Stedman and Charles Swindoll shared the platform with Reformed Presbyterians such as Richard Halverson and James Boice. Pentecostals such as Jack Hayford and Gordon Fee shared the platform with high church Anglicans such as John Stott. These individuals could have found much about which to disagree, but what they all had in common was a conviction that expositional preaching must be at the heart of the church's ministry.

At the 1986 congress in Anaheim, Ray preached in one of the general sessions on "The Purpose of Preaching," an exposition of 2 Timothy 3:10–17 in which he likened the godless cultural conditions of Paul and Timothy's day to today. "How can pastors make a difference in the midst of such decadence?" he asked. And his answer came in two points: "a model to follow" and "a message to preach." Ray spent little time on the first point, although he did mention the impact that Dr. H. A. Ironside had upon his life, both as a man and as a preacher. The bulk of his sermon dealt with the second point, and he spoke of the origin of the Scriptures as "the breathing out of God," as well as the nature of Scripture as that which builds character, imparts wisdom, and discloses the thoughts of God. Finally, he outlined the different ways Scripture produces change: teaching, rebuking, correcting, and training in righteousness.

Ray's style was characteristically mellow, but as he neared the conclusion of his sermon, his voice increased in intensity and with unusual passion as he promised his audience that careful and relevant exposition would bear the fruit they longed to see in their churches: "When you change a person's thinking, you change their behavior. You can't help it. Once they begin to think the thoughts of God . . . and the whole congregation begins to catch on, you'll find the behavior of that congregation automatically beginning to change. And it will result in a whole people becoming whole persons, and when that happens you will have a flood of eager workers who are ready for any good work."[10]

After the congress in Anaheim, Ray was reluctant to conduct another because the first conference suffered from inadequate funding. He agreed to lead the second congress in Houston only after a prominent pastor in the Houston area guaranteed that his church would cover the entire cost of the conference. Besides Ray, the plenary speakers at the Houston conference included James Boice, Tony Evans, Howard Hendricks, J. I. Packer, John Stott, Charles Swindoll, Richard Halverson, and Ed Young of the Second Baptist Church, Houston, the host church.

In a message entitled "A Declaration on Biblical Exposition," Dr. James Boice stated: "Preaching in the latter decades of the twentieth century exhibits a strange contradiction. On the one hand, there is acknowledgment of the need for great preaching, usually defined as expository preaching. But on the other hand, good expository preaching has seldom been more lacking. Evangelical (and even liberal) seminaries exhort their young men, 'Be faithful in preaching. Spend many hours in your study poring over the Bible. Be sure you give the people God's Word and not merely your own opinions.' But in practice these admonitions are usually not heeded, and ministers who emerge from the seminaries—whether because of poor instruction, lack of focus, a low view of the Bible's authority, or some other undiagnosed cause—often fail in this primary area of responsibility."

In addition to these two national conferences, there were also several regional conferences on biblical exposition between 1982 and 1986. These were held at Ontario Bible College in Canada, Mount Hermon Conference Center, Fuller Seminary, Wheaton College, Cedar Falls Bible Conference, Elmbrook Church, and Idaho Mountain Ministries in Boise, Idaho.

Eventually, the COBE committee disbanded. In the minutes from a conference call of the COBE board on May 9, 1986, it is stated: "Ray Stedman personally expressed the desire to cut back on the amount of leadership he could provide to COBE. It was discussed and agreed that there is no 'heir-apparent' to assume the leadership role. Without leadership, the organization cannot continue." No one knows exactly why Ray desired to withdraw from the leadership of COBE at this point, but Ray always tried to avoid institutionalizing events or ministries of any kind. Perhaps he simply felt COBE's usefulness had run its course.

Was COBE successful? Did it revive biblical exposition in America's churches? For many young pastors the answer would be yes, because COBE was the encouragement they needed to make exposition their top priority. After the Houston congress, 225 participants were asked to evaluate the experience, and the overall evaluation was positive. "As a young pastor I have found myself under tremendous pressure," wrote one participant. "I had to compete to be successful in a culture crying out for quick fixes. Painfully, I'd almost given up the task of careful Bible study. That's what leads to practical exposition. It became too easy to rely on human cleverness and popular psychology. I'm glad for the impact COBE has made on my life."[11]

On the other hand, one can hardly imagine that Ray expected COBE to end after a few short years and just two national congresses. Howard Hendricks, who served on the committee with Ray, remembers that COBE suffered the same plight that prayer often suffers: "You cannot promote prayer.... It's not until the person understands they have a need that they want to pray, which is why most of it comes out of desperation at some point. Well, the same thing with preaching. Everybody wants good preaching, but who wants to pay for it?"[12]

With the disbanding of COBE, Ray also began thinking that he was nearing the finish line in his ministry at PBC.

A New Base of Operations

THE 1980S BROUGHT CHANGES in Ray's personal life as he and Elaine spent increasing amounts of time in the Rogue River area of southern Oregon. Ray and Elaine had purchased a house on the river in August of 1979. Lynn and Della Berntson, close friends of the Stedmans from their days at PBC, lived on the Rogue River in Grants Pass. Lynn had been an elder at PBC, and when Ray and Elaine visited them, Lynn took Ray to see an old house two properties away from theirs. It was a badly used house, but Ray saw the potential, and he fell in love with the setting on the river. "It was at a time when he was beginning to think the young men needed him to move out so they could stretch their wings," Elaine recalls. "So when we had a week or two of vacation, we would go to the river house, and Ray would get a how-to book and work on renovation. In the late 1980s we spent as much as two or three weeks at a time there, and gradually as we approached the retirement year, as much as a month." Two of their daughters, Linda and Susan, lived in northern Oregon at the time Ray and Elaine bought the house; eventually, Linda and her boys moved to Medford, Susan and her girls to Ashland, and Laurie and family to Grants Pass. In the intervening years they had multiple family gatherings, greatly enjoying the river and one another.[13]

For Ray, though, the idea of retirement was hard to swallow. "I have always been sensitive about the word *retirement*," he remarked in his sermon "The Passing of the Torch" on June 6, 1982. "I do not like it. When I suggested a couple of years ago that I might be changing my base of operations from Palo Alto to southern Oregon, the word went out that I was retiring. Everywhere I travel around the country now, somebody will say to me, 'How are you enjoying your retirement?' No, I am not retired, and I hope I never do retire in that sense. Although it is perfectly proper for those who grow older—which I perhaps will someday—to slow down a bit, and take time to do other things, we must never forget that we have a ministry until we die. Our ministry is to be a Christian, to live as a Christian, to walk and talk as a Christian wherever we are, whatever we do."[14]

By April 1990, however, Ray Stedman was finally ready to make an official step toward changing his "base of operations." After forty years of ministry at PBC, he announced that he was moving on.

It is a testimony to Ray's vision for team ministry and his working out of that vision that when he retired the church did not set out to search for another "superstar" preacher or senior pastor, as a church that large and influential would normally do. For years Ray had shared leadership with the men around him, and they were more than ready to have the torch passed to them when Ray moved into retirement.

On April 29, 1990, Ray Stedman preached his last sermon as "senior pastor" at PBC from the final chapter of Revelation. In "The City of Glory" he spoke of the glories of the new heaven and the new earth, quoting from a poem he had learned as a young Christian:

> *There's no disappointment in heaven,*
> *No weariness, sorrow, no pain,*
> *No hearts that are bleeding and broken,*
> *No song with a minor refrain.*
> *The clouds of our earthly horizon*
> *Shall never appear in the sky.*
> *But all will be sunshine and gladness,*
> *With never a sob nor a sigh.*[15]

Little did Ray know that in three short years that city would become his permanent home.

ELEVEN

Ready For Something Tremendous

A year after Ray Stedman retired, he returned to PBC as a guest preacher. As he taught from Ephesians, he commented on Paul's prayer that the church at Ephesus would see and understand "the hope of his calling."

"We must not look at life as the world around us does, as being all that we'll ever get, as the only chance you are going to have to find fulfillment. The world says, 'If you don't take it now, you are never going to get another chance.' I have seen that misunderstanding drive people into forsaking their marriages after thirty or forty years and running off with another, usually younger, person, hoping that they can still fulfill their dreams because they feel life is slipping away from them.

"Christians are not to think that way. We are being told that life is a school, a training period. It is where we are being prepared for something that is incredibly great, but it is yet to come. I don't understand all that is involved in that, but I believe it, and sometimes I can hardly wait until it happens.

"We are told in Scripture (and certainly our experience agrees with it) that these bodies of ours are growing old and will lose their powers. Ever since I moved to Oregon I have noted a few streaks of gray in my hair. I can tell by the way I feel, many times, that my body is losing its elasticity, its ability to function, and I grow weary and weak. I don't know why, because in my mind I don't feel that way at all. But, as I get older, I remember that it is all aimed at something tremendous which I am being readied for."[1]

Little did Ray or the congregation know how strangely prophetic his words were that morning. Little did he know that before long he would experience that "something tremendous" that had been the goal of his life since the time he began preaching to the cows sixty-three years earlier.

Life on the Rogue

WHEN RAY RETIRED IN May of 1990, he and Elaine left Palo Alto for good and moved into the house they had renovated on the Rogue River in southern Oregon. Ray reveled in the unspoiled beauty of southwestern Oregon as he revealed in an unpublished paper entitled "Spiritual Survival":

> My home is on the Rogue River in southwestern Oregon. As the river flows by my door it is a quiet, happily murmuring stream. But ten miles downstream it is a raging torrent, sweeping through the walls of Hellgate Canyon with unbelievable power and white-capped display. The varied assortment of rafters, kayakers, and boatsmen who challenge its course through the coast range have but one thought in mind—survival! A few hardy, experienced souls dare it on their own, but most rely on river-wise guides who thoroughly know the dangers, can instruct in the techniques of survival, and are able to build implicit trust in their knowledge and leadership.[2]

Living on the Rogue River also brought back vivid memories of Ray's boyhood adventures in the Montana wilderness, prompting him to make a return trip to Montana with his cousin Wendell Sheets. The two men spent five days recapturing about a ten-year period of Ray's childhood as they visited Great Falls and Winifred, where Ray attended high school, and attempted to find one of the ranches where Ray had worked during the summer. Ray took Wendell to one of his favorite spots on earth: a high desert crest overlooking the Missouri River, which Ray said was the only place in the world he had ever been that had not been polluted or corrupted in any way. He called it God's natural, unspoiled creation. They also went on to Fort Benton and Fort Shaw, following the Lewis and Clark trail into Oregon. The entire time, Ray provided Wendell with a running narrative of the history of the entire area, as if he had not been gone for some fifty years.[3]

Neither the passing years nor his retirement had diminished Ray's love for the outdoors and his interest in, and amazing ability to recall, historical facts. Nor did it mean the end of his ministry. Ray remained active, speaking several times at both PBC Palo Alto and PBC Cupertino, as well as continuing to teach at many retreats and conferences. He also continued to write, completing a book on John's gospel, *God's Loving Word*, and a commentary on the book of Hebrews, which was part of the *IVP New Testament Commentary Series*.

Ray also was one of the founding members of a group called the Rogue River Fellowship. Initiated by Doug Shearer, senior pastor of New Hope Christian Fellowship of Sacramento, California, this group of evangelical leaders sought to address various practices and beliefs in the church. Their burden was to address such contemporary church issues as demonic deliverance, political involvement, inner healing, modern-day prophecy, and worship styles. "The name 'Rogue Fellowship' may come from the character of the participants," Shearer writes, "the character of the heterodoxies and heteropraxies we hope to define, or from the fact that we first met in Ray Stedman's house overlooking the Rogue River in Grants Pass, Oregon."[4] Other members of the group included Gerry E. Breshears of Western Theological Seminary; Zenas Bicket, president of Bercan College; Rick Booyes, pastor of Trail Christian Fellowship; Bob Bonner, pastor of Calvary Crossroads Church; and Garry Friesen, dean of the faculty of Multnomah School of the Bible.

Perhaps the most significant aspect of Ray's ministry during retirement, however, was simply the relationships he continued to nurture with younger men. Although by now a well-known, seasoned veteran of ministry himself, Charles Swindoll still considered Ray one of his most valued mentors, as revealed in his memories of his last meeting with Ray.

"There we sat, a cluster of six. A stubby orange candle burned at the center of our table. Flickering eerie shadows crossed all our faces. One spoke; five listened. Every question was handled with such grace, such effortless ease. There was no doubt that each answer was drawn from deep wells of wisdom, shaped by tough decisions and nurtured by time. Like forty years in the same church. And seasoned by travel. Like having ministered around the world. And honed by tests, risks, heartbreaks, and failures. But, like the best wines, it was those decades spent in the same crucible year after year that made Ray's counsel invaluable. Had those years been spent in the military, he would have a chest full of medals.

"His age? Seventy-four. His face? Rugged as fifty miles of bad road. His eyes? Ah, those eyes. Piercing. When he peered at you, it was as if they penetrated to the back of your cranium. He had virtually seen it all; weathered all the flack and delights of the flock. Outlived all the fads and gimmicks of trendy generations, known the ecstasy of seeing many lives revolutionized, the agony of several lives ruined, and the monotony of a few lives remaining unchanged. He has paid his dues. And he has the scars to prove it. What a creative visionary!

"But this is not to say he's over the hill. Or to suggest that he has lost his zeal for living, his ability to articulate his thoughts, or his keen sense of humor. There we sat for well over three hours, hearing his stories, pondering his principles, questioning his conclusions, and responding to his ideas. The evening was punctuated with periodic outbursts of laughter followed by protracted periods of quiet talk. All six of us lost contact with time."[5]

Times of Restoration

ALTHOUGH RAY REMAINED ACTIVE in ministry, his primary focus in retirement became his family. For forty years Elaine had had a sense that Ray was not hers to possess, that she was called to release him to be a blessing to others. But now, together in Oregon, she and the girls felt that this husband and father was "theirs" again. Susan Stedman believes that in order for that to be possible, Ray needed to be out of the public eye.

"I saw Dad and Mom's move up here to Oregon as an attempt to move out of that position and rekindle the family bonds, to allow us to get to know each other now, past those tumultuous times, and to allow for a new, more mature relationship to develop between us. And I felt like that really happened. I saw Dad moving away from those very busy, busy years. I remember as a child . . . most of my memories of Dad are of this person in an office that I was not to disturb . . . I understand that it was necessary, that he needed that time because in order for him to do what he did he needed unbroken blocks of concentrated time to put into his studies . . . but as a child I felt like, first, my mother, and then people in the congregation were constantly keeping me from my father, and I resented it. So those last years here in Oregon with us as a family spending unrestricted time together, not just on holidays, but being able to have Mom and Dad over for dinner, just to have them all to myself . . . was a really important thing to me. It meant a tremendous amount to me."[6]

These times not only meant a lot to his daughters, they also meant a good deal to Ray. Linda Stedman Teshima remembers how important it was to her father that she and her children join him on another return trip to Montana.

"It was . . . June of 1991. I had taken my boys to visit Mom and Dad at their river house in Grants Pass and I was getting ready to leave and head back to Medford. Dad and I were standing in the driveway and he asked me if I could attend a family conference in Montana that August, where he was the speaker. It was to be held at Clydehurst Ranch, which is located between Billings and Bozeman. He asked if I would bring the boys. . . . I told him I already had plans to go to Santa Barbara to visit my friends. . . . For some reason he was very insistent about me going to this conference. I was very reluctant to change my plans and told him I really couldn't see how it would work. . . . But, no matter what excuse I presented, he was very insistent about me going. Finally he took me gently by the arm and said, 'I don't know how much longer I'll be with you, Linda, and I really want you to see Montana.' At that point, I simply said, 'OK, I'll go.' Something about his plea was so sincere and so important, I couldn't say no.

"Dad paid for my travel expenses, and the kids and I packed our bags and took off in my Ford Bronco for Montana. . . . Dad flew to Montana and we met him there at Clydehurst Ranch, a beautiful family conference center located in a small canyon underneath the BIG Montana sky. Already enchanted by the rugged beauty of Montana, I knew why he wanted to share this with me and his grandchildren. But what was to come was even more special.

"Many families had come there to hear Dad teach the book of Revelation. He taught every night, the messages very similar to each chapter in his book *God's Final Word*. With no distractions, other than the peaceful, majestic canyon and the warm, loving atmosphere of the family camp, I felt like Dad and I were as close as we'd ever been. I was amazed at his insight into Revelation and soaked in everything he taught. We would have meals together and talk about so many things. He made sure that the kids could take any fun class they wanted, and knowing how much I love horses, he paid for all of us to have horseback rides together. He took the boys fishing—as he often did—and they even saw a bear one day that crossed the river right in front of them!

"One night, toward the end of the week, I met Dad at his cabin just before the dinner bell rang. We were sitting together on the porch, enjoying the summer Montana evening when he suddenly said to me 'Linda, Mom and I are so grateful for your restored faith in our Lord,' and then he asked me, 'Is there anything I could have done differently as a father that would have helped you girls more and kept you from straying?'

"I was so touched by his candor and vulnerability. I thought for a moment and just said, 'No, Dad, I don't think there is anything you could have done differently. We were all taught the truth, and were loved so well by you and Mom, but times were hard when we became teenagers, and the culture was so influential on our lives. We were strong-willed children, and we made a choice as to what direction we would take. You and Mom did the best you could, and now, what you taught us all makes sense and God has won us back by His kindness and grace. The Lord never let us stray too far and your prayers kept us alive, I'm sure. You have loved us unconditionally through all our years of rebellion, and that's more than any child could ask for. You never turned away from us.' He expressed regret about having to be away so much when we were young. I told him I never had a problem with that because I just knew he was doing the Lord's work, and I never questioned that. I gave him a big hug and we headed up to dinner.... As always, being with Dad was fascinating and fun, educational and enlightening, sweet and safe. This trip to Montana was one that was meant to be. Dad knew it. I knew it. And best of all, the Lord knew it."[7]

Some of Ray's most meaningful times in those later years were spent with his eleven grandchildren. Known to them as "Papa,"

Ray especially enjoyed fishing and boating with his grandchildren, and these outings allowed him to express his mischievous side. On one occasion, Ray attempted to take several of his grandsons on an ill-advised journey down the Rogue River in a flat-bottomed aluminum rowboat he had just purchased. Partway through the trip, after fishing, Ray forgot to pull up the anchor as the boat started down the rapids. When the anchor caught the bottom, the boat quickly filled with water, forcing Ray and the boys to hang on to the side of the boat for dear life. Ray calmly pulled out his pocketknife, disappeared into the water, and cut the anchor loose. When he emerged and saw all were safely back in the boat, instead of being overjoyed by their deliverance from danger, Ray was upset about losing a fifteen-dollar anchor![8]

Times like these meant a great deal to Ray and his family, and probably would have been cherished even more if they had known that his days on earth were coming to an end.

Nearing the End

IN THE EARLY MONTHS of 1992, Ray began to feel increasingly tired. His appetite decreased, and he lost a great deal of weight. For a long time he resisted seeing a doctor, and when he finally did, he was diagnosed with an inoperable tumor of the kidney. Ray now had just a few months to live.

Many believe that Ray had a strong sense that he was dying even before the diagnosis. Jeanne Hendricks recalls talking with him at their annual gathering with the Stedmans, Heatons, and Ropers in the early part of 1992. "The last time we were in Mendocino with him, we were asking about his health, and he said he'd been healthy all his life, but now he had a few questions—he was going to the doctor right after that. But I think, at that point, he knew in his heart that there was something wrong, something really wrong."[9]

When Jeanne spoke with Ray on the phone after he had been to the doctor, he told her that the diagnosis was not good. It was cancer. "But his whole tone of voice," says Jeanne, "was that he knew it all along."[10]

A few weeks later, Howard received a postcard from Ray. "It brings tears to my eyes," says Howard. "It was such a gentle, loving note, and at the end he said how things were with him, and how he would have a little attack now and then, but that the Lord was in charge. Just a postcard, handwritten by Ray on both sides. Believe me I cherish that."[11]

Ray spent most of the last few months of his life seeing only his family, although he did have some communication with cherished friends. David Roper spoke with him several times on the phone and remembers Ray being very subdued and quiet. Luis Palau received a cherished handwritten note inside a copy of Ray's recently published commentary on Hebrews, which read, "To my dearly beloved son in the faith, with grateful memories that stretch from Argentina to the whole world. May God richly bless you and Pat and your four wonderful boys—until the Sun rises and every shadow fades away."[12]

Howard and Jeanne Hendricks visited Ray during this time and found him in good humor. He insisted that they watch a Victor Borge video together. Howard confesses that he never laughed harder in his life, and Ray was literally rolling on the floor with laughter. "It was like, the reality of heaven is coming, man, and I'm in a position to laugh—you know, I'm leaving here, baby! I remember his last words to me, 'Carry on, Howie. Carry on.'"[13]

Just a few weeks before his death, Ray and Elaine traveled to Mexico so that Ray could undergo an experimental treatment. Ray might not have gone, but Elaine urged him to try every possible avenue to prolong his life. Although the treatment was unsuccessful, this trip turned into a sweet time for Ray and Elaine to be alone together and, in essence, to say their own special goodbyes.

When Laurie and Linda met their parents at the airport upon their return, they were grieved to see that their father was very frail and so weak that he could hardly speak. "I knew my father's days on earth were almost done," says Linda.

On October 5, 1992, Ray celebrated his seventy-fifth birthday surrounded by his family. As Elaine read to him from the many cards he had received, Ray asked, "Could we just read the rest later? I'm so tired." Elaine responded, "Oh, Ray, you have been a blessing to so many and they just want to thank you." In characteristic humility he replied, "Oh, it's so undeserved. I just did what I was sent to do."[14]

As a birthday gift, Ray's family gave him a new recording of Handel's Messiah, which he had always loved. Unable to get out of bed, and with his legs swollen to twice their normal size, Ray listened and allowed the music to bolster his spirit. When Linda reminded him that he would soon get to talk with Moses and Paul, Ray responded, "I just want to see my Jesus."[15]

Even in pain and on the brink of death, Ray did not lose his sense of humor. Just before slipping into a coma, he fell forward while being lifted up from his bed. The hospice nurse caring for him asked rhetorically, "Where are you going, Ray?" His response broke up the others in the room with laughter. "I'm going to heaven!"[16]

On October 7, Linda and Laurie were at his bedside and Linda was reading from 1 Corinthians 15:50–55 (NASB). As she read those triumphant words, "Death is swallowed up in victory. 'O death, where is your victory? O death, where is your sting?'" she and Laurie felt a holy presence in the room. And at that moment Ray Stedman took his last deep breath and slipped away to glory. It was a fitting homegoing for one who for so long had anticipated this day.[17]

A few weeks after his death, the memorial service for Ray was held at PBC. Bob Roe, Ray's good friend and fellow elder, gave the eulogy. There was the joyful singing of Ray's favorite hymn, "And Can It Be." And David Roper preached from the life of Elijah, comparing Ray to Elijah, for both had lived according to unseen realities. Then, as had been the practice in the days of Body Life, the microphone was passed around and many of Ray's sons in the faith shared what Ray meant to them. One of these men, Brian Morgan, who had also worked alongside Ray as a pastor, read a moving poem he had written in Ray's honor:

O Ray,

> *you were the good scribe*
> *who took out of your treasure*
> *things old and made them new,*
> *as glorious as Emmaus!*

> *You were the loving disciple*
> *whose warmth could disarm*
> *the most awkward legalist; and rebuild*
> *from that ancient rubble a heart of flesh.*

> *You were our bright illumined star,*
> *the Luther of our generation,*
> *with earthly genius removing the papal scepter,*
> *and fearing none, returned it to the saints.*

> *No rank of man was able to stand*
> *before your penetrating eye;*
> *nor was there a garrison strong enough*
> *to protect one's heart from your piercing gaze.*

> *You were the orphan of old*
> *who sang in Adullam,*
> *and in that cave gathered*
> *the outcasts of a new age.*

> *You transformed us*
> *by the simplicity*

of the Sacred page,
into a multitude of royal sons.

Now we say, "Everything from Him,
nothing from us!"
Yes, any old clay pot will do,
but it first must be broken.

And in the end, when you could have it all,
when all others were playing the role of King,
you arose and said, "It shall not be so among you."
And taking your towel, sat down as a brother.

Now the dream of life is over,
morning of eternity doth succeed,
Away the shadows of time
to eternal substance—Yeshuah.

And while we remain, our tears
shall bear constant witness
that it was you who faithfully taught us
The New Covenant.
We love you, Papa.[18]

The service was concluded by Howard Hendricks, who had journeyed with Ray since their days at Dallas Seminary, giving the benediction before a bagpipe solo of "Amazing Grace." A fitting way to bid farewell to the Scotsman from Montana.

A Faithful Steward

HOW SHOULD RAY STEDMAN be remembered? When he was seventy-three and one of his daughters reminded him of all that he had accomplished in his those years, he turned to her and said, "I just wanted to be a faithful steward." And it is those words that are engraved on his gravestone in Grants Pass, Oregon: "He was a faithful steward."

Yes, Ray Stedman was, above all else, a faithful steward. He was the steward of a family. His willingness to offer up to the Lord his own wounded past of abandonment, refusing to play the victim, and somehow receive back a more tenacious and redemptive love for his own wife and four daughters is one of his greatest but least recognized accomplishments. He was the steward of a ministry. His legacy of investing in young men, who today are proud to call him their spiritual father, is unsurpassed. He was a steward of the truth. His commitment to the church as the body of Christ, and to the reality of "Christ in you" as described in his teaching on the New Covenant, truths that he felt the church needed to recover, continues to bear fruit today. Above all, he was a steward of the Scriptures. His model of faithful exposition, while serving for over forty years in the same church, is increasingly rare.

A few years before he died, Ray reflected candidly on the ministry God had entrusted to him years earlier. "Thirty-five years ago this year I came as a pastor to Peninsula Bible Church. I didn't realize it at the time, but, looking back now, I must confess that I was motivated more by personal ambition than any other thing. I thought I was dedicated to the work of the Lord, and to some degree I was. But, on reflection, I can see how much of it came from an urge to be a well-known pastor, to make a name as a Christian leader, to see an effective ministry begin with a great congregation. Through these thirty-five years, through much pain and struggle, those dreams have been fulfilled. But I want to tell you this: They do not mean very much to me right now! As I look back, what means more to me are the hundreds of lives that have been changed as people heard the Word of truth.... Homes have been revitalized, marriages have been restored, young people have been turned from hurtful and destructive practices, such as drug addiction, alcoholic abuse, false doctrines, and led into purity, and righteousness.

"I think of the great number of printed messages that have gone out to the far corners of the earth, and the hundreds of letters that keep coming back telling of dramatic, life-altering circumstances that have come out of reading these messages. I want to tell you, that is not my work, nor is it the work of anybody associated with us here, loyal and helpful as they have been. That is the work of Jesus, His mighty work, conducted from the throne of power at the right hand of the Majesty on high, carried out through the Spirit by means of willing men and women who saw themselves in the same relationship to Him as He is to the Father: 'You in me and I in you.' That is the greatest truth in the Bible."[19]

APPENDIX

———⟶⟨▌⟩⟵———

MEMORIES OF WINIFRED

I FIRST SAW IT in the summer of 1931, riding over the hill on a blistering hot day in my uncle's 1929 Chevrolet. Along with my aunt and their two small boys, Lowell and Wendell, we were coming to live there where my Uncle Fred would be superintendent of schools for the coming years.

We had driven the 42 miles north from Lewistown on a gravel road, skirting the edge of the Moccasin Mountains where the old mining camp of Maiden lay, and heading steadily north through the Dog Creek Valley. Far on the northern horizon and across the Missouri, the Bearpaws marked the site of Chief Joseph's last stand, and east of them the sharp edges of the Little Rockies broke the skyline.

I was just about to turn 14 and already Montana and the West was an exciting place to me. Though I missed my grade school friends back in the Red River Valley of North Dakota, I now looked forward eagerly to my first year of high school, and what life in Winifred would be like.

In those days the frontier seemed close at hand. The town was the center of a large, still sparsely settled area, stretching from the Missouri River, 25 miles to the north, to the lilting waters of the Judith River, 20 miles west, and to the east the small ranches and open range that reached to the mouth of the Musselshell, some 70 miles away, with the nearest city of any size, Lewistown, just beyond the Moccasins.

At that time Winifred served as a center for the whole vast area. It was still primitive in many ways, having no electricity, no phones except one line from Turner's Haberdashery to Lewistown. There was no modern plumbing and every house had its outside privy, even the high school, which sat at the top of the hill at the west end of main street. The nearest doctor was in Lewistown and though there once had been a drugstore, it had closed its doors during the Depression.

Nevertheless, it was an exciting place in which to live. Ranchers, cowboys, dryland farmers, all came to town to buy groceries, or to ship cattle or grain on the little Milwaukee train that came up on a spur line twice a week, or oftener when needed. Though Prohibition was the law, everyone knew where liquid refreshment was available. As Will Rogers remarked, "Prohibition was certainly a lot better than not having any liquor at all!"

Winters were often bitterly cold with great blizzards shutting down the little town's social life for days on end. Yet when the Chinooks [warm, moist winds] would blow, the snow could all disappear overnight. School was the center of the town's activity, for all the surrounding ranch and farm families would send their children into town to rent a house and live, often by themselves without adult supervision, for weeks on end. But these ranch children were for the most part well-disciplined, eager students who stayed away from immoral activities, and did well in their studies. There were some exceptions, of course, but they were all my acquaintances and friends and it was not difficult to sort out the few bad ones and avoid them.

There were two families, however, that usually provided some excitement. They had adjoining ranches north of town, and owned adjoining houses in town, which they occupied for the school season. For some reason which I never discovered, there was bad blood between them, and this would erupt from time to time in clashes between the family members. I recall walking home from school one spring day and passing the two houses in time to see one boy from one family lying prone on the ground, with one of the older girls of the other family standing over him with a raised axe, about to split his skull in two. Perhaps she was only threatening, but my arrival led her to lower the axe and let the boy up. Unfortunately, that wasn't the end, for occasionally they would take pot shots at one another with rifles at their ranches, though I never knew anyone to be hit.

Though lawmen were few and far between (there being a sheriff in Lewiston, but only an Irish constable named Nels in Winifred) there were surprisingly few major crimes. One notorious murder was that of a part-Mexican farmer named Turkey Joe, who lived by himself a few miles out of town. One day his body was found in his one-room cabin, and an attempt had been made to burn the cabin but the fire had gone out. Two brothers from a Hungarian immigrant family nearby were suspected of trying to rob Turkey Joe of the store of gold he had reputed to have hidden in the cabin, but to my knowledge no one was ever arrested for the crime.

Summers were the most fun for me. Two families who had children my own age had ranches, one on the edge of a deep canyon in the Breaks, and the other a wheat ranch northwest of town. One family had horses and cattle and ran a typical western cattle ranch where we would often ride in parties of ten or more, down the deep canyons to the creek and practice calf-roping, etc. The other family grew wheat and hay but had a large house where families would often gather for a full night of dancing, to the tunes of a fiddler, a piano, and whatever other instruments anyone cared to bring and play. Memories of those colorful evenings still rise fresh in my mind. The dancing would not stop till the sky began to lighten in the east.

Another ranch couple, just a mile out of town, had no children of their own, and virtually adopted me as a son. I got my first job with them, making hay during the summer, at 50 cents a day! They too had horses and cattle, and I learned much of the cowboy life with them, sometimes riding east to the open range, to brand calves that had been born during the spring months.

The main sport played at high school was basketball and the whole town would turn out in support of the local team. We played teams from Denton and Roy and sometimes as far away as Grass-range and Winnett. Though I played on the varsity my last two years I have not followed basketball much since then. My attraction was not to the game itself, but to the excitement that accompanied it and to the intense rivalry that would build up between towns.

My second job was driving a truck up from the isolated Stafford ranch on the Missouri, up through the steep Breaks to bring produce grown on the ranch to the Stafford grocery store in town. My days at the ranch were often lonely ones, as the only other person around was a part-French ex-sheepherder who served as manager of the ranch. I spent my hours after work resurrecting a leaky rowboat which I found, and rowing across the rapid-flowing Missouri to fish. I caught several catfish around two to three feet long and they were a welcome change to our diet. I also had to be on constant watch for rattlesnakes, as I killed several large ones that summer.

Many years later (in 1989) I drove back to that ranch and found it abandoned. But my cousin and I took the free ferry across the river and, parking the car on the dirt road out of sight, we climbed a nearby hill and looked out over the river and surrounding hills. For 360 degrees we could not see anything that was manmade or changed since Lewis and Clark had camped at that spot in 1805. There are few places left in the United States of which a claim like that could be made.

Though the school I attended was in an isolated town far from the fine amenities of civilization, yet the education I received was first-class. The knowledge I was given of classical literature was far beyond anything now taught in the high schools of California. Though we only had a primitive chemistry laboratory I went on from there to become so proficient in chemistry that my professor in college asked me to take over the class if he could not show up someday. The typing and shorthand which I learned at Winifred High School kept me employed through most of the Depression, and led to my serving as a court reporter in the Navy, taking shorthand records of the Navy court-martials at Pearl Harbor during World War II.

When I graduated in the spring of 1935 I was only 17, but though I soon left Winifred for college and then on into various parts of the world, I have never ceased to value the things I learned and the people I knew in that strategic little central Montana town. In 1989 I was honored to be invited to launch the Montana Centennial Celebration as speaker at the Billings Civic Arena in November. It was a great delight to me to do so as it brought flooding back the happy memories I had of those days on the Great Plains when Montana was still young and its skies were always blue!

———

(From The Ray Stedman Library Index, the archives of Elaine Stedman, July 30, 1996. Used by permission.)

AUTHENTIC CHRISTIANITY

A COVENANT IS AN arrangement between people. All life operates or arises out of a covenant. When two people want to go into business together the first thing they do is draw up a contract or a partnership. That is the basic covenant that defines the terms of their operation. A marriage is that kind of a covenant. It is an agreement between a man and a woman to stick together against all odds, to work out their problems, to share their resources.

Life itself is the most fundamental covenant of all. Life is the agreement or the arrangement that God has already made with us that He will provide for us what it takes to operate, to act. None of us really supplies our own energy; God does. But God does this so continually that we get the illusion that we are supplying it, that it is something inherent in us. We are so used to making a decision, and then promptly starting to do something, that we never realize that if God didn't give us power to act we could not do what we decided to do. We could not even move a muscle, raise an arm or wink an eye if it weren't for power supplied from something outside of us. All men operate on this principle, but they are blind to this basic truth. It's a funny thing that truth that is really basic is very hard to discover because we take it for granted. It is so much a part of us that we hardly even think about it.

In the Scriptures we have what the apostle Paul calls an Old Covenant and a New Covenant. Now the passage I use oftentimes in teaching the whole truth of both of these Covenants, or arrangements for life, is found in 2 Corinthians. In chapter 3, verse 4, Paul says some interesting words:

> Such is the confidence that we have through Christ toward God.

What kind of confidence? Obviously, that is referring back to something. Paul is referring to the boldness, the confident sense of adequacy he has in his life that makes him able to function as a human being, and even in his work as an apostle. He says this confidence, this adequacy, comes from a certain source. I am not going to take time to expound this at any length, but I want to show you what kind of confidence Paul is talking about. In chapter 2, verse 14, Paul says,

> Thanks be to God who in Christ always leads us in triumph (2 Corinthians 2:14a RSV).

Now that is confidence. You are always going to be led in triumph not in defeat, not in failure, not in weakness even, but in triumph.

> . . . and through us spreads the fragrance of the knowledge of him everywhere we go. For we are the aroma of Christ to God among those who are being saved and among those who are perishing. To one a fragrance from death to death and to another a fragrance from life to life. (2 Corinthians 2:14b–16a RSV).

Then Paul asks this question:

> Who is sufficient for these things? (2 Corinthians 2:16b RSV).

Where do you get that kind of ability and adequacy? What kind of a study course will give you that? What kind of chemical compound will produce that? I am always fascinated by magazine ads. They are forever offering the secret of adequacy. If you get a certain deodorant you will be adequate to handle whatever comes your way. Or if you would use the right mouthwash, or the right toothpaste, it will help tremendously. Now everybody knows those ads are fake. Nobody even takes them seriously, although people do buy the product, which is what these ads seek. But if you really took seriously the claims of the newspaper advertising and billboard advertising you would think you had discovered the elixir of life in some of these things. They are offering adequacy because that is what human beings long for: how to be able to cope, how to handle situations. And not only are chemical compounds offered, but also courses. One says, "Have you discovered all the hidden powers of your personality? Do you know the secrets of the ancients, now rediscovered? Send ten dollars for this course. Read this and you will get all these secret powers." Again, it is the offer of the secret of adequacy. In a hundred ways today the world is offering this.

Paul continues, verse 17:

> For we are not like so many, peddlers of God's word; but as men of sincerity, as commissioned by God, in the sight of God we speak in Christ. Are we beginning to commend ourselves again? Or do we need, as some do, letters of recommendation to you, or from you? (2 Corinthians 2:17–3:2 RSV).

It is hard to believe, but these people in Corinth had been misled by some teachers who came down from Jerusalem and taught them that they ought to do like everybody else and boast about their accomplishments. These teachers even suggested that the apostle Paul was not much of an apostle because he did not do this; and that he really was not one of the true apostles because he was not part of the Twelve. They actually had the effrontery to suggest that these people write to Paul and suggest that the next time he came to Corinth he bring a letter of recommendation from the apostle Peter, or James or John, or others of the real Twelve, the real apostles.

Paul says, in effect, "Do you really mean that? Are you serious about that? Have you ever thought that you yourselves are our letter of recommendation?"

> You yourselves are our letter of recommendation, written on your hearts, to be known and read by all men; and you show that you are a letter from Christ delivered by us, written not with ink, but

with the Spirit of the living God, not on tablets of stone but on tablets of human hearts (2 Corinthians 3:2–3 RSV).

How were they a letter of recommendation? Paul says, "Look what has happened to you. Look at the changes that have happened in your lives since we came and preached to you the word of truth. Has anything happened?" In his first letter to the Corinthians, there is a beautiful passage, which says, "Do you not know that the unrighteous will not inherit the kingdom of God?" (1 Corinthians 6:9a RSV). It goes on to list such things as idolaters, adulterers, homosexuals, thieves, drunkards, etc. Paul goes on to say, "Such were some of you, but you were washed, you were sanctified, you were justified" (1 Corinthians 6:11a RSV). Some amazing things had happened to them. So Paul says, in effect, "Take a look at your life. Do you think that these changes could happen if what we were saying was not the truth of God? Your own life is our letter of recommendation."

Now I have listed in the study I have made on 2 Corinthians certain qualities of this kind of life. First, there is a kind of unquenchable optimism. "Thanks be unto God," Paul says (2 Corinthians 2:14a RSV). That marks the kind of life Paul lived. He was always giving thanks for everything that happened, no matter how rough and tough it was.

Then there is a pattern of unvarying success: "Who always leads us in triumph," Paul says (2 Corinthians 2:14b RSV). Never in failure. That is, not triumph in his (Paul's) plan, but Christ's plan.

Then there is an unforgettable impact, as brought out in the last part of verse 14 through verse 16. Everywhere Paul goes he is like a perfume which fills a room, a fragrance of Christ. To some who are rejecting him, this fragrance is an odor of death unto death, but to those who accept him, it is an odor of life unto life.

Then there is this unimpeachable integrity, in verse 17. It is summed up in the words, "We are men of sincerity, commissioned of God, living in the sight of God, speaking in Christ to you."

And then finally, this note of undeniable reality. In chapter 3, verses 1–3, Paul says, "Your own lives are proof that what we say and what we do is by the power of the Spirit of God."

That is what Paul means when he says, "Who is sufficient for these things?" (2 Corinthians 2:16b). Where do you find the secret of that kind of living? His answer is the New Covenant. In chapter 3, verses 4–6, he says,

> Such is the confidence that we have through Christ toward God. Not that we are sufficient of ourselves to claim anything as coming from us; our sufficiency is from God, who has qualified us to be ministers of a new covenant, not in a written code but in the Spirit; for the written code kills but the Spirit gives life (2 Corinthians 3:4–6 RSV).

Everyone is born into this world operating on the Old Covenant, as contrasted with the New, which we can learn when we become Christians. Now being a Christian does not mean that you automatically operate in the New Covenant. That is why you find Christians who are just as mixed up, just as torn up inside, just as unable to handle life as non-Christians are. Though they are Christians they have not learned the value of being a Christian. They have not learned how to operate on the New Covenant, which they have available to them in the Lord Jesus. They are still operating, for the most part, on the Old Covenant. That is what is fouling up their lives.

Now what do I mean when I say, "The Old Covenant"? Paul links this with the Law of Moses. He calls it, "the written code which kills, which was written on tablets of stone" (cf. 2 Corinthians 3:6, and so on). Why would Paul associate this with the Law of Moses? The reason is that Law was given to us in order to show us that the basis of our human life, inherited from Adam, is all wrong. It won't work. The Law makes that clear to us and nothing else will do it. The Law makes a demand upon us and when we try to fulfill that demand, we find out we can't, ultimately. Nobody has ever lived up to the Ten Commandments by trying his best to do so. If you doubt that, give yourself twenty-four hours in which you seek with all your strength and might to live up to the Ten Commandments. I will guarantee you will have broken one of them before fifteen minutes is over. If not any others, the last one: "Thou shalt not covet." That means you must not look around this room and see anything that anybody has that you would like to have. That is the Law! It is given to show us that the way we are living now, the resources of our life in Adam, is not workable.

The New Covenant Paul describes consists of this: Nothing coming from us, everything from God:

> Not that we are sufficient of ourselves to claim anything as coming from us [nothing coming from us, but]; our sufficiency is from God [everything from God] (2 Corinthians 3:5 RSV).

It is God at work in us that makes us act and produce this kind of living, if we are going to do it at all. If that is the New Covenant, what do you think the Old Covenant is? "Everything coming from us; nothing coming from God."

At any given moment you are operating as a Christian on one or the other of those two. You never can draw from both at once. Jesus said so: "No man can serve two masters. Either he will love the one and hate the other or cling to one and despise the other" (cf. Matthew 6:24). You cannot cling to both; you cannot draw from both. The only time you have to live is right now: The present is all there is; the future is not yet come; the past is gone.

You only can live in the present, and therefore the present moment is either being lived in the Old Covenant or the New, but not both.

"But," you say, "I don't understand that. How could a believer in Jesus Christ even act as though nothing depended on God? Of course we depend on God." It's amazing how easy it is to do this.

We all know that God is there, but we really don't expect Him to do anything. That is the problem. And that is the great problem with the church today.

As I travel around the world I am continually astonished at how little Christians expect God to do anything, how churches are run and operated exactly like businesses, never expecting God to do a thing. Everything depends on us. It all has to be organized. It all has to be carried out by men alone.

Now God is a God of order, but He is not a God of organization, particularly. Organizations can often become the substitute for the Holy Spirit. Somebody well said that if the Holy Spirit were suddenly removed from most of the churches of this country, nobody would know that anything had happened because they were not depending on Him anyway.

Let me illustrate how this can be. Think of that story of Jesus feeding the five thousand. The scene is by the seashore in the evening hours. The crowd has been listening all day and they are hungry. Philip came to Jesus and said, "Send them away. We have no bread to feed them with" (cf. Matthew 14:15b). Jesus said to him, "You give them bread. Give them to eat" (cf. Matthew 14:16). And what was Philip's reaction? "We do not have money and the stores are all closed and we cannot get a loan from the bank and there is no way we can do this" (cf. John 6:7). Philip is counting on his human resources. Here is the Lord Jesus, whom he had just seen do wonderful things, standing in front of him, but he did not reckon on Him at all. His reckoning was on the normal resources of life. Now, if Philip had been an atheist and Jesus had said to him, "Give ye them to eat" (KJV) he would have said the same thing exactly. In other words, there is no difference between the believer and the unbeliever in the way he acts in that situation.

How often and how easily we do this. God tells us to do something and we start immediately saying, "Have I got the training, the background, the skill, the necessary knowledge? Have I had the course? Can I do this? Have I got the personality?" Now I am not implying that you don't have to do some planning because God does direct us to do certain things and not to do other things. But the point is, whom do you reckon on when you do decide to do something? Is it you, or God in you?

That is the difference between the Old and the New Covenant. The Old is, everything comes from me, it all depends on me. If I don't have what it takes, it can't get done. On the other hand, your attitude can be that everything depends on God. He has called you and asked you to be His agent by which this comes. That is the New Covenant. That produces the kind of life Paul has been describing in 2 Corinthians 2:14–17. The Old produces what Paul calls in Galatians "the works of the flesh." That is what the Old Covenant is: the flesh at work. Thus it produces the works of the flesh which he says are evident, manifest, easily visible: "The works of the flesh are plain: immorality, impurity, licentiousness, idolatry, sorcery enmity, strife, jealousy, anger, selfishness, dissension, party spirit, envy, drunkenness, carousing, and the like" (Galatians 5:19–21a RSV).

That explains the struggle that Paul records for us in his own experience in Romans 7: "The thing that I would not do, that I do, and the thing that I would do, I do not" (cf. Romans 7:15). Have you ever felt that way? Have you ever seen a zealous, eager young Christian or older Christian desperately trying to do something for God and ending up after awhile so discouraged and defeated he just wants to quit? In fact, he probably does. But that is a very hopeful stage. Jesus said, "Blessed are the poor in spirit, who have come to the end of their resources" (cf. Matthew 5:3). Why? "For theirs is the kingdom of heaven." That is the time when God can give you something. When you have ended your own resources, then He can give you His. That is why the Old Covenant is, "Nothing coming from God, everything coming from me," while the New Covenant is, "Everything coming from God, nothing coming from me."

You only have to look at yourself to see how much of your life is lived in that Old Covenant. You expect success by virtue of something resident in you: your ancestry, your training, your personality, your good looks or something like that. This attitude produces the extrovert, the kind that reckons on his resources: "I've got what it takes, I can do that." Now he may be very modest in his language. We learn all kinds of little subtle tricks to hide this kind of egoism. We say, "I have never really had any special training for that, but I have had some experience in it, and I will do my best." Thus we are subtly saying to people, "I have got what it takes." Or we look at the demands, the problem, the situation we are asked to enter into or perform, and we say, "I don't have what it takes. I can't do that. Don't ask me to do a thing like that. I am one of those people who was behind the door when the gifts were passed out, and I just can't do anything like that." But who are you looking at when you say something like that? Yourself! You are reckoning on your "unresources" but your eye is fixed on the same person, yourself. So both the introvert and the extrovert are wrong.

Most of us introverts always envy the extroverts and wish we could be like them; but, if we did, we would only switch to the extreme which is just as bad. So we don't improve our position by being that. What we need to discover is how to get off any trust in ourselves at all and trust in the activity of God, who has promised that He would be in us and work through us.

Philippians 2:13 has a beautiful promise in which Paul says, "Go to work to work out your own solution." (That is what he means when he says to "work out your own salvation" not in the sense of going to heaven, but of solutions to problems that beset you.) "Work out your own solutions," he says, "knowing that God is at work in you, both to will and to work that which pleases him." Now the only thing that pleases God is what God Himself does. Anything a man does apart from God never pleases God. It is always a failure; it is always insufficient in some area. The only thing that can please God is perfection, and the only one who can perfectly work is God Himself. Therefore, the only thing, the only life that is ever pleasing to God is the life lived by faith, that is, by expecting God to be at work in you. That is what faith is. That is why Hebrews tells us, "without faith it is impossible to please God" (cf. Hebrews 11:6), and why God tells us Himself that the only life that is pleasing to Him is that which He Himself does. That is the New Covenant.

It helped me a great deal to learn that the apostle Paul did not know this for at least ten years of his life as a Christian. After he was converted on the Damascus Road, he made the same mistake that every one of us makes. He started out with a bit of knowledge of who Christ was and set out to convert the world for Christ by using the brilliance of his mind, the background and training he had, and even his ancestry as a Jew to convince the Jews. He thought he had what it took and he lists a most impressive array of credentials for us in Philippians, chapter 3. "If any of you think that you are men of the flesh," he says, "I've got something more to glory in. I was a Hebrew of the Hebrews, born a Jew, circumcised on the eighth day, raised up as a Pharisee, trained as a Pharisee. I was blameless before the law. My morality was without rebuke in the eyes of the religious world in which I lived. My activity was zealous. I even persecuted the church" (cf. Philippians 3:4–6a). He had all these things going for him. So even after he became a Christian, he reckoned on the same things for success. But, when he tried it in Damascus, not one convert is recorded. Instead they organized a lynch party! Paul had to sneak out over a wall in a basket at night, just like a criminal.

Then he came up to Jerusalem, he tells us, and there he tried the same thing. He went in and out among the Hellenists (the Greek-speaking Jews) and tried to persuade them that Jesus was the Christ. This was his own crowd. He was so sure that he had what it took to reach them. But they organized another lynch party in Jerusalem.

Finally, discouraged and defeated, Paul went into the temple to pray. The Lord Jesus appeared to him and said to him, "I want you to leave Jerusalem because they will not receive your testimony about me" (Acts 22:18). And what did Paul say? He tells us in Acts 22. I am going to paraphrase a little bit, but in essence what he said was,

"Lord, you don't understand this situation. You are going to miss the greatest opportunity of your life. Do you realize the equipment I have to reach these people? I was one of them. I know their language. I know their customs. I know their attitudes. If anybody has what it takes to reach these Jews it is me. You don't know what you are doing sending me away from here. Why, this is the greatest opportunity you have ever had" (cf. Acts 22:19–20).

But Jesus replied in one word: "Depart!" (Acts 22:21a). Then He said, "Don't argue with me. I am going to send you far hence to the Gentiles" (cf. Acts 22:21b).

So Paul was sent to the hardest place on earth, his hometown, Tarsus. For ten years we never hear of him again, until Barnabas goes down to Antioch where a great awakening has broken out; but he comes down to help him, he is a different man now. He has learned to shift from the Old Covenant to the New Covenant. He tells us in Philippians he learned a tremendous truth: that the things he once counted gain he now counts nothing but a pile of manure, compared with the richness and greatness of trusting in Christ to be at work in him (cf. Philippians 3:8).

Now that is the secret of life. That is the way man was intended to live. That is the way he did live in the beginning. When Adam was created he was a man indwelt by the Spirit of God, and therefore everything he did, he did by the power of God. Whenever Adam planted a tree, or weeded the garden, or picked up a shrub, or named the animals, or whatever it was, he did it by the wisdom and power of God. Therefore it was right. It fit the situation. It was done by God at work in him. Adam had a tremendous exhilarating sense of doing things right, knowing they were right, and doing so by virtue of the fact that he expected God who lived within him to supply what it took to do it. That is the New Covenant. When God gave him the choice of obedience, which involved Adam continuing to expect God to supply him with all the knowledge that he needed, Adam chose to disobey and he lost that whole relationship. The Spirit of God was withdrawn from his human spirit. He was plunged into the condition in which we are all born, that of counting on something in us for success. That is what destroys us.

This is basic to an understanding of human activity and the problems of human life. We have to teach people that the problem with them is that they are counting on the wrong resource. This is a painstaking lesson, one not easily learned. We must patiently set it forth and carefully show how it lies in the Scriptures, and then help people to recognize the flesh (the old life at work within them) and analyze various situations to see whether it was the Old or the New Covenant they are drawing on.

Nothing is more basic to getting people operating rightly than this. The Old Covenant is totally rejected by God. It is what the Bible calls "the flesh," and the "flesh cannot please God" (Romans 8:8 KJV). The flesh results in death, which is the experience of negative qualities in life, like boredom, worry, anxiety, hostility, anger, greed, etc. That is death and that comes by trusting in something you think you have got in yourself.

This does not mean that people become robots. The choosing is left up to us, just as it was to Adam. The power of choice is what is given to men, not the power to do. The minute you choose to act, something else must supply the power within you. Either it is the old twisted form of life called "the flesh," or it is the new life from the Spirit which will produce "the fruit of the Spirit" (Galatians 5:22). But the key is that you must reject the old, then you can choose the new.

Most of us know something about this life in the Spirit. We try to live this way, but the trouble is that we try to hang on to both.

I find this everywhere. Talk to people about Body Life, for instance, in a church beginning to function this way, and you find they want to keep the whole program the way it is now and add Body Life to it. Nobody ever wants to tear down anything or get rid of anything, but until they do so they cannot put in anything new. That is what Jesus meant when He said, "You cannot put new wine into old wine skins. You cannot put new patches onto old garments" (cf. Matthew 9:15–16). You have got to get rid of it and start with everything fresh, in a sense. But we want to cling to the old, a dependence on something in us, and add God to it.

Do you ever see that in your prayers? Do you ever come to God and say, "Lord, I have worked this all out, I want you to bless it"? What is that saying? "It all depends on me. I want you to make it work, that's all." That is trying to mix the old and the new, and it will never work. You cannot do it. God will never go along with that process. He just folds His arms and says, "If that is the way you want to do it, you do it. I'll watch you." And He watches us until we fall flat on our faces. But when we are discouraged, after finding out it did not work, and cry out, "Lord, help me," He says, "Here I am. I have been here all along and I am willing to work through you right now, as long as you quit working, depending on yourself."

This means that we are agents, not instruments. God allows us to make the choices and He works through us. We very definitely have decisions to make in these matters, and without these decisions it won't work. But once we decide something, once we feel that we know what God wants us to do, then what do we count on to do it? That is the great question. That is what this New Covenant is all about.

Replies to comments and questions from the audience:
BOTH BOREDOM AND ANGER are fleshly reactions. The fruit of the Spirit is love, joy, peace, longsuffering, gentleness, patience, etc., and

also excitement. God is exciting and His kind of life is exciting. But when you are living in the Spirit, it does not mean that you are keyed up to a high pitch all the time; I don't want to give that idea. But life in the Spirit is never boring. It may be frightening, almost. Life can be filled with such intense problems that you hardly know how you are going to get through them, but you are not bored. You may even be scared, for fear and trembling is part of the Christian life. But not boredom, or anger. There is a right kind of anger, but there is also an impatient anger that is wrong. For example, we will see somebody operating in the flesh and we get upset or irritated with them, so then we are operating in the flesh. This is why, in that beautiful story of the woman taken in adultery, Jesus judged the judges. He would not let them sit there and self-righteously point their fingers at this woman. He pointed His finger at them and said, "Let him who is without sin cast the first stone" (cf. John 8:7).

Q. Is there a point in your life when you really come into the New Covenant, and you can recognize it, and live in it for days or weeks?

A. I would say that it is very unlikely that you would live for days and weeks in the New Covenant, simply because the enemy we are up against is very clever. The flesh is very deceitful. It is very unlikely, in my judgment, that you would live even a full day in the Spirit. Be glad if it is a few hours. But you never have to live long in the flesh. That is the point. You may catch yourself living in the flesh. (I do not mean tempted to live in it, that is a different thing. We must distinguish between the temptation to get angry, or to envy or lust or whatever it is. That is not sin in itself. It is how we deal with it that makes the difference.) But if we yield to it, we ought not to yield very long. We ought to learn to quickly recognize the flesh. That is the point. Irritability, upset, impatience, anxiety, whatever it may be, immediately recognize it, renounce it as being no longer necessary to us, immediately flee to the Lord and lay it before Him. Then we are returned to the Spirit immediately, and we go on until the next fall occurs (which may not be very far down the road).

So the Christian life is not a continual life of unbroken victory, although ideally that would be possible. Jesus undoubtedly lived that way, but we don't have that kind of understanding and recognition of the flesh, so we are apt to be trapped more. That is why the grace of forgiveness is provided for us, because those falls do not impede our progress if we return to the Lord. We have not lost it all by falling, since it did not depend on us in the beginning. If we ever begin to think, "Here I have been making it now for two-and-a-half days—and now look at me. I have fallen again and all that time is wasted." That shows you that you do not understand the New Covenant. It was not coming from you all that time anyhow. Return to your source of strength, thank God for being shown what was wrong, and then go on.

Notice how Paul often speaks of himself as approaching a demand made upon him with fear and trembling. Jesus did so too. When He went into the Garden of Gethsemane, He said, "My soul is deeply troubled within me" (cf. Matthew 26:38). He asked the disciples to pray with Him because of this. Fear and trembling is simply a recognition of weakness, of inability. It is a normal thing in human life. It is the way we ought to approach every situation. But don't stop there. It isn't just fear and trembling; it is fear and trembling that leads us to faith, to the confidence that God is there and He will do it. Therefore we need no longer fear and tremble. But to be frightened and feel a bit nervous or upset by any demand made upon us is a proper thing and not one that we should try to cure.

Q. It is easy to think of the New Covenant in terms of the Lord and the apostles, the New Testament, etc., but how about Moses and the Old Testament?

A. Moses is the symbol of the Old Covenant, but he lived by the New. The Old Testament saints did understand and live by the New Covenant, even though it had not yet been historically laid. The New Covenant is laid in the blood of Jesus: "This blood of the New Covenant which was made with many for the remission of sin" (cf. Matthew 26:28). But as the Old Testament saints were saved by the death of Christ, just as much as we, so they lived by His life, just as much as we. When Moses, therefore, was reckoning upon God to empower him to speak to Pharaoh and trusted God to fulfill His word that He would put His words into Moses' lips, he was living by the New Covenant. Now there were failures in Moses' life, just as there are in ours. He disobeyed God when he struck the rock, when he should have spoken to it. As a result, he was not permitted to enter into the Promised Land. But he himself was restored by the activity of God at work in him, even though a limitation was set upon his leadership. As Moses himself was restored to God at work in him and went on, so we can go on to be productive and effective persons.

Yet as a type, Moses stands as a symbol of the Old Covenant because he is associated with the Law, and the Law is always linked to the flesh. If there were no flesh, there would never have been any Law. Adam and Eve were never given the Law. They did not need it. They had the Law written in their hearts, as they were trusting the work of God within them. They knew what was the right thing to do in any given situation and that is the way we are to live too— by the Spirit. This is why Paul argues that the Law is ended the minute we believe. But the minute we disbelieve, the Law comes in again in order to show us our unbelief.

The Law as a standard of life will never change. The Law is nothing but an expression of the character of God, and God never changes His character. If we are to be like God, then that demand is always upon us, no matter how long the world, the heavens, and the earth last. Jesus said, "Heaven and earth will pass away, but these words [the words of the law] will never pass away" (cf. Matthew 24:35; Mark 13:31; Luke 21:33), because they reflect the character of God. In that sense, the Law remains always. But when you believe in Christ, it is the end of the Law for you. You do not need the Law making demands upon you then. I am not talking about becoming Christian when I say, "believe in Christ," I mean trusting Him as a Christian. In any moment that you expect Him to be at work in you and to supply you with his life in you and you are counting on that, then you do not need any law. But the minute you stop doing that, you need law again. It is right there waiting to correct you.

In that sense, the Law only ends by faith. This is what Paul says in Romans: "Christ is the end of the law to everyone who believes" (cf. Romans 10:4 KJV). Now don't quote that as, "Christ is the end of the Law." That would contradict what Jesus said in the Sermon on the Mount: "The law shall never pass away" (cf. Matthew 5:18). Christ is the end of the Law to everyone who believes. The minute you act by faith you are not acting by law, because faith and works are exactly contrary to one another. When you try to obey the Law because it is there, that is works. But when you respond to the God who is in you, and act on that basis, that is faith. Then you will fulfill the Law another way.

—◁◁◁▷▷▷—

(This special early paper by Ray C. Stedman is further developed and expanded upon in Ray's popular, best-selling book, *Authentic Christianity*. The book is in print and also available online at The Ray Stedman Library, © 1995, Discovery Publishing, a ministry of Peninsula Bible Church. Used by permission.)

A PASTOR'S AUTHORITY

"Those who are supposed to rule over the Gentiles lord it over them, and their great men exercise authority over them [Jesus said to His disciples]. But it shall not be so among you" (Mark 10:42b–43a RSV).

RATHER THAN BEING LORDS, He went on to say, disciples are to be servants of one another and the greatest is the one who is servant of all.

By these words Jesus indicates that an entirely different system of government than that employed by the world should prevail among Christians. Authority among Christians is not derived from the same source as worldly authority, nor is it to be exercised in the same manner. The world's view of authority places men over one another, as in a military command structure, a business executive hierarchy, or a governmental system. This is as it should be. Urged by the competitiveness created by the Fall, and faced with the rebelliousness and ruthlessness of sinful human nature, the world could not function without the use of command structures and executive decisions.

But as Jesus carefully stated, ". . . it shall not be so among you." Disciples are always in a different relationship to one another than worldlings are. Christians are brothers and sisters, children of one Father, and members one of another. Jesus put it clearly in Matthew 23:8: "One is your Master, and all you are brethren" (RSV).

Throughout twenty centuries the church has virtually ignored these words. Probably with the best of intentions, it has nevertheless repeatedly borrowed in toto the authority structures of the world, changed the names of executives from kings, generals, captains, presidents, governors, secretaries, heads, and chiefs to popes, patriarchs, bishops, stewards, deacons, pastors, and elders, and gone merrily on its way, lording it over the brethren and thus destroying the model of servanthood which our Lord intended. Christians have so totally forgotten Jesus' words that they frequently have set up the world's pattern of government without bothering to change the names, and have operated churches, mission organizations, youth organizations, schools, colleges, and seminaries, all in the name of Jesus Christ, but with presidents, directors, managers, heads, and chiefs in no way different from corresponding secular structures.

It is probably too late to do much about altering the many structures that are commonly called "para-church" or "quasichurch" organizations, but certainly Jesus' words must not be ignored in the worship and training functions of the church itself. Somewhere, surely, the words of Jesus, ". . . it shall not be so among you," must find some effect. Yet in most churches today an unthinking acceptance has been given to the idea that the pastor is the final voice of authority in both doctrine and practice, and that he is the executive officer of the church with respect to administration. But surely, if a pope over the whole church is bad, a pope in every church is no better!

It is clear from the Scriptures that the apostles were concerned about the danger of developing ecclesiastical bosses. In 2 Corinthians 1:24a (RSV), Paul reminds the Corinthians concerning his own apostolic authority: "Not that we lord it over your faith; we work with you for your joy. . . ." In the same letter he describes, with apparent disapproval, how the Corinthians reacted to certain leaders among themselves: "For you bear it if a man makes slaves of you, or preys upon you, or takes advantage of you, or puts on airs, or strikes you in the face" (2 Corinthians 11:20 (RSV)). Peter, too, is careful to warn the elders (and he includes himself among them) not to govern by being "domineering over those in your charge, but being examples to the flock" (1 Peter 5:3 RSV). And John speaks strongly against Diotrephes "who likes to put himself first, and takes it on himself to put some out of the church" (cf. 3 John 1:9–10). These first-century examples of church bosses indicate how easily churches then, as in the 20th century, ignored the words of Jesus, "it shall not be so among you."

But if the church is not to imitate the world in this matter, what is it to do? Leadership must certainly be exercised within the church, and there must be some form of authority. What is it to be? The question is answered in Jesus' words: "One is your Master" (Matthew 23:8b KJV). All too long churches have behaved as if Jesus were far away in heaven, and He has left it up to church leaders to make their own decisions, and run their own affairs. But Jesus Himself had assured them in giving the Great Commission, "Lo, I am with you always, even unto the end of the age" (cf. Matthew 28:20b). And in Matthew 18:20 (RSV) He reiterated, ". . . where two or three are gathered together in my name, there am I in the midst of them." Clearly this indicates that He is present not only in the church as a whole but in every local church as well. It is Jesus Himself, therefore, who is the ultimate authority within every body of Christians, and He is quite prepared to exercise His authority through the instrument He Himself has ordained—the elderhood.

The task of the elders is not to run the church themselves, but to determine how the Lord in their midst wishes to run His church. Much of this He has already made known through the Scriptures, which describe the impartation and exercise of spiritual gifts, the availability of resurrection power, and the responsibility of believers to bear one another's burdens, confess sins to one another, teach, admonish, and reprove one another, and witness to and serve the needs of a hurting world.

In the day-to-day decisions which every church faces, elders are to seek and find the mind of the Lord through an uncoerced unanimity, reached after thorough and biblically-related discussion. Thus, ultimate authority, even in practical matters, is vested in the Lord and in no one else. This is what the book of Acts reveals in its description of the initiative actions of the Holy Spirit, who obviously planned and ordered the evangelizing strategy of the early church (Acts 8, 13, etc.). The elders sought the mind of the Spirit, and, when it was made clear to them, they acted with unity of thought and purpose. ("For it has seemed good to the Holy Spirit and to us to lay upon you no greater burden . . ." Acts 15:28a RSV.) The authority, therefore, was not the authority of men, but of God, and it was expressed not through men, acting as individuals, but through the collective, united agreement of men whom the Spirit had led to eldership (see Acts 20:28).

The point is: no one man is the sole expression of the mind of the Spirit: No individual has authority from God to direct the affairs of the church. A plurality of elders is necessary as a safeguard to the all-too-human tendency to play God over other people. Even then, the authority exercised is not one of domination and arbitrary decree over anyone. The ability of a servant to influence anyone else does not lie in ordering someone around, but by obtaining their voluntary consent. This is the nature of all authority among Christians, even that of the Lord Himself! He does not force our obedience, but obtains it by love, expressed either in circumstantial discipline or by awakening gratitude through the meeting of our desperate needs.

The true authority of elders and other leaders in the church, then, is that of respect, aroused by their own loving and godly example. This is the force of two verses which are often cited by those who claim a unique authority of pastors over church members. The first is found in 1 Thessalonians 5:12–13a (RSV), "But we beseech you, brethren, to respect those who labor among you, and are over you in the Lord and admonish you, and to esteem them very highly in love because of their work." The key phrase is "and are over you in the Lord." The Greek word in question is *prohistamenous.* Though this is translated "over you" in both the Revised Standard and King James versions, the word itself contains no implication of being "over" another. The New English Bible more properly renders it, ". . . and in the Lord's fellowship are your leaders and counselors." The thought in the word is that of "standing before" others, not of "ruling over" them. It is the common word for leadership. Leaders can lead only if they are able to persuade some to follow.

Another verse used to support command authority is Hebrews 13:17a, which the Revised Standard Version renders, "Obey your leaders and submit to them, for they are keeping watch over your souls, as men who will have to give account." The imperative translated "obey" is from the word *peitho,* "to persuade." In the middle voice, used here, Thayer's lexicon gives its meaning as "to suffer one's self to be persuaded." Again there is no thought of a right to command someone against his will, but the clear thrust is that leaders are *persuaders* whose ability to persuade arises not from a smooth tongue or a dominant personality, but from *a personal walk which evokes respect.*

At this point many may be tempted to say, "What difference does it make? After all, the pattern of command authority is too widely established to alter now, and, besides, many churches seem to be doing all right as it is; why try to change now?"

In response, consider the following:

1. The Bible indicates that any deviation from the divine plan inevitably produces weakness, division, strife, increasing fruitlessness, and, ultimately, death. The present low state of many churches is testimony to the effects of ignoring, over a long period of time, God's way of working.

2. A command structure of authority in the church deprives the world of any model or demonstration of a different way of life than the one it already lives by. Worldlings see no dif-

ference in the church, and can see no reason why they should change and believe.

3. A command authority inevitably produces resentment, repression, exploitation and, finally, rebellion. It is the law, which Scripture assures us we can never redeem or restore, but which must, by its very nature, condemn and repress.

4. The desire of the Lord Jesus to show to the world a wholly new form of authority which is consistent with grace, not law, is nullified by a command structure among Christians, and the gospel of dying-to-live is denied even before it is proclaimed. This means that God is robbed of His glory and distorted before the watching world. Nothing could be more serious than this!

Admittedly, a call for a change of this nature is radical, even revolutionary. But since when was the church called to be a conforming society? Is it not high time we took seriously our Lord's words: "it shall *not* be so among you"? (emphasis added).

HOW TO KILL A LION ON A SNOWY DAY

I WANT TO DO SOMETHING this morning which I have done only once or twice before in all my twenty-three years at Peninsula Bible Church—to repeat a message I have given here before. I do this for two reasons. First, this has been a very heavy week for me. I have already preached or taught or lectured some twenty-two hours this week, and so have had very little time to work on proper preparation of a message. Rather than present one half-prepared I would much rather do this. Second, I feel this message is much needed. I do not think I have known a time when more people have been going through deep trouble and tribulation and pressure. We have seen a sample of it this morning in the prayer requests over which we have just prayed. And I feel this would be an appropriate message for such a time.

So I apologize to those of you who have heard this message before—and remember that you have — but I hope that, like wine and cheese, it will improve with age!

I have chosen this passage in 1 Chronicles because it deals with a very practical problem in our lives, one which every one of us wrestles with from time to time. I want to be both practical and helpful—that is what Scripture is for. And this passage deals with the problem of how to kill a lion on a snowy day.

Now, you have had that problem this week, I know! You may not have recognized it, but I am sure you have had it. As we get on into this text I am sure you will agree with me. It deals with that problem, along with a couple of others, and I think we will find it helpful.

And Benaiah the son of Jehoiada was a valiant man of Kabzeel,
a doer of great deeds; he smote two ariels of Moab. He also

went down and slew a lion in a pit on a day when snow had fallen. And he slew an Egyptian, a man of great stature, five cubits tall. The Egyptian had in his hand a spear like a weaver's beam; but Benaiah went down to him with a staff, and snatched the spear out of the Egyptian's hand, and slew him with his own spear. These things did Benaiah the son of Jehoiada, and won a name beside the three mighty men. He was renowned among the thirty, but did not attain to the three. And David set him over his bodyguard (1 Chronicles 11:22–25).

You notice this is in the days of David the king. There are two groups of men mentioned—the thirty, and the three. These three mighty men, whose names are given in preceding texts, were the leaders of all the armed forces of Israel, the "Joint Chiefs of Staff," if you like. Then there was another band of thirty men who were the commanders of various divisions within the military. It was among these thirty men, chosen from throughout the ranks of Israel, that our man Benaiah the son of Jehoiada became prominent. He was made captain of David's bodyguard. He was chosen for that position of honor close to the person of the king because of three great events which had happened in his life; three deeds of valor for which he was widely known throughout the nation.

The first was that he smote two ariels of Moab. If you are reading from the King James Version you will notice that it says "two lion-like men of Moab." This is because the King James translators did not know what this word meant. Nor, in fact, did the translators of the Revised Standard Version. For this word in Hebrew is one of the very few of which we have lost the meaning. We do not know what it means. The King James translators noticed that it was somewhat similar to the word for lion. So they translated it *lion-like*, feeling that this would be as close as they could come. But it does not mean exactly that. So when the Revised translators worked on this passage they said, "Well, let's not translate this word at all. We don't know what it means, so let's just admit it, and anglicize it, i.e., take the sound of it in Hebrew and put it in English." So that is why it is *ariel*, for that is what it sounds like in Hebrew.

But no one knows what an ariel is. The King James translators made what you might call a "holy guess" at it. If I may take an unholy guess, I would suggest that the word probably is some kind of military term, referring to a troop unit of a particular size, like a company or a platoon, and that this man had won fame because he encountered these two units, whatever they were, of the military of Moab, and singlehandedly put them down. Whatever it does mean, it was a notable deed. He was widely recognized as a mighty man because he had smitten these two ariels of Moab.

Another deed for which he was known was that he went down and slew a lion in a pit on a day when snow had fallen. That, too, was a notable deed. A lion is a very ferocious adversary. He met him in a very difficult place and slew him, and was recognized as a man of valor because he had dared to face a lion in a pit on a day when snow had fallen. We are going to come back to that incident in a moment.

The third great deed for which he was known was that he met an Egyptian, a man of great stature, five cubits (about nine feet) tall. That is about the same size as Goliath, for slaying whom David won fame. This man had a tremendous spear, like a weaver's beam. Unfortunately we are not acquainted with that terminology. A weaver's loom had a tremendous beam on it, usually about six or seven inches thick. That is what this man's spear was like. We might liken it to a flagpole or a telephone pole. At any rate it was a formidable weapon. And Benaiah the son of Jehoiadah met this huge man with this great spear, and, using only his staff, somehow knocked the spear out of the Egyptian's hand, seized it, and slew the giant with his own spear, for which he won great fame in Israel as a man of valor.

"Well now," you say, "that's all very interesting. But what on earth does it have to do with me? How does this relate in any sense to me? It is an interesting story, and certainly he was a great man, but I don't see how this helps me." But, you see, this is one of the glories of Scripture. Paul tells us in Romans 15:4a (RSV), "For whatever was written in former days was written for our instruction," and these tales in the Bible are not merely Sunday school stories, or even myths and legends recorded for our entertainment. They have meaning and purpose for us. They apply to us.

For instance, it is interesting to note that these three enemies whom Benaiah overcame are all used in Scripture as types, or symbols, of enemies of the believer today:

"Benaiah smote two ariels of Moab." Who was Moab? In the Old Testament we find that the Moabites were a tribe living on the borders of Israel who were related to the Israelites. Back in the book of Genesis we are told that Lot, when he fled from Sodom, hid with his two daughters in a cave. There, in a rather shadowed episode, we are told that Lot was made drunk by his two daughters and that, in his drunken stupor, he sired children by each of his own daughters. One was Ammon, and the other was Moab. Ammon, by the way, is the one for whom the capital city of present-day Jordan was named. So the Moabites were closely related to the Israelites and grew up beside them. But they were always enemies of Israel, wherever you read of them. This is used throughout the Old Testament as a picture of something which is true of us. We have an enemy within us, to which we are related. In the New Testament it is called "the flesh." It is referred to as our "self-life," the "old life," and by other terms like that. But it is related to us. It is part of us. We cannot get rid of it. It lives in the back room of the house of our life, like a poor relative. We are ashamed of it, but we cannot get rid of it. And so Moab is a picture of the flesh throughout Scripture.

"And he slew an Egyptian." Egypt also is used as a type, or picture, of an enemy throughout the Scriptures. Do you know what it is? Egypt was the leading nation of the world of that day, the country which was looked up to as the source of worldly power, with its vast armies and tremendous temples, its pharaohs and their pomp and circumstance, its libraries and accumulated wisdom. All this is a picture of the superficial impressiveness, the empty glory of the world and its ways. When Jesus was tempted by Satan in the wilderness, He was taken up on a high mountain and shown all the kingdoms of the earth, with all their power and glory. That is what is symbolized by Egypt. The Israelites, many of them, longed to return to Egypt. They had forgotten the bondage, the slavery, the cruelty, the tears and the heartache of Egypt, and remembered only its comforts, its conveniences, the leeks and onions and garlic and melons of Egypt. What a picture Egypt is of the world and its ways— its philosophies, its pursuit of pomp and prestige and pride and status! So this incident is used as a vivid figure of a man who overcame the world.

But then there was the lion. I am sure you have guessed by now what the lion symbolizes. Remember that Peter tells us outright: "Your adversary the devil prowls around like a roaring lion, seeking some one to devour" (1 Peter 5:8 RSV). Here is an enemy who is sinister, and who, like a lion, has tremendous majesty and authority and power, and is out licking his chops, looking for something to eat, "seeking whom he may devour." What a picture!

Who among us has not been confronted with these enemies? There they are: the world, the flesh, and the devil. We have felt the pressure of them, seen the attack of the flesh, our relative, Moab, sneaking up on us when we are least aware. We have felt the pull of the world, its attractiveness, and have wanted to be involved in it and thought we were missing something if we were not. We have felt it draw us away as we have longed to go back to Egypt. And at times, I am sure, we have sensed a tremendous dread of the devil, felt frightened, terrified by this powerful adversary.

We don't have time this morning to deal with all three of these in detail, so I would like to focus on this central story of the killing of the lion, as I think it has great significance for us. Certainly this was the most dangerous of the enemies recorded here, for a lion is the most powerful of beasts, the most ferocious of adversaries. There are several things said about it which we want to note. We read that Benaiah slew a lion—a lion, not a leopard, not a wild hyena or a boar or a buffalo, but a lion.

Why a lion? Well, it is not for nothing that the lion is called the king of beasts, because it is indeed a very powerful animal. I have read that a lion is able, with one blow of his paw, to smash the human skull just as you would break an egg. He would slap you and your skull would cave in. Yet the bones of the skull are among the strongest structures of the body. A lion is able, with his teeth, to bite through any bone of the human body, including even the thigh bone. With one crunch of those jaws he could smash that bone. And to face that kind of ferocious beast at close quarters is a tremendously daring thing to do. That is what Benaiah did.

As a boy I used to wonder what would happen if a lion and a tiger got into a fight. For years I would play that over in my imagination and speculate about the outcome. Until one day I happened to see a movie exhibited by Dr. Louis Talbot. He had been in India on an occasion when a lion and a tiger had somehow accidentally fallen into the same pit. Someone was there with a movie camera and filmed the whole thing. I tell you, I watched with great interest as this battle went on! These cats circled one another, one would lash out at the other, they would spit and snarl and leap about in that light way cats have. Then suddenly they would grapple together and roll about, spitting and biting. It was tremendous to watch! Then, quicker than the eye could follow, something happened, and the tiger appeared to cave in. He simply fell down. The lion had caught it at just the right moment, had slapped it on the side of the head, and had crushed its skull. That was the end of the battle. So that was the adversary Benaiah the son of Jehoiada met on the day when he slew this lion.

Do you know that every one of us has a lion in our life? This, for Benaiah was the worst possible foe he could meet. And you and I have something like that don't we? You have something—and it flashes into your mind as I say these words—which is the worst possible foe. It is something you have dreaded, something you have been afraid of, something you have thought might happen but have wished would not. It had been there on the horizon of your thinking, always threatening, and you have been wondering if it were ever going to happen. The worst possible foe, the thing you have dreaded more than anything else—that is the lion in your life.

Maybe it is a quite different lion for the person sitting next to you, or for me. Maybe it is a physical disease or affliction—a heart attack, brain surgery, cancer. It may be some terrible, crushing disappointment, some loved one taken from you so that you are left alone. Maybe it is the fear of being financially ruined. Whatever it may be, the lion is the worst possible foe in your life.

Benaiah met this lion, and he met him in the worst possible place. He met him in a pit. If you are going to fight a lion, certainly the one place not to choose is a pit, where you cannot get away, where you are at close quarters with this lion and there is no escape.

If I were to fight a lion, I at least would want to be out on a plain where I could take certain steps—preferably long ones—to get away! I would feel like the man who was caught stealing watermelon out of a patch. The farmer fired at him, and when his friends asked him, "Did you hear those bullets?" he said, "Yes sir, I heard them twice—once when they passed me, and then again when I passed them!" That is the way I would feel about a lion. I would want to be out where I could run. But you cannot run in a pit. Benaiah met the worst possible foe in the worst possible place.

Have you ever been there? Have you ever run into this terrible thing you dreaded to have happen, and found there was no way to avoid it? You could not go home to mother, could not take a vacation, could not do a thing. You had to face up to it. There was no way to get away.

But also notice that Benaiah met this lion in a pit on a day when snow had fallen. That made it a very treacherous situation— the worst possible foe, in the worst possible place, under the worst possible circumstances.

You folks who grew up here in California have no idea what snow is like. I grew up in Montana where, as we often said, we have only two seasons: Winter and August! We know what snow is like, and what snow does. I have been in snow up to my chest—cold, numbing snow—just walking out in the backyard. One of my favorite delights, ever since I came to California, is to sit on my patio on a warm winter afternoon and read all about the blizzards back east! Snow numbs the fingers and makes it difficult to handle weapons. Snow makes footing treacherous and slippery. And snow blinds the eyes. You have all read about snow-blindness. The brightness of the sun upon the snow can actually destroy your vision temporarily. All these factors were involved in this battle when Benaiah the son of Jehoiada met the lion in a pit on a day when snow had fallen. He met the worst possible foe, in the worst possible place, under the worst possible circumstances.

And do you know, as I speak of this, I think that right now this is where God has me. I am going through something like this right now in my own experience. Something I have dreaded all my life has happened. Something I did not want to see happen, felt would be the most hurtful thing which could happen, has happened. I cannot escape it, and have to deal with it at a time when I have lots of other pressures, lots of problems. It is not an easy time to do it. It is the worst possible foe, in the worst possible place, under the worst possible circumstances. Are you there too?

Well, the thing we want to know is, how did he win? The whole focus of this story is that Benaiah the son of Jehoiada was able to kill this lion. He slew him! How did he do it? Is that the question you are asking? The passage does not seem to tell us, does it? The account seems merely to give us the incident without telling us anything about how it happened. There again is the wonder of the Scriptures. We are told in the book of Proverbs, "The glory of God is to conceal a thing, but the glory of kings is to search it out" (cf. Proverbs 25:2). And God never tells us something like this without hiding the answer for us to find, if we will but look for it. And this is what He has done here. He has hidden certain clues in this story which tell us how Benaiah the son of Jehoiada won this battle.

The answer, of course, if you think about it, is that Benaiah was able to do this because that is the kind of man he was. He was indeed a mighty man of valor. It was not the deeds he did which made him that way. He was already a mighty man of valor. The deeds simply revealed what he already was. He had what it took. He was that kind of man. These deeds simply made it clear to everybody else that he was that kind of man.

In the Bible, when you want to know what a man is like, look at his name, because biblical names are deliberately designed to give you a clue to the character of the individual. There is much evidence for this throughout the Scriptures. You know how God often changed a man's name when he changed his character.

Jacob meant "usurper, supplanter," and God changed his name to *Israel*, "prince with God," when Jacob went through a transforming experience in his life. He changed Abraham's name from *Abram*, "exalted father," to *Abraham*, "father of a multitude." He changed Sarah's name from *Sarai*, "dominating," to *Sarah*, "princess." Jesus changed Peter's name. He said, "Your name is Simon, but I'm going to call you Peter, for I'm going to make you into a rock." *Peter* means "rock" (cf. Matthew 16:18). And Saul (which means "asked") of Tarsus was changed to *Paul*, which means "little," when he became a Christian. So God changes names when character changes. If you want to know the meaning of a man, look at his name.

In the book of Isaiah we learn that Isaiah had two sons to whom he gave special names in order to teach the people something. One was called "Shearjashub," the other "Maher-shalal-hashbas." Can you imagine calling that boy in to lunch? His name means "hasting (is he) to the booty, swift (to the) prey," and it was a testimony to the people of Israel that God had declared Israel to be a spoil and a prey to the nations around, and that He was inviting the nations to hasten in, to hasten to the spoil and to the prey. "Now is the time to come in and take this nation." Ah yes, that was the word of warning. But the other boy's name was a note of hope. It means "a remnant shall return." That is what God taught His people through those names.

There is a similar instance in the book of Genesis in a name which God chose to teach a lesson to a whole generation. The whole world was taught by the name of a single man. His name was Methuselah. He was given that name by his father, Enoch, the one who "walked with God, and was not, for God took him" (Genesis 5:24). Enoch didn't start walking with God until he was sixty-five years old, when his son was born. He named him because of something God taught him at that time. The name signifies it: It means "when he dies it will come." What will come? The Flood. Can you imagine how they watched him everywhere he went? "Where's Methuselah? Keep your eye on him. We don't want him falling off a cliff, because when he dies it will come." Everybody knew that. Sure enough, you can see from the account that the very year Methuselah died, the Flood came. And the grace of God is revealed in the fact that Methuselah was the oldest man who ever lived! Nine hundred and sixty-nine years they watched him. But when he died, the Flood came.

What does this name mean—"Benaiah the son of Jehoiada"? That is a clue to the kind of man he was. Well, there is an interesting thing about it. This man was well-known in David's day, and is mentioned often in Scripture. But in almost every instance, with only one or two exceptions, his name is listed as "Benaiah the son of Jehoiada." So his father's name is important too. If you take the meaning of those two names, in the order of seniority, you get the secret of how to kill a lion on a snowy day. Jehoiada means "God knows," and Benaiah means "God builds." Those twin truths are the secret of how to meet a lion, the worst possible foe, in the worst possible place, under the worst possible circumstances, and win. Remember to rest upon the facts that God knows, and God builds.

God knows where you are. He chose that place for you. That is the revelation of Scripture. God put you where you are, and, therefore, He knows. He knows all about you. Jesus said that the hairs of your head are numbered. He knows what you are going through, and He brought it about. "We know that in everything God works for good with those who love him, who are called according to his purpose," Paul tells us in Romans (8:28 RSV). And He not only knows what you are going through, but He feels what you feel. God knows how you feel. That is one of the most comforting things to realize when you are upset, when somebody has done you dirt. When you are angry, or remorseful, or impatient, or are tempted to be bitter, or have been betrayed, or have been hurt—God knows how you feel. The writer of Hebrews tells us, "We have not a high priest who is unable to sympathize with our weaknesses" (Hebrews 4:15a RSV). We do not have the kind of God to come to who says, "Oh, don't bother me! Your little troubles—what are they to me?" No, no. We have one who "in every respect has been tempted as we are" (Hebrews 4:15b RSV), who has been where we have been, and knows how we feel.

On my way to Europe recently I was reading the story of Corrie ten Boom, that remarkable Dutch woman who has traveled around the world telling the story of her years under the occupation of the Nazis in Holland, when she and her family were put in a concentration camp. I was reading this account because I was going to visit her home there in Holland. (In fact, I bought a watch at her watch shop.) The Nazis had taken her and her sister and had put them in a concentration camp under horrible conditions, along with thousands of other women. One day, after a terrible series of degrading experiences, these women were marched out single-file and, one by one, were made to take off all their clothes and stand absolutely naked before a group of Nazi doctors, arrogant men, who showed their contempt for them. These modest, refined women had to stand stark naked before these examining doctors, and it was a terrible wrench to their spirit. Corrie says that she turned to her sister, Betsie, and said, "Betsie, remember, Jesus was naked on the cross." And her sister turned, and her face lit up with a smile, "Oh, that's right. Oh, that helps!" God knows. He knows how you feel.

Ah, but more than that, He builds. He has a purpose in mind. He knows what is happening and He is using it to work toward an end. That is the glorious thing, isn't it? Out of all the record of Paul's heartache and sorrow and privation and pain and suffering, "This light affliction," he said, "is but for a moment, and is working for us a far more exceeding and eternal weight of glory" (cf. 2 Corinthians 4:17 KJV), and, "I reckon that the sufferings of this present time are not worthy to be compared with the glory which shall be revealed in us" (Romans 8:18 KJV). And this is not only in heaven someday, but now. Those who go through heartaches, pressure, problems, tribulation, always emerge, when they are in God's hand, softened, chastened, mellowed, more loving, warmer, more compassionate. God is building—that is the whole point. This is the secret of survival: God knows, God builds.

In 1895 Andrew Murray was in England suffering from a terribly painful back, the result of an injury he had incurred years before. He was staying with some dear friends. One morning while he was eating his breakfast in his room, his hostess told him of a woman downstairs who was in great trouble and wanted to know if he had any advice for her. Andrew Murray handed her a paper he had been writing on and said, "Just give her this advice I'm writing down for myself. It may be that she'll find it helpful." This is what was written:

In time of trouble, say, "First, He brought me here. It is by His will I am in this strait place; in that I will rest." Next, "He will keep me here in His love, and give me grace in this trial to behave as His child." Then say, "He will make the trial a blessing, teaching me lessons He intends me to learn, and working in me the grace He means to bestow." And last, say, "In His good time He can bring me out again. How, and when, He knows." Therefore say, "I am here (1) by God's appointment, (2) in His keeping, (3) under His training, (4) for His time."

That is how to kill a lion on a snowy day.

Prayer:

Thank you for this truth, Lord, which leaps at us from an obscure incident in the Scriptures, which shows us that all these things have been designed for our instruction, that we may know how to face life and live as you want us to live. May it strengthen us in the hour of trial. In Jesus' name, Amen.

THE PRIMACY OF PREACHING

—◆—

I BELIEVE IN PREACHING! The fall of 1987 will mark my 37th year in one pulpit, and for all of those years I have considered preaching to be my primary task. I have been greatly encouraged in this commitment by the example of great preachers of the past and of the present. Among the latter have been Dr. Martyn Lloyd-Jones, Dr. J. R. W. Stott, and Dr. Stephen Olford. The fact that these are all British preachers speaks well of the quality of British preaching, and, perhaps, of the relative weakness of the American pulpit. To the degree that this is so I would attribute it to the fact that British evangelicals tend more toward expository preaching than their American counterparts. For it is expository preaching that constitutes, in my judgment, the only true form of preaching!

Expository sermons are those which derive their content from Scripture itself. They borrow their structure and thrust from a specific passage. They make the same point that the passage makes, and apply that point with directness and urgency to contemporary life. What other modes of preaching often lack is biblical content. Those in the pews are often drowning in words, but thirsting for knowledge. John Stek, of Calvin Seminary, puts it well: "Preachers who rummage through the Bible to find texts on which to hang topical sermons are often guilty of substituting their word for the biblical Word."* This soon results in an unconscious trivializing of preaching.

Proof of this trivializing is found in the widespread biblical illiteracy that exists today. Many persons in the average congregation do not know the meaning of terms like justification by faith, or sanctification, or the kingdom of God, or the new covenant, or the

---

* Quoted from an article in *Christianity Today*, 1986.

walk in the Spirit, the flesh, or even faith, love, and peace! Worse yet, because they don't know the biblical meaning of "flesh," for instance, they do not know how to recognize it in themselves, and the flesh therefore rages in unrestrained destructiveness throughout their thinking and living. Because they know nothing of the nature of the new covenant, they live continually in the legal bondages of the old. Because they do not understand the wisdom of God, they succumb constantly to the pompous pretensions of the wisdom of the world. Because they do not know how to use the shield of faith, they are besieged daily by the fiery darts of the wicked one.

What is essential therefore in preaching is, first of all, content! It is what Paul calls "the unsearchable riches of Christ." In a verse that has meant much to me personally, Paul calls himself and other first-century preachers: "stewards of the mysteries of God" (1 Corinthians 4:1). He sees himself as entrusted with a fabulous deposit of truth which he is responsible to dispense to others. It ought to be the supreme business of a preacher to discharge that responsibility with utter faithfulness. Paul adds: "It is required of a steward that one be found faithful." So he says, in another place, he sought always "to declare the whole counsel of God."

In my opinion, much of the present weakness in preaching is due to the failure of preachers to understand the uniqueness of what they are to preach, and its remarkable power to change a congregation, a community, a city, or even a nation. When Paul came to Corinth, as he tells us in 1 Corinthians 2, he came "in weakness and fear and much trembling." He was, in actual fact, intimidated by Corinth! He knew these Greek cities well, and they frightened and discouraged him. He saw the terrible degradation of Corinth and it looked incurable. Sexual depravity, centered in the temple of Aphrodite perched on the AcroCorinth overlooking the city, was so widespread and so popular it seemed impossible to oppose. Paul knew the superstitious fears of the masses in Corinth; he was aware of the devious dishonesty of its politicians, and the shameless injustice of the city courts.

He had often himself felt the tyranny of Rome in its iron-fisted control of the whole known world, especially evident in Corinth because of its past history of rebellion. He saw daily the hopeless despair of the citizenry: one half slave to the other half and living in misery and near starvation. Yet, in contrast, he felt the pride of Corinth in its beautiful location; the arrogance of its philosophers as heirs of the great thinkers of Greece; the wealth which the city's commerce brought; the acclaim it enjoyed as one of the chief cities of the empire. How could he reach it? How could he change it? It looked impenetrable, unassailable!

But then he remembered his message—and his resource! He began to preach, "not with persuasive words of human wisdom, but in demonstration of the Spirit and power." That demonstration derived from what, in the subsequent verses, he describes in some detail as "the wisdom of God." It is also that which in chapter 4 he terms, "the mysteries of God." It has several outstanding characteristics, of which I now take but three.

1. The wisdom of God is in sharp contrast to the world's wisdom: "Not the wisdom of this age, nor of the rulers of this age, who are doomed to pass away" (NIV, "coming to nothing"). When he speaks of the rulers of this age he means more than government officials. The phrase refers to the leaders of thought in any age, the movers and shakers, the mind-benders—not only statesmen, but philosophers, thinkers, scientists, educators. "Doomed to pass away," describes their transient character. Their plans and ideas are in a constant flux. They swing from one extreme to another, or flow in cycles of acceptance like fads in fashion. Everyone knows that no science textbook more than ten years old is worth owning today. Economic theories change like the tides, ebbing and flowing with the Dow-Jones averages. Educational policies come in cycles, alternating between extremes of permissiveness and heavy control. Polit-

ical programs, all promising boundless prosperity, appear every election year. (I have now lived through the New Deal, the Fair Deal, the Great Society, Camelot, Peace with Honor, the Camp David process, and now Reaganomics—all promising much, but delivering little.)

This constant change gives rise to much of the rush and restlessness of modern living. It is all "doomed to pass away" or is "coming to nothing." Perhaps its effect has been best caught by a modern jingle that reads:

This is the Age of the Half-read Page
And the Quick Bash, and the Mad Dash
The Bright Night, with the Nerves Tight
The Plane Hop, with a Brief Stop
The Lamp Tan in a Short Span
The Big Shot in a Good Spot
And the Brain Strain and the Heart Pain
And the Cat-Naps, till the Spring Snaps
And the Fun's Done!

In sharp contrast, the Word of God remains unchanged and unchangeable. Always relevant, always up-to-date, always perceptive and penetrating—eternally accurate!

2. The truth of God's wisdom is unique and unrivaled: "We impart a secret and hidden wisdom of God, which God decreed before the ages for our glorification." The paramount glory of the gospel is that there is nothing like it anywhere else. It is without rival, either in the scientific laboratory, in the psychologist's office, or the philosopher's study. It is this factor that constitutes the supreme value of preaching. It simply does what nothing else can do! Here in this chapter, Paul calls this truth, "the deep things of God," "the thoughts of God," "spiritual truth," and "the mind of Christ"! Since it originates in God alone, it stands in sharp contrast with the thinking of men.

When Jesus came He told His disciples that He "would utter things kept secret since the foundation of the world" (Matthew 13:35). He said, "Many prophets and righteous men have longed to hear what you hear, but did not hear it." In 1 Corinthians 2, Paul declares these truths have now been revealed to us through the Spirit, and he sums it all up in the arresting phrase, "the secret and hidden wisdom of God." Since I preach in a university community, this has always meant to me that when I open this Book on a Sunday morning, I am offering to the physicists, the scientists, the high-tech engineers, the doctors, lawyers, bankers, and captains of industry present, as well as artisans, secretaries, plumbers, and many others, essential knowledge about themselves and about life, which they never learned, nor could learn, in any secular college or graduate school! I am privileged to give them an understanding of reality unattainable from any other source.

It is the business of preaching to change the total worldview of every member of the congregation; to dispel the secular illusions which are widely believed around, and to identify and underscore the concepts and practices that are right, and to do this for each member. Perhaps the most amazing statement of all in this amazing verse is that this hidden truth is "for our glorification"! The Westminster Confession properly states that the chief end of man is to glorify God, and to enjoy Him forever. But this verse declares that God plans and works "for our [that is, human] glorification."

To glorify anyone or anything is to make openly manifest the hidden values within. God glorifies Himself when He reveals Himself to us. John says of Jesus, "The Word was made flesh . . . and we beheld his glory." What was that glory? John tells us precisely, ". . . full of grace and truth." That was the glory of Jesus: grace and truth!

What, then, is the glory of man—of ourselves? It is to display outwardly all that God made us to be! To be (to use a modern term) a whole person! The truly fascinating thing is that this is what every person, without exception, wants to be! Listen to people talking and you will hear it expressed everywhere. "I want to be me!" "I'm looking for fulfillment." "I'm trying to get my act together." What we are sent to preach is clearly what everyone everywhere desperately wants to find!

But right here is the tragedy of much modern preaching. Preachers have lost sight of this great fact. They actually have come to believe that the average person no longer has any religious interest. They seek to reach him or her by appealing to their respect for knowledge or science or philosophy. If this lack of religious interest appears to be true, it is because preaching has failed to make clear that what men eagerly want to find—the secret of human fulfillment—is what God is lovingly offering to give! True preaching, the preaching of "the secret and hidden wisdom of God" will result in human glorification, the actual fulfillment of man's deepest desires.

This hidden wisdom, as Paul declares plainly in verse 2, is: "Jesus Christ and him crucified." In chapter one Paul terms it, "the word of the Cross." It is a message so totally different from the thinking of the world that it constitutes, "the offense of the Cross." It declares that until man is changed by a gracious act of God, his highest efforts and most clever schemes for self-improvement will not only prove ineffective—they will actually make things worse! By trying to control his own destiny and run his own world, he will end by not only destroying himself, but his world as well. Do we need anything else but history or the newspaper to confirm that? On a recent visit to Stanford University, Malcolm Muggeridge summed up the approaching end of Western civilization in this remarkable quote from an American critic, Leslie Fiedler:

"The final conclusion would seem to be that whereas other civilizations have been brought down by attacks of barbarians from without, ours had the unique distinction of training its own destroyers at its own educational institutions and providing them with facilities for propagating their destructive ideology far and wide, all at the public expense.

"Thus did Western man decide to abolish himself, creating his own boredom out of his own affluence, his own vulnerability out of his own strength, his own impotence out of his own erotomania, himself blowing the trumpet that brought the walls of his own city tumbling down. And, having convinced himself that he is too numerous, labors with pill and scalpel and syringe to make himself fewer, until at last, having educated himself into imbecility and polluted and drugged himself into stupefaction, he keels over, a weary, battered old brontosaurus, and becomes extinct."**

Though brilliantly stated, this is scarcely hyperbole. It is happening all around us, and is an inescapable result of "human wisdom."

3. The wisdom of God exposes the incredible blunders which human wisdom makes: "None of the rulers of this age understood this; for if they had, they would not have crucified the Lord of Glory." Here were keen, intelligent men, priding themselves on their ability to govern, to make decisions, and to understand men. Yet when Truth Himself appeared before them they could not recognize Him, totally misunderstood and mishandled Him, and ended by nailing Him to a Cross. That tendency to commit terrible blunders is characteristic of the wisdom of the world. It is the reason why we live on a polluted planet today, torn by strife and schism, and threatened by violence and meaninglessness on all sides. It is the business of preaching to identify such blunders and to give help to those who fail to see these unrecognized errors in society today.

Listen to any television news broadcast and in the course of it you will be exposed to 15 or 20 commercials, urging you to buy a

---

** Quoted in "The Trousered Ape" by Duncan Williams.

product, to take a trip, or to spend your money in some other way. Note how many times you hear the word, "deserve." "You deserve this—you've got it coming to you—you're the kind of person who has a right to expect this." "You deserve a break today!" Gradually listeners begin to believe this subtle propaganda. The end result of it is to remove all possibility of gratitude. You don't feel grateful when you finally get what you feel you have long deserved—you are only angry that you didn't get it sooner, or you didn't get as much as the next fellow. And if you don't get it at all, you can only feel resentful and abused.

What the media is unknowingly producing is a nation of angry, resentful people, dissatisfied with all they have. And since gratitude is the chief ingredient of joy, we find ourselves in the midst of a joyless people, seeking fun continually, but unable to know joy. And this includes thousands of Christians! It is the business of the preacher to point out these effects and direct people to the true sources of joy. The truth is, we do not deserve any good thing! We belong to a race that deserves to be eliminated from the earth. Because we live in continual enmity against God, and in rebellion to His laws, we deserve death. But that is not what we are given! By the grace and mercy of a loving God, we are given life—often long lives—and we are given beauty, and family love, and food and shelter and many, many other blessings. Even more, we are given opportunities to learn the truth, and if we follow them, we are given forgiveness, and acceptance, and love and peace—and joy!

Because of these undeserved gifts, everyone's normal attitude should be one of intense gratitude. This is why Scripture exhorts us continually to thanksgiving. Every good gift, and every perfect gift, for which men are properly thankful, comes, as James tell us, "from above, from the Father of lights, with whom is no variableness, even the shadow of turning." Even those gifts we call trials, are from the same source, sent to make us do what we don't want to do, in order to be what we've always wanted to be!

223

When Paul began to preach this message in Corinth, in dependence on the power of the Spirit, Corinth began to change. Acts 18 says, "Many of the Corinthians hearing Paul believed and were baptized." There sprang up in that pagan city a group of changed people. They lost their fears and their despair. Under the impact of new life from within, they were gradually changed into loving, caring, wholesome people. Some still struggled with the residues of their past, but the city was never the same again. And because of that, the history of the world has been changed as well.

There is much more I could say, but perhaps this is enough to help us see the enormous consequences of true preaching, and the terrible blight that falls upon a congregation or community which is deprived of these "unsearchable riches of Christ." My plea is, let preachers stop feeding people with moral platitudes and psychological pablum. Let us say once more, with Jeremiah,

"Your words were found, and I ate them, and Your Word was to me the joy and rejoicing of my heart."

(From The Ray Stedman Library and the archives of Elaine Stedman, July 30, 1996. Used by permission.)

THE POWER YOU ALREADY HAVE

WHEN I WAS A STUDENT at Dallas Seminary back in the 1940s right after World War II, Elaine and I lived in a tiny trailer on the campus of the seminary. It was the only housing that we could find in Dallas at that time. A number of families, 17 all together, moved trailers right onto the campus, and we lived there throughout the four years of our seminary training. In a trailer directly behind us, Don and Bea Campbell lived. Don is now the president of Dallas Seminary, so you can see that trailer life is a very good beginning for somebody. On the next row over were Howard and Jeanne Hendricks, and many of you know of their ministry. Howard is probably widely known all over the world today as a speaker and as a Christian educator. They lived in a trailer identical to ours. We were all poor as church mice. In fact our trailer was so small that the mice were humpbacked trying to fit into it! Seventeen families shared two bathrooms! I remember standing outside one day, waiting in line, singing the old hymn, "Why do you wait, dear brother? Why do you tarry so long?"

I'll never forget the day, in our extreme poverty, when there was a letter in my mailbox from a man whom I had never met, but whose name I knew. When I opened it there fell out a ten-dollar bill and a note from him that said he had heard about our ministry among the servicemen, during the war, teaching the Bible. He said he wanted to help us financially and was praying for us. To this day I can recall the immense feeling of gratitude that I felt because some man, unknown to me, had thought of us, and was praying for us, and wanted to help us.

We find a similar situation here in the letter to the Ephesians. The apostle Paul had started the church at Ephesus (you can read about it in Acts 19), and he had been away from it for a number of years. Evidently many other people had come into new life in Christ, and a great many new Christians had joined the church. It was now filled with people that he didn't know. In fact he tells us in this opening paragraph that he had heard about their faith, but he had never met them yet. Nevertheless he was praying for them and was hoping to help them in their spiritual growth. So this passage is very appropriate, especially for me, when I come back and find a lot of people that I have never seen or yet met in the church, and yet we've been praying for you as well. The apostle says, in verse 15:

> For this reason, ever since I heard about your faith in the Lord Jesus and your love for all the saints, I have not stopped giving thanks for you, remembering you in my prayers (Ephesians 1:15–16 NIV).

That must have been a wonderful word of encouragement to them. You perhaps are asking, "What does he mean, 'for this reason'?" I don't want to go back into the opening verses of this chapter, but there you will find a magnificent statement from the apostle Paul. It is actually only one sentence long in the Greek, but it covers several paragraphs in English translation. In them the apostle is describing all that they possess in God, all that Christ has done in their lives, and all the great doctrinal foundations of Christianity. And it is all addressed to the mind, in order that they might understand with their intellect what God had done for them. It is for that reason, he says, that he has been praying for them.

But now in this paragraph he goes on in verse 17 to give the content of his prayers:

> I keep asking that the God of our Lord Jesus Christ, the glorious Father, may give you the Spirit of wisdom and revelation, so that you may know him better (Ephesians 1:17 NIV).

Now, that is really the major objective of a Christian life—to know God better. We need to ask ourselves, "Is this happening with us? Are we really getting to know God better?"

There is a principle in the Scripture that is very important for us to understand. We are all familiar with the phrase that says we are made in the image of God, which means in some way that humanity reflects God. But that fact means that we cannot learn who we are until we begin to know and learn who God is. It is the revelation and understanding of the nature of God that will tell us what we are like.

I believe that this is one of the major reasons why many people today never seem to discover who they are. They never learn what they can do, what possibilities lie within, and what potential is theirs because they have never discovered who God is. We reflect Him, and therefore it is extremely important that we come to know God better.

Remember that Jesus said this in His great prayer to the Father in John 17: "This is eternal life: that they may know you, the only true God, and Jesus Christ, whom you have sent" (cf. John 17:3 NIV).

This is the reason that we exist—that we may know God better. I hope this is happening to you, young and old alike. You never get over knowing more about God. He is such a fantastic being that revelations about His character and nature keep coming to us and we discover that as we know Him better we suddenly realize we know ourselves better too.

So Paul prays for them. He doesn't know their circumstances. He can't pray for their daily problems and pressures as you can when you know somebody personally. But he can pray, and does pray, that they may know God better. That will take care of everything.

All of this is addressed to their minds. They need to understand the great facts about God—to understand with their thinking the being and majesty of God. But now, in verse 18, he adds another thought:

> I pray also that the eyes of your *heart* may be enlightened in order that you may know the hope to which he has called you, the riches of his glorious inheritance in the saints, and his incomparably great power for us [to us or in us literally] who believe (Ephesians 1:18–19a NIV, emphasis added).

That is a different idea. The eyes of the mind can grasp the doctrine and teaching about God for we *see* with our minds.

Perhaps somebody has said something to you and you have replied, "Oh, yes, I see what you mean." You didn't see it with your eyes; you saw it with your mind—with the eyes of the mind. But Scripture declares that your hearts have eyes too. And Paul prays that the eyes of your heart may be enlightened.

In the Scriptures the heart is the seat of the emotions. The apostle's prayer is that they (and we) may so grasp the revelation that is made to the mind—that it begins to enlighten, move, and motivate our hearts. That is when we become vital Christians— turned on, ready to serve, and highly motivated because we have begun to feel the power and the wonder of the truth that we have been taught. That is why Paul prays for the eyes of your heart, that you may *feel* the truth—not just in your intellect, but also deep in your emotions—and that you may reflect and rejoice on who God is and what He is like.

There are three specific things, He says, that we need to know about God: First, the hope to which He has called us, second, the riches of His glorious inheritance in the saints, and third, His incomparably great power.

Let us take a closer look at those three things because they are designed to keep us steady under pressure. They will grip our feelings, turn us on, motivate us highly, and make our lives effective and influential. Everyone wants to be significant. We all want our lives to count for something, and these are the three ingredients, says the apostle Paul, that will keep us turned on, excited, and anticipating the adventure of walking with God.

The first one is that we may remember the hope to which we have been called. This is clearly the hope of being changed into His likeness, the hope of glory. Paul speaks of it many places in the Scripture. He says, "This light affliction which is but for a moment is working for us an exceeding great and eternal weight of glory" (2 Corinthians 4:17 KJV). And he also says, "The sufferings of this present time are not worthy to be compared with the glory which shall be revealed in us" (Romans 8:18 KJV). In other words, we must not look at life as the world around us does, as being all that we'll ever get, as the only chance you are going to have to find fulfillment. The world says, "if you don't take it now, you are never going to get another chance." I have seen that misunderstanding drive people into forsaking their marriages after 30 or 40 years and running off with another, usually younger, person, hoping that they can still fulfill their dreams because they feel life is slipping away from them.

Christians are not to think that way. We are being told that life is a school, a training period. It is where we are being prepared for something that is incredibly great, but it is yet to come. I don't understand all that is involved in that, but I believe it, and I can hardly wait until it happens sometimes. We are told in Scripture (and certainly our experience agrees with it) that these bodies of ours are growing old and will lose their powers.

Ever since I moved to Oregon I have noted a few streaks of gray in my hair. I can tell by the way I feel, many times, that my body is losing its elasticity, its ability to function, and I grow weary and weak. I don't know why, because in my mind I don't feel that way at all. But, as I get older, I remember that it is all aimed at something tremendous which I am being readied for.

It is important not to forget that. Don't succumb to the philosophy around that you have got to have it now or you will never have a chance. You can pass by a lot of things now and be content because you know that what you are getting, what God is sending you in terms of your present experience, is just what you need to get you ready for what He has waiting for you when life is over. One of my favorite quotations from literature is the words of Robert Browning, which you sometimes see on sundials:

> Grow old along with me.
> The best is yet to be.
> The last of life,
> for which the first was made.

So don't lose hope. You are headed for hope, headed for life, headed for glory. All of this life is working toward that end; it's playing its part in that process. That's the first thing to hang on to. You don't need to be depressed or feel that everything is useless, that you can't do anything—you are getting older, you have lost your ability to function, and so on. That is not true. Paul prays that these Christians may feel in their hearts the great hope to which he has called them. It is all waiting for them beyond death, it is the shining hope that they are moving inevitably toward.

The second aspect is the "riches of his glorious inheritance in the saints." Now this is such an important truth that I despair sometimes of trying to get it across to people. When people hear the word *inheritance*, everyone thinks in terms of the inheritance that we have in God, and Scripture teaches that. He is our inheritance. He is like a great bank deposit of resources from which we can draw strength, comfort, encouragement, correction, and whatever else we need as we face problems in our lives. We can draw on God—daily, moment by moment. We have all sung hymns about it, and you have experienced it yourselves. But that is not what Paul is talking about here. He is talking about God's inheritance *in us*, and the enrichment that will come to our lives when we discover what it means to let God have what is His—His inheritance in us.

What is that?

All through the Scriptures we are being told that, when we became Christians, God gave us gifts which we never had before. Every Christian has one or more, and they are given to us in order that, when we begin to exercise them, we will find that we can help others and life becomes an exciting adventure of faith. I could spend the rest of the day up here telling you stories about individuals who have found this to be true: I am thinking right now of retired people from this congregation who have started a Bible class in their home and have begun to reach out into their communities. Though their bodily health is failing, they nevertheless are being tremendously influential in reaching some of the leaders of a community—the mayor of a city in one case, the chief of police in another—and influencing the whole community by the exercise of the gifts that God has given them.

God's inheritance in us is the joy He feels in using us to accomplish His work of changing people, of bringing them from death to life, using the gifts He has given us. The apostle is saying that he wants us to discover how exciting and enriching that can be for us.

Do you know that the greatest thrill that any human being can have is the sense that God has just used you to help somebody else? That is the most wonderful feeling that you can ever have. And God has given each of us gifts for that purpose.

I hope that, if you haven't done so by now, you will seriously think about the gift God has given you and will put it to work in helping someone. Some have the gift of helps, some teaching, some administration, some wisdom, and some knowledge, etc. All of these things are gifts that the Spirit of God has given to us. When we begin to exercise them, we lose the dullness and routine of our lives because we are caught up in an exciting ministry.

I have never been able to appreciate the kind of retirement that many people desire, where all they do is sit around and play bridge or golf or bingo or something like that. They try to just fill up their time until they die. What a waste that is of all the lessons of life and of all the possibilities that God has given! I hope that young and old alike will begin to put this to work and find out the exciting riches of His glorious inheritance in the saints.

You may say, "Well, that all sounds good, but I don't have the strength to do that. I don't seem to be able to begin to do anything like that." That is why Paul goes on to pray that you may know "his incomparably great power [which is at work in us] who believe." Power is the word of the hour today. Everyone is talking about it. You hear about power evangelism, and power living—power lunches. Everybody is looking for power.

I am afraid that the search for some kind of power sends many people off on wild goose chases. They look for either some kind of internal strengthening, so that they feel adequate and competent, or perhaps even some miraculous event that is going to enable them to do things that ordinarily would not be possible for anyone—miracles of some sort—an ability to heal people, or an ability to change our circumstances. But that is because they do not understand the model that Paul gives us here of what the power of God is like.

Did you know that when you became a Christian you were immediately equipped with power? It came with the Spirit of grace who came into your heart. If you do not already have the Spirit of Christ, you are not yet a Christian. When we receive the Lord Jesus, He gives us the Spirit of love and grace and of power; and all of that comes when we believe in Him. What we need to understand is the way that power works. This is the example that the apostle gives, in verses 19–21, to describe this power:

> That power is like the working of his mighty strength, which he exerted in Christ when he raised him from the dead and seated him at his right hand in the heavenly realms, far above all rule and authority, power and dominion, and every title that

can be given, not only in the present age but also in the one to come (Ephesians 1:19b–21 NIV).

The resurrection of Jesus is the model of the power we possess.

Unfortunately, again, we have very confused ideas about this power. We don't listen and look carefully at what the text says about the resurrection. We focus upon the angel's rolling away of the stone, and upon the earthquake, and the terror of the Roman guards as they realize that some tremendous event has taken place. But what we don't realize is that all those events *followed* the resurrection. They were results of it, not the thing itself.

It didn't take the rolling of the stone, and the overpowering of the Roman guards, to allow Jesus to be resurrected. If you think about it, He was already resurrected when those things took place. His body lay in the tomb wrapped in the grave clothes, and yet at a moment that God determined, the body left those grave clothes; it evaporated out of them. They were left lying there, crumpled up and sunken down, with no body in them. Jesus passed through the great stone while it was still standing before the door of the tomb. It was later rolled away to let the disciples in! In some way He was alive and standing in the garden, where Mary mistook Him for a gardener, before any of those events had taken place.

What I am trying to say is that the power of God, the resurrection power of God, is not a power that makes a great demonstration. It is quiet. We are so used to power that makes noise that we don't think we have power if we don't have noise. Things buzz, hum, pulsate, pound, explode, and bang; and these are seen as power. But this is power that you don't feel. You don't have any sense that it is happening, but it is happening.

This power has a peculiar characteristic: It only happens when you begin to act! When you begin to exercise the gifts that God has given you, then the power begins to flow, not before. Then God will work through you to accomplish things that will leave you gasping, sometimes, at what He has done. You didn't feel this power. You don't suddenly feel strong, capable, and mighty. No, you felt weak; Paul says that God's power is made perfect in weakness, but we pay no attention, sometimes, to such a statement. If you feel weak, if you feel inadequate, if you feel ineffectual, this is no hindrance to being used of God and exercising the power of God—not in the least! That is what this is teaching us.

Many people never discover what God could do in their lives because they keep waiting to feel powerful before they act. No, you won't feel powerful. Begin to reach out and act to meet the needs around, and suddenly you discover that there is unusual power at work.

I have a power toothbrush that runs by a battery. It has an unusual characteristic. When you get the toothpaste on the toothbrush and you are ready to brush your teeth, you look around for the button to turn it on. But you don't need a button to turn it on. The directions instruct you to put it up to your teeth and press, and suddenly the power will be there. I remember with what unbelief I tried this the first time, but, to my amazement, it worked. I put the toothbrush up and began to press against my teeth, and, suddenly, the brush began to move up and down—there was power available.

This is a trivial (and even silly), example of what the power of God is like, but resurrection power works much the same way. It works when you reach out to somebody. It works when you sit down to exercise a teaching gift, to comfort someone who is in trouble, or to confront someone who is taking a wrong course. It works *when you expect it to be there.* That is, it works by faith! That is when the power of God is available, and it is wonderful power. It is beyond anything that earth can match.

There are Bible stories that help us understand this. All through the Old Testament, God is teaching His people how He works in power. One of these stories is when Joshua crossed the Jordan River into the Promised Land. The people of Israel were lined up, and the priests were told to go first and bear on their shoulders the ark of the covenant. They were to walk down to the River Jordan, which was flowing in flood before them, and trust in God that something would happen by the time they got to the river. And so they did. In faith they believed that God would do what He said He would do. When the priests put the ark of the covenant on their shoulders, it says, they walked down, and, when the soles of their feet actually touched the water, the water parted, and they went through on dry ground to the other side. That is the way God's power works. When you put it to work, when you begin to act yourself, expecting Him to be with you, then His power begins to work. There is no noise, no flash, and no movement. The power is already there, and God is waiting for you to trust.

Remember the verse later on in Ephesians that says:

> Now unto him who is able to do exceedingly abundantly above all that you can ask or think according to the power that is at work in us ... (cf. Ephesians 3:20).

This is the explanation. You will never find out what God can do with you until you begin to step out and take on some activity that you need power for. Then you will discover His power. That is why Paul prays for these Ephesians and says that the secret of a vital congregation is that you never forget the hope to which God has called you and the enriching adventure that awaits you when you begin to use the gifts God has given you. You will be overwhelmed by the extent of change that God will work through you when you expect that He will act in power when you begin to act.

In closing, I will point out some of the wonderful things this power can do: First of all, Scripture tells us that it is power to face our inner hurts and fears. I find so many people locked into uselessness by dwelling on their past. It helps to know your past and to acknowledge it; I am not disparaging that. But once you know the things that set you on a wrong path, you also have to remember that Scripture says we are to forget the things that are past and press on because *we are new creatures in Christ Jesus.* We are no longer what we once were, and therefore we can set aside that past, having once faced it and seen its impact upon us. We can set it aside and day by day begin to walk with God as His newly created child. We will discover that this power will enable us to overcome all the dysfunctions of a bad past. I have seen it happen many times. It means that no dysfunctional background can keep us from fulfilling what God wants.

Second, it is power to abandon evil habits. I know Christians who are still in bondage to habits that have held them in an iron grasp—alcoholism, drug use, an evil temper, lustful practices, and bad attitudes. Here is a power that enables you to say "No!" to these things, and to go on saying "No." It can break the grip of these things upon us.

One of Charles Wesley's great hymns includes the words,

He breaks the power of cancelled sin,
He sets the prisoner free;
His blood can make the foulest clean;
His blood availed for me.

That's the power of God. It is a power to restore broken relationships. There may be members of your family or friends that you haven't spoken to for a long time; the relationship is entirely broken. You may be bitter over some experience that you had long ago, and you never want to forgive somebody for what they have done. Here is power to forgive, power to remember that you have been forgiven. Therefore, you can forgive, and you can heal those broken relationships, and give a word of acceptance to somebody who has been estranged from you for a long time.

It is power to change bad attitudes, and stop obnoxious behavior. I know some Christians that I can't stand to be around because they are so obnoxious and are constantly acting in such a way that they hurt people and demolish relationships. No Christian needs to go on being like that. We often excuse it, saying, "Well, I'm Irish, I can't help it," or "I'm Italian, that's the way we all are." But we have no right to use those excuses because we have a power that can break every dominion known to man. That is what this verse says: "It is far above all rule or authority and power and dominion and every title that can be given, not only in the present age but also in the one to come."

Finally, it is power to reach out to others to help them in their need. It is power to respond to people's hurts around you and power to take some of your own time to minister to them. This is what makes a church function as God intended it to in society. That is what these last verses say. Verses 22–23 says:

> And God placed all things under his [Jesus'] feet and appointed him to be head over everything for the church [it is all for the church now], which is his body, the fullness of him who fills everything in every way (Ephesians 1:22–23 NIV).

Everything takes place through the church now. The church is God's great funnel through which all this great power flows.

My prayer for you is that with the eyes of your hearts you may come to know the hope to which He has called you, the riches of His glorious inheritance in the saints, and the incomparable power which He has already given you.

——◦∮◦——

(Last sermon preached by Ray C. Stedman at Peninsula Bible Church in Palo Alto, © 1995 Discovery Publishing, a ministry of Peninsula Bible Church. Used by permission.)

NOTES

INTRODUCTION

1. Howard Hendricks, interview by author, Summer 2001.

2. R. Kent Hughes, *Colossians and Philemon, The Supremacy of Christ,* 2nd edition (Westchester: Crossway Books, a division of Good News Publishers, 1995). Quotation is from the back of the book jacket.

3. Galatians 6:2 NASB

4. Lecture at Glen Eyrie, unpublished article, n.d.

5. Charles Swindoll, "Of Servants and Mentors," unpublished article, n.d.

CHAPTER ONE: A Father to Me

1. Elaine Stedman, interview by author, July 15, 2001, Grants Pass, Ore., tape recording.

2. Wendell Sheets, interview by Susan Stedman, August 4, 1994, Grants Pass, Ore., tape recording.

3. Laurie Stedman, interview by author, July 15, 2001, Grants Pass, Ore., tape recording.

4. Susan Stedman, interview by author, July 14, 2001, Grants Pass, Ore., tape recording.

5. Alan Stedman, letter to author, December 16, 2003.

6. Wade Whitcomb, "The Passing of the Torch: A Homiletical Biography of Ray Stedman," [1998], photocopy, 18.

7. Elaine Stedman, interview, July 15, 2001.

8. Ray Stedman, "The Sons of God Among Men," sermon preached on October 24, 1976; online on Peninsula Bible Church Web site, The Ray C. Stedman Memorial Library, Discovery Paper #3520.

9. Ibid.

10. Ibid.

11. Ray Stedman, "Memories of Winifred," July 30, 1996; online on Peninsula Bible Church Web site, The Ray C. Stedman Memorial Library Index, Archives of Elaine Stedman.

12. Ray Stedman, "What You See Is What You Can Be," sermon preached on May 16, 1982; online on Peninsula Bible Church Web site, The Ray C. Stedman Memorial Library, Discovery Paper #3790.

13. Wendell Sheets.

14. Elaine Stedman, interview, July 15, 2001.

15. Stedman, "Sons of God Among Men."

16. Wendell Sheets.

17. Elaine Stedman, interview, July 15, 2001.

18. Ibid.

19. Stedman, "Memories of Winifred."

CHAPTER TWO: Learning the Ground Rules

1. Rocky Mountain College is the oldest college in Montana and represents the blending of three distinct religious traditions. In 1877, a small group of Methodists met in Bozeman to establish a school. After encountering roadblocks, another group from Deer Lodge, Montana, established the Montana Collegiate Institute in 1878. Four years later, the Presbyterian Church assumed control of the institute and chartered the College of Montana, with three brick buildings and a student population of 160. A few years later, in 1889, the Methodist Episcopal Church opened Montana Wesleyan University in Helena. In 1923 these institutions merged under the aegis of Intermountain Union College in Helena, which was renamed Rocky Mountain College in 1947. (College History & Heritage section, Web site of Rocky Mountain College, Billings, Montana.)

2. Ray Stedman, "God Is Light," sermon preached on September 18, 1966; online on Peninsula Bible Church Web site, The Ray C. Stedman Memorial Library, Discovery Paper #135.

3. Ray Stedman, letter to Beulah Sheets, October 18, 1935.

4. Ibid.

5. *Electric City Collegian,* Great Falls, Montana, December 20, 1935.

6. Ibid.

7. Elaine Stedman, interview by author, July 15, 2001, Grants Pass, Ore., tape recording.

8. Ibid.

9. Ray Stedman, "Sons of God Among Men."

10. Ray Stedman, letter to his family, October 18, 1936.

11. Ibid.

12. Ray Stedman, letter to Fred Sheets, January 23, 1937.

13. Ibid.

14. Ray Stedman, "The True Lord's Prayer," sermon preached on April 26, 1964; online on Peninsula Bible Church Web site, The Ray C. Stedman Memorial Library, Discovery Paper #64.

15. Elaine Stedman, interview by author, July 15, 2001, Grants Pass, Ore., tape recording.

16. Ray Stedman, "The Incredible Hope," sermon preached on April 7, 1985; online on Peninsula Bible Church Web site, The Ray C. Stedman Memorial Library, Discovery Paper #3876.

17. Ray Stedman, "The Promise of Life," sermon preached on February 7, 1982; online on Peninsula Bible Church Web site, The Ray C. Stedman Memorial Library, Discovery Paper #3782.

18. Ray Stedman, "The Death of Death," sermon preached on April 14, 1968; online on Peninsula Bible Church Web site, The Ray C. Stedman Memorial Library, Discovery Paper #275.

19. Ray Stedman, "The Fact of Facts," sermon preached on Easter [1967]; online on Peninsula Bible Church Web site, The Ray C. Stedman Memorial Library, Discovery Paper #177.

20. Ray Stedman, "Soul and Spirit," sermon preached on March 17, 1963; online on Peninsula Bible Church Web site, The Ray C. Stedman Memorial Library, Discovery Paper #35.

21. Ray Stedman, letter to his family, April 4, 1939.

22. Allen Stedman had changed the spelling of his name from Allen to Alan after an incident at the orphanage in Denver when he was mistakenly called Helen Stedman. (Letter from his son, Alan Stedman, to author, December 16, 2003.)

23. Donald Stedman served with the 9th Armored Division, 52 Armored Infantry Battalion, A Company, Second Platoon of the US Army.

He was killed on March 27, 1945, near Limburgh, Germany. After the war, a fellow soldier/medic, Elmer M. Orr, wrote to Mrs. Stedman, explaining how Donald had died and expressing his own joy at finding a fellow believer in the midst of a war. Orr assured Mrs. Stedman that Donald had said that he was ready to meet the Lord should he be killed. (Letter from Ray's nephew, Alan Stedman, December 16, 2003.)

24. Ray Stedman, letter to his family, April 4, 1939.

25. Ray Stedman, letter to Elaine Smith, September 24, 1940.

26. Ray Stedman, letter to Elaine Smith, December 30, 1940.

27. Ray Stedman, letter to Elaine Smith, January 10, 1941.

28. Ray Stedman, letter to Elaine Smith, August 28, 1940.

29. Ray Stedman, letter to Elaine Smith, September 24, 1940.

30. Ray Stedman, letter to Elaine Smith, December 30, 1940.

31. Ibid.

32. Ray Stedman, letter to Elaine Smith, January 10, 1941.

33. Ray Stedman, letter to Elaine Smith, September 24, 1940.

CHAPTER THREE: A Soldier in Active Service

1. Ronald H. Bailey and William K. Goolrick, ed., *World War II: The Home Front (U.S.A.)*, vol. 8 (Alexandria, Va.: Time-Life Books Inc., 1978), 45.

2. Maurice Isserman and John Bowman, gen. ed., *World War II* (New York: Facts on File, Inc., 1991), 76.

3. Ray Stedman, letter to Beulah Sheets, July 5, 1942.

4. Ibid.

5. Ray Stedman, letter to Elaine Smith, December 26, 1942.

6. Ray Stedman, letter to Elaine Smith, February 15, 1943.

7. Ray Stedman, letter to Elaine Smith, March 27, 1944.

8. Ray Stedman, letter to Elaine Smith, April 12, 1944.

9. Ray Stedman, letter to Elaine Smith, May 12, 1944.

10. Betty Lee Skinner, *Daws* (Grand Rapids, Mich.: Zondervan Publishing House, 1974), 163–164, 260–261.

11. Ray Stedman, "Behind Divisions," sermon preached on March 19, 1978; online on Peninsula Bible Church Web site, The Ray C. Stedman Memorial Library, Discovery Paper #3572.

12. Skinner, *Daws*, 262–263.

13. Elaine Stedman, interview by author, July 15, 2001, Grants Pass, Ore., tape recording.

14. Ray Stedman, "Can We Trust Government?" sermon preached on November 21, 1982; online on Peninsula Bible Church Web site, The Ray C. Stedman Memorial Library, Discovery Paper #3812.

15. Ray Stedman, letter to Dawson Trotman, July 26, 1945.

16. Skinner, *Daws*, 267–270.

17. Elaine Stedman.

18. Elaine Smith, letter to Ray Stedman, April 5, 1944.

19. Ray Stedman, letter to Elaine Smith, April 12, 1944.

20. Ibid.

21. Stedman, "Behind Divisions."

22. Sydney E. Ahlstrom, *A Religious History of the American People*, vol. 2 (Garden City, N.Y.: Image Books, a division of Doubleday, 1975), 279–280.

23. Ray Stedman, letter to Elaine Smith, December 26, 1942.

24. Ray Stedman, letter to Elaine Smith, April 21, 1944.

25. Elaine Stedman.

26. Martin E. Marty, "The Electronic Church," in *Eerdmans' Handbook to Christianity in America* (Grand Rapids, Mich.: William B. Eerdmans Publishing Company, 1983), 478.

27. Elaine Stedman, e-mail to author, November 11, 2003.

28. Elaine Stedman.

CHAPTER FOUR: Equipped for Every Good Work

1. Betty Lee Skinner, *Daws*, 270.

2. Harold H. Rowdon, "Hudson Taylor," Dr. Tim Dowley, ed., *Eerdmans' Handbook to the History of Christianity* (Hertz, England: Lion Publishing, 1977), 554.

3. Elaine Stedman, interview by author, July 15, 2001, Grants Pass, Ore., tape recording.

4. "A Rich Tradition: A Brief History" section, Web site of Dallas Theological Seminary, Dallas, Texas.

5. C. Norman Kraus, "Dispensationalism," Mark A. Knoll, ed., *Eerdmans' Handbook to Christianity in America* (Grand Rapids, Mich.: William B. Eerdmans Publishing Company, 1983), 327–330.

6. Howard Hendricks, interview by author, March 15, 2001, Gleneden Beach, Ore., tape recording.

7. Elaine Stedman, interview by author, July 15, 2001, Grants Pass, Ore., tape recording.

8. Ray Stedman, "The Power You Already Have," sermon preached on September 29, 1991; online on Peninsula Bible Church Web site, The Ray C. Stedman Memorial Library, Discovery Paper #4308.

9. Elaine Stedman.

10. Howard Hendricks.

11. Ibid.

12. Ibid.

13. Elaine Stedman.

14. Ibid.

15. Ray Stedman, "Wage the Good Warfare," sermon preached in 1981; online on Peninsula Bible Church Web site, The Ray C. Stedman Memorial Library, Discovery Paper #3767.

16. Mark S. Mitchell, letter to Ray Stedman, August 1992.

17. Ray Stedman, letter to Elaine Stedman, May 20, 1947.

18. Ray Stedman, letter to Elaine Stedman, June 7, 1947.

19. Ibid.

20. Ibid.

21. Ray Stedman to Elaine Stedman, June 18, 1947.

22. Ray Stedman, letter to Elaine Stedman, May 24, 1947.

23. Ray Stedman, letter to Elaine Stedman, June 7, 1947.

24. Ray Stedman, "Liberated!" sermon preached on August 13, 1972; online on Peninsula Bible Church Web site, The Ray C. Stedman Memorial Library, Discovery Paper #3003.

25. Ray Stedman, "False Consecration," sermon preached on July 22, 1962; online on Peninsula Bible Church Web site, The Ray C. Stedman Memorial Library, Discovery Paper #12.

26. Elaine Stedman, e-mail to author, November 11, 2003.

27. Ray Stedman, "Why I Am An Expositor," *Theology, News and Notes* XXXII, no. 4 (December 1985): 4.

28. Ray Stedman, letter to Elaine Stedman, June 8, 1950.

29. Ray Stedman, "Who Is Jesus?" sermon preached on March 20, 1983; online on Peninsula Bible Church Web site, The Ray C. Stedman Memorial Library, Discovery Paper #3831.

CHAPTER FIVE: Laying a Foundation

1. Howard Hendricks, interview by author, March 15, 2001, Gleneden Beach, Ore., tape recording.

2. Joanie Burnside, "A Stone's Throw: Peninsula Bible Church 1948–1998," September 1998, written to commemorate Peninsula Bible Church's 50th anniversary (photocopy).

3. Ibid.

4. Elaine Stedman, interview by author, July 15, 2001, Grants Pass, Ore., tape recording.

5. Burnside, "A Stone's Throw."

6. Elaine Stedman.

7. Ibid.

8. Ibid.

9. Ibid.

10. Sheila Brekke, e-mail to author, August 23, 2002.

11. Ray Stedman, *Body Life* (Grand Rapids, Mich.: Discovery House Publishers, 1995), 208–209.

12. Ray Stedman, "The Christian and Worldliness," first published in *The King's Business* magazine, 1957; online on Peninsula Bible Church Web site, The Ray C. Stedman Memorial Library, Discovery Paper #2.

13. Ray Stedman, "The Lord and His Church," sermon [preached in 195?]; online on Peninsula Bible Church Web site, The Ray C. Stedman Memorial Library, Discovery Paper #3.

14. Ray Stedman, "The True Baptism of the Spirit," sermon preached on June 20, 1976; online on Peninsula Bible Church Web site, The Ray C. Stedman Memorial Library, Discovery Paper #3514.

15. Lewis Sperry Chafer, *Grace* (Findley, Ohio: Dunham Publishing, 1947), 336.

16. Ray Stedman, letter to Miles Stanford, September 26, 1957.

17. Ray Stedman, letter to Miles Stanford, August 5, 1957.

18. Ray Stedman, letter to Miles Stanford, September 12, 1957.

19. Ray Stedman, letter to Miles Stanford, August 25, 1961.

20. Elaine Stedman.

21. Ray Stedman, "The Goal of Revelation," sermon preached on November 24, 1963; online on Peninsula Bible Church Web site, The Ray C. Stedman Memorial Library, Discovery Paper #188.

22. Ray Stedman, "A Father's Joy," sermon preached on December 27, 1987; online on Peninsula Bible Church Web site, The Ray C. Stedman Memorial Library, Discovery Paper #4092.

23. Elaine Stedman, "Body Language," message given on March 8, 1998; online on Peninsula Bible Church Web site, The Ray C. Stedman Memorial Library, Discovery Paper #8157.

CHAPTER SIX: A Steward of the Mysteries of God

1. Ray Stedman, "Why I Am An Expositor," *Theology, News and Notes* XXXII, no. 4 (December 1985): 4.

2. Ray Stedman, lecture at Glen Eyrie, unpublished article, n.d., quoted by Wade Whitcomb, "Passing of the Torch," 27.

3. Ray Stedman, "On Expository Preaching," July 30, 1996; online on Peninsula Bible Church Web site, The Ray C. Stedman Library Index, archives of Elaine Stedman.

4. Ibid.

5. Ibid.

6. Ibid.

7. Ibid.

8. Ibid.

9. Ibid.

10. David Roper, interview by author, March 15, 2001, Gleneden Beach, Ore., tape recording.

11. Wade Whitcomb, "Passing of the Torch: A Homiletical Biography of Ray Stedman" [1998], photocopy, 72.

12. Ibid., 77.

13. Ibid.

14. David Roper, interview, March 15, 2001.

15. Whitcomb, "Passing of the Torch," 39.

16. Ray Stedman, "Jesus and the Priests," sermon preached on September 21, 1975; online on Peninsula Bible Church Web site, The Ray C. Stedman Memorial Library, Discovery Paper #3328.

17. Whitcomb, "Passing of the Torch," 42.

18. Ibid., 41.

19. Ibid., 42–43.

20. David Roper, interview, March 15, 2001.

21. Ray Stedman, "Hebrews: All About Faith," sermon preached on March 31, 1968; online on Peninsula Bible Church Web site, The Ray C. Stedman Memorial Library, Discovery Paper #259.

22. Ray Stedman, "What You See Is What You Can Be."

23. Ray Stedman, "Exhibit A," sermon preached on June 3, 1962; online on Peninsula Bible Church Web site, The Ray C. Stedman Memorial Library, Discovery Paper #10.

24. Ray Stedman, "*Why Pray?*" sermon preached on February 2, 1964; online on Peninsula Bible Church Web site, The Ray C. Stedman Memorial Library, Discovery Paper #56.

25. Ray Stedman, "Wage the Good Warfare."

26. Ray Stedman, "Stand Firm," sermon preached on February 21, 1988; online on Peninsula Bible Church Web site, The Ray C. Stedman Memorial Library, Discovery Paper #4099.

27. Stedman, "Wage the Good Warfare."

28. Whitcomb, "Passing of the Torch," 61.

29. David Roper, interview, March 15, 2001.

30. Whitcomb, "Passing of the Torch," 37.

31. Stedman, "Why I Am An Expositor," 6–7.

32. Whitcomb, "Passing of the Torch," 34.

33. Charles Swindoll, "The Picture of Integrity: Ray Stedman," *Insight for Living* broadcast, February 1994.

34. David Roper, interview, March 15, 2001.

35. Ray Stedman, *Body Life* (Grand Rapids, Mich.: Discovery House Publishers, 1995), 128–129.

36. Ray Stedman, "Good Grief," sermon preached on March 10, 1963; online on Peninsula Bible Church Web site, The Ray C. Stedman Memorial Library, Discovery Paper #34.

37. Whitcomb, "Passing of the Torch," 73.

38. Ray Stedman, "Let's Get On with It," sermon preached on April 11, 1965; online on Peninsula Bible Church Web site, The Ray C. Stedman Memorial Library, Discovery Paper #88.

39. Whitcomb, "Passing of the Torch," 73.

40. David Roper, interview, March 15, 2001.

41. Ray Stedman, "The Secrets of God," sermon preached on July 16, 1972; online on Peninsula Bible Church Web site, The Ray C. Stedman Memorial Library, Discovery Paper #3000.

42. Stedman, "Why I Am An Expositor," 6.

43. Ray Stedman, "The Desperate Need for Biblical Truth in Our Churches," unpublished article, n.d.: 2.

44. Ibid.

45. Ibid.

46. Whitcomb, "Passing of the Torch," 77.

CHAPTER SEVEN: The Winds of Change

1. Author unlisted, "An Unruly Time (1960–1980)," Mark A. Knoll, ed., *Eerdmans' Handbook to Christianity in America* (Grand Rapids, Mich.: William B. Eerdmans Publishing Company, 1983), 464.

2. Ibid., 465–468.

3. Ibid., 469.

4. Ray Stedman, *Body Life* (Glendale, Calif.: Regal Books, 1972), 131–132.

5. David Roper, interview with author, March 15, 2001, Gleneden Beach, Ore., tape recording.

6. Ibid.

7. Ibid.

8. Ibid.

9. Ibid.

10. Ibid.

11. Wade Whitcomb, "Passing of the Torch", 73

12. Luis Palau, interview by author, September 9, 2002, by telephone, tape recording.

13. Howard Hendricks, interview by author, March 15, 2001, Gleneden Beach, Ore., tape recording.

14. Charles Swindoll, "The Picture of Integrity: Ray Stedman," *Insights Newsletter,* vol. 2, no. 6, December 1992.

15. Bill Lawrence, quoted by Joanie Burnside in "A Stone's Throw," 21.

16. Ibid., 13.

17. David Roper.

18 Elaine Stedman, "Body Language."

19. Ted Wise, quoted by Joanie Burnside, "A Stone's Throw," 23.

20. Whitcomb, 42–43.

21. Ray Stedman, "The Child in Our Midst," sermon preached on March 2, 1975; online on Peninsula Bible Church Web site, The Ray C. Stedman Memorial Library, Discovery Paper #3317.

22. David Roper.

23. Elaine Stedman, "Body Language."

24. Quoted from *Christianity Today* in *Body Life,* 139–143.

CHAPTER EIGHT: Treasure in a Clay Pot

1. Susan and Linda Stedman, interviews by author, July 14, 2001, Grants Pass, Ore., tape recording.

2. Ibid.

3. Laurie Stedman, interview by author, July 15, 2001, Grants Pass, Ore., tape recording.

4. Susan, Linda, and Laurie Stedman, interviews by author.

5. Ibid.

6. Laurie Stedman, interview.

7. Ibid.

8. Susan and Linda Stedman, interviews by author.

9. Elaine Stedman, interview by author, July 15, 2001, Grants Pass, Ore., tape recording.

10. Ray Stedman, letter to Elaine Stedman, October 22, 1968.

11. Elaine Stedman, interview by Wade Whitcomb, November 17–18, 1994, Grants Pass, Ore., transcript.

12. Linda Stedman, interview.

13. Sheila Stedman, letter to author, August 26, 2002.

14. Elaine Stedman, inteview.

15. Ibid.

16. Susan Stedman, interview.

17. Sheila Stedman, letter.

18. Linda Stedman, interview.

19. Sheila Stedman, letter.

20. Jim Heaton, interview by author, March 15, 2001, Gleneden Beach, Ore., tape recording.

21. Luis Palau, interview by author, September 9, 2002, by telephone, tape recording.

22. Ray Stedman, *Spiritual Warfare* (Peninsula Bible Church Web site, Ray C. Stedman Memorial Library, Discovery Publishing, Internet edition 1999), Chapter 3: "The Strategy of Satan."

23. Linda Stedman, e-mail to author, September 1, 2002.

24. Stedman, *Authentic Christianity* (Grand Rapids, Mich.: Discovery House Publishers, 1996), 122.

25. Ibid., 125.

26. Susan Stedman, interview.

27. Laurie Stedman, interview.

28. Linda Stedman, e-mail to author, September 1, 2002.

29. Sheila Stedman, e-mail to author, August 26, 2002.

CHAPTER NINE: Contending for the Faith

1. Ray Stedman, "Tell It to the Church," sermon preached on September 30, 1984; online on Peninsula Bible Church Web site, The Ray C. Stedman Memorial Library, Discovery Paper #3952.

2. Ray Stedman, "The Church That Lost Its Love," sermon preached on November 12, 1989; online on Peninsula Bible Church Web site, The Ray C. Stedman Memorial Library, Discovery Paper #4190.

3. Quoted by Ray Stedman, "The Signs of an Apostle," sermon preached on March 25, 1980; online on Peninsula Bible Church Web site, The Ray C. Stedman Memorial Library, Discovery Paper #3697.

4. Ibid.

5. Ray Stedman, "The Message of Romans," sermon preached on January 22, 1967; online on Peninsula Bible Church Web site, The Ray C. Stedman Memorial Library, Discovery Paper #246.

6. Elaine Stedman, interview by author, July 15, 2001, Grants Pass, Ore., tape recording.

7. Ray Stedman, "Guard the Teaching," sermon preached on unknown date in 1981; online on Peninsula Bible Church Web site, The Ray C. Stedman Memorial Library, Discovery Paper #3764.

8. Ray Stedman, letter to colleague, August 30, 1989.

CHAPTER TEN: Passing the Torch

1. Bev Forsyth, unpublished document, 1992.

2. Joanie Burnside, "A Stone's Throw: Peninsula Bible Church 1948–1998."

3. Ibid., 12–13.

4. Ray's speaking calendar from 1982–1984 reveals the extent to which he made himself available to the body of Christ at large. He spoke to various groups at retreat centers such as Mount Hermon (Calif.), Mission Springs (Calif.), The Firs (Wash.), Hume Lake (Calif.), The Ozarks (Ark.), Ridgecrest (N.C.), and Glen Eyrie (Colo.). He taught at pastors' conferences for Presbyterians in Washington D.C., Evangelical Free pastors in Florida, and interdenominational pastors in Texas, Colorado, Oregon, Washington, and California. He ministered to Christian organizations such as Young Life, Bible Study Fellowship, America's Keswick, Overseas Crusade, and Challenge Unlimited. He taught at Bible colleges and seminaries such as Big Sky Bible College (Mont.), Westmont College (Calif.), Talbot Seminary (Calif.), Fuller Seminary (Calif.), Dallas Seminary (Tex.), Westminster Seminary (Pa.), and Regent College (Vancouver, B.C.). He also traveled internationally several times to Asia, Europe, and Canada.

5. Jim Heaton, interview by author, March 15, 2001, Gleneden Beach, Ore., tape recording.

6. Joanie Burnside, "A Stone's Throw," 6.

7. Ray Stedman, quoted in "Unsheathing the Sword," *Eternity*, March 1986, 14.

8. Ibid.

9. Ibid.

10. Ray Stedman, "The Purpose of Preaching," sermon at COBE Conference, March 1986, Multnomah Ministries, Portland, Ore., audiotape #CB6003.

11. Wade Whitcomb, "Passing of the Torch," 95

12. Howard Hendricks, interview by author, March 15, 2001, Gleneden Beach, Ore., tape recording.

13. Elaine Stedman, e-mail to author, January 29, 2004.

14. Ray Stedman, "The Passing of the Torch," sermon preached on June 6, 1982; online on Peninsula Bible Church Web site, The Ray C. Stedman Memorial Library, Discovery Paper #3793.

15. Ray Stedman, "The City of Glory," sermon preached on April 29, 1990; online on Peninsula Bible Church Web site, The Ray C. Stedman Memorial Library, Discovery Paper #4211.

CHAPTER ELEVEN: Ready for Something Tremendous

1. Ray Stedman, "The Power You Already Have."

2. Ray Stedman, "Spiritual Survival," unpublished document, undated (photocopy).

3. Wendell Sheets, interview by Susan Stedman, August 4, 1994, Grants Pass, Ore., transcript.

4. Doug Shearer, quote on The Rogue River Fellowship section; online on Peninsula Bible Church Web site, The Ray C. Stedman Memorial Library.

5. Charles Swindoll, "Of Servants and Mentors," unpublished article, n.d. (photocopy).

6. Susan Stedman, in transcript of Wendell Sheets interview.

7. Linda Stedman, e-mail to author, August 29, 2002.

8. Linda Stedman, Susan Stedman, and Stedman grandchildren, interviews by author, July 14, 2001, Grants Pass, Ore., tape recording.

9. Jeanne Hendricks, interview by author, March 15, 2001, Gleneden Beach, Ore., tape recording.

10. Ibid.

11. Howard Hendricks, interview by author, March 15, 2001, Gleneden Beach, Ore, tape recording.

12. Luis Palau, interview by author, September 9, 2002, by telephone, tape recording.

13. Howard Hendricks, interview by author.

14. Elaine Stedman, e-mail to author, January 22, 2003.

15. Linda Stedman, interview by author.

16. Ibid.

17. Ibid.

18. Brian Morgan, quoted in Joanie Burnside, "A Stone's Throw," 15.

19. Ray Stedman, "The Cure for Heart Trouble," sermon preached on March 17, 1985; online on Peninsula Bible Church Web site, The Ray C. Stedman Memorial Library, Discovery Paper #3868.

Sources Consulted

INTERVIEWS

Heaton, Jim. Interview by author, March 15, 2001, Gleneden Beach, Ore. Tape recording.

Hendricks, Howard. Interview by author, March 15, 2001, Gleneden Beach, Ore. Tape recording.

Hendricks, Jeanne. Interview by author, March 15, 2001, Gleneden Beach, Ore. Tape recording.

Palau, Luis. Interview by author, September 9, 2002, by telephone. Tape recording.

Roe, Robert. Interview by author, September 24, 2002, Sunnyvale, Calif. Tape recording.

Roper, David. Interview by author, March 15, 2001, Gleneden Beach, Ore. Tape recording.

Sheets, Wendell. Interview by Susan Stedman, August 4, 1994, Grants Pass, Ore. Transcript.

Stedman, Elaine. Interview by author, July 15, 2001, Grants Pass, Ore. Tape recording.

Stedman, Elaine. Interview by Wade Whitcomb, November 17–18, 1994, Grants Pass, Ore. Transcript.

Stedman, Susan. Interview by author, July 14, 2001, Grants Pass, Ore. Tape recording.

Stedman Martin, Laurie. Interview by author, July 15, 2001, Grants Pass, Ore. Tape recording.

Stedman, Linda. Interview by author, July 14, 2001, Grants Pass, Ore. Tape recording.

LETTERS FROM RAY C. STEDMAN

Stedman, Ray, to Beulah Sheets, October 18, 1935. Collection of Elaine Stedman.

_____, to Beulah Sheets, July 5, 1942. Collection of Elaine Stedman.

_____, to confidential recipient, August 30, 1989. Collection of recipient.

_____, to Dawson Trotman, July 26, 1945. Collection of Elaine Stedman.

_____, to Elaine Smith, August 28, 1940. Collection of Elaine Stedman.

_____, to Elaine Smith, September 24, 1940. Collection of Elaine Stedman.

_____, to Elaine Smith, December 30, 1940. Collection of Elaine Stedman.

_____, to Elaine Smith, January 10, 1941. Collection of Elaine Stedman.

_____, to Elaine Smith, December 26, 1942. Collection of Elaine Stedman.

_____, to Elaine Smith, February 15, 1943. Collection of Elaine Stedman.

_____, to Elaine Smith, March 27, 1944. Collection of Elaine Stedman.

_____, to Elaine Smith, April 12, 1944. Collection of Elaine Stedman.

_____, to Elaine Smith, April 21, 1944. Collection of Elaine Stedman.

_____, to Elaine Smith, May 12, 1944. Collection of Elaine Stedman.

_____, to Elaine Stedman, May 20, 1947. Collection of Elaine Stedman.

_____, to Elaine Stedman, May 24, 1947. Collection of Elaine Stedman.

_____, to Elaine Stedman, June 7, 1947. Collection of Elaine Stedman.

_____, to Elaine Stedman, June 18, 1947. Collection of Elaine Stedman.

_____, to Elaine Stedman, June 8, 1950. Collection of Elaine Stedman.

_____, to Elaine Stedman, October 22, 1968. Collection of Elaine Stedman.

_____, to Fred Sheets, January 23, 1937. Collection of Elaine Stedman.

_____, to his family, undated. Collection of Elaine Stedman.

_____, to his family, October 18, 1936. Collection of Elaine Stedman.

_____, to his family, April 4, 1939. Collection of Elaine Stedman.

_____, to Miles Stanford, August 5, 1957. Collection of Elaine Stedman.

_____, to Miles Stanford, September 12, 1957. Collection of Elaine Stedman.

_____, to Miles Stanford, September 26, 1957. Collection of Elaine Stedman.

_____, to Miles Stanford, August 25, 1961. Collection of Elaine Stedman.

LETTERS FROM OTHERS

Mitchell, Mark, to Ray Stedman, August 1992. Collection of Mark S. Mitchell.

Smith, Elaine, to Ray Stedman, April 5, 1944. Collection of Elaine Stedman.

Stedman, Elaine, e-mail to Mark Mitchell, January 22, 2003. Collection of Mark S. Mitchell.

Stedman Brekke, Sheila, letter to Mark Mitchell, August 26, 2002. Collection of Mark S. Mitchell.

Stedman, Susan, e-mail to Mark Mitchell, August 23, 2002. Collection of Mark S. Mitchell.

Stedman, Linda, e-mail to Mark Mitchell, August 29, 2002. Collection of Mark S. Mitchell.

_____, e-mail to Mark Mitchell, September 1, 2002. Collection of Mark S. Mitchell.

PUBLISHED SERMONS BY RAY C. STEDMAN

Stedman, Ray C. "Behind Divisions." Discovery Paper #3572. Peninsula Bible Church Web site (www.pbc.org), The Ray C. Stedman Memorial Library. Sermon preached on March 19, 1978. Database online.

_____. "Can We Trust Government?" Discovery Paper #3812. Peninsula Bible Church Web site (www.pbc.org), The Ray C. Stedman Memorial Library. Sermon preached on November 21, 1982. Database online.

_____. "The Child in Our Midst." Discovery Paper #3317. Peninsula Bible Church Web site (www.pbc.org), The Ray C. Stedman Memorial Library. Sermon preached on March 2, 1975. Database online.

_____. "The Christian and Worldliness." First published in *The King's Business* magazine, 1957. Discovery Paper #2. Peninsula Bible Church Web site (www.pbc.org), The Ray C. Stedman Memorial Library. Database online.

_____. "The Church That Lost Its Love." Discovery Paper #4190. Peninsula Bible Church Web site (www.pbc.org), The Ray C. Stedman Memorial Library. Sermon preached on November 12, 1979. Database online.

_____. "The City of Glory." Discovery Paper #4211 Peninsula Bible Church Web site (www.pbc.org), The Ray C. Stedman Memorial Library. Sermon preached on April 29, 1990. Database online.

_____. "The Cure for Heart Trouble." Discovery Paper #3868. Peninsula Bible Church Web site (www.pbc.org), The Ray C. Stedman Memorial Library. Sermon preached on March 17, 1985. Database online.

_____. "The Death of Death." Discovery Paper #275. Peninsula Bible Church Web site (www.pbc.org), The Ray C. Stedman Memorial Library. Sermon preached on April 14, 1968. Database online.

_____. "Doing What Comes Unnaturally." Discovery Paper #4. Peninsula Bible Church Web site (www.pbc.org), The Ray C. Stedman Memorial Library. Sermon preached prior to May 10, 1959. Database online.

_____. "Exhibit A." Discovery Paper #10. Peninsula Bible Church Web site (www.pbc.org), The Ray C. Stedman Memorial Library. Sermon preached on June 3, 1962. Database online.

_____. "The Fact of Facts." Discovery Paper #177. Peninsula Bible Church Web site (www.pbc.org), The Ray C. Stedman Memorial Library. Sermon preached on Easter [1967]. Database online.

_____. "False Consecration." Discovery Paper #12. Peninsula Bible Church Web site (www.pbc.org), The Ray C. Stedman Memorial Library. Sermon preached on July 22, 1962. Database online.

_____. "A Father's Joy." Discovery Paper #4092. Peninsula Bible Church Web site (www.pbc.org), The Ray C. Stedman Memorial Library. Sermon preached on December 27, 1987. Database online.

_____. "The Goal of Revelation." Discovery Paper #188. Peninsula Bible Church Web site (www.pbc.org), The Ray C. Stedman Memorial Library. Sermon preached on November 24, 1963. Database online.

_____. "God Is Light." Discovery Paper #135. Peninsula Bible Church Web site (www.pbc.org), The Ray C. Stedman Memorial Library. Sermon preached on September 18, 1966. Database online.

_____. "Good Grief." Discovery Paper #34. Peninsula Bible Church Web site (www.pbc.org), The Ray C. Stedman Memorial Library. Sermon preached on March 10, 1963. Database online.

_____. "Guard the Teaching." Discovery Paper #3764. Peninsula Bible Church Web site (www.pbc.org), The Ray C. Stedman Memorial Library. Sermon preached on unknown date in 1981. Database online.

_____. "Hebrews: All About Faith." Discovery Paper #259. Peninsula Bible Church Web site (www.pbc.org), The Ray C. Stedman Memorial Library. Sermon preached on March 31, 1968. Database online.

_____. "The Incredible Hope." Discovery Paper #3876. Peninsula Bible Church Web site (www.pbc.org), The Ray C. Stedman Memorial Library. Sermon preached on April 7, 1985. Database online.

_____. "Jesus and the Priests." Discovery Paper #3328. Peninsula Bible Church Web site (www.pbc.org), The Ray C. Stedman Memorial Library. Sermon preached on September 21, 1975. Database online.

_____. "Let's Get On with It." Discovery Paper #88. Peninsula Bible Church Web site (www.pbc.org), The Ray C. Stedman Memorial Library. Sermon preached on April 11, 1965. Database online.

_____. "Liberated!" Discovery Paper #3003. Peninsula Bible Church Web site (www.pbc.org), The Ray C. Stedman Memorial Library. Sermon preached on August 13, 1972. Database online.

_____. "The Lord and His Church." Discovery Paper #3. Peninsula Bible Church Web site (www.pbc.org), The Ray C. Stedman Memorial Library. Sermon [preached in 195?]. Database online.

_____. "The Message of Romans." Discovery Paper #246. Peninsula Bible Church Web site (www.pbc.org), The Ray C. Stedman Memorial Library. Sermon preached on January 22, 1967. Database online.

_____. "On Expositional Preaching." Sermon preached on July 30, 1996. Peninsula Bible Church Web site (www.pbc.org), The Ray Stedman Library Index. From the Archives of Elaine Stedman. Database online.

_____. "One Thousand Years of Peace." Discovery Paper #4210. Peninsula Bible Church Web site (www.pbc.org), The Ray C. Stedman Memorial Library. Sermon preached on April 22, 1990. Database online.

_____. "The Passing of the Torch." Discovery Paper #3783. Peninsula Bible Church Web site (www.pbc.org), The Ray C. Stedman Memorial Library. Sermon preached on June 6, 1982. Database online.

_____. "The Power You Already Have." Discovery Paper #4308. Peninsula Bible Church Web site (www.pbc.org), The Ray C. Stedman Memorial Library. Sermon preached on September 29, 1991. Database online.

_____. "The Promise of Life." Discovery Paper #3782. Peninsula Bible Church Web site (www.pbc.org), The Ray C. Stedman Memorial Library. Sermon preached on February 7, 1982. Database online.

_____. "The Secrets of God." Discovery Paper #3000. Peninsula Bible Church Web site (www.pbc.org), The Ray C. Stedman Memorial Library. Sermon preached on July 16, 1972. Database online.

_____. "The Signs of an Apostle." Discovery Paper #3697. Peninsula Bible Church Web site (www.pbc.org), The Ray C. Stedman Memorial Library. Sermon preached on March 25, 1980. Database online.

_____. "A Song of Realities." Discovery Paper #386. Peninsula Bible Church Web site (www.pbc.org), The Ray C. Stedman Memorial Library. Sermon preached on September 28, 1969. Database online.

_____. "The Sons of God Among Men." Discovery Paper #3520. Peninsula Bible Church Web site (www.pbc.org), The Ray C. Stedman Memorial Library. Sermon preached on October 24, 1976. Database online.

_____. "Soul and Spirit." Discovery Paper #35. Peninsula Bible Church Web site (www.pbc.org), The Ray C. Stedman Memorial Library. Sermon preached on March 17, 1963. Database online.

_____. "Stand Firm." Discovery Paper #4099. Peninsula Bible Church Web site (www.pbc.org), The Ray C. Stedman Memorial Library. Sermon preached on February 21, 1988. Database online.

_____. "Tell It to the Church." Discovery Paper #3952. Peninsula Bible Church Web site (www.pbc.org), The Ray C. Stedman Memorial Library. Sermon preached on September 30, 1984. Database online.

_____. "The True Baptism of the Spirit." Discovery Paper #3514. Peninsula Bible Church Web site (www.pbc.org), The Ray C. Stedman Memorial Library. Sermon preached on June 20, 1976. Database online.

_____. "The True Lord's Prayer." Discovery Paper #64. Peninsula Bible Church Web site (www.pbc.org), The Ray C. Stedman Memorial Library. Sermon preached on April 26, 1964. Database online.

_____. "Wage the Good Warfare." Discovery Paper #3767. Peninsula Bible Church Web site (www.pbc.org), The Ray C. Stedman Memorial Library. Sermon preached in 1981. Database online.

_____. "What You See Is What You Can Be." Discovery Paper #3790. Peninsula Bible Church Web site (www.pbc.org), The Ray C. Stedman Memorial Library. Sermon preached on May 16, 1982. Database online.

_____. "Who Is Jesus?" Discovery Paper #3831 Peninsula Bible Church Web site (www.pbc.org), The Ray C. Stedman Memorial Library. Sermon preached on March 20, 1983. Database online.

_____. "Why Pray?" Discovery Paper #56. Peninsula Bible Church Web site (www.pbc.org), The Ray C. Stedman Memorial Library. Sermon preached on February 2, 1964. Database online.

OTHER PUBLISHED WORKS BY RAY C. STEDMAN

Stedman, Ray C. "Memories of Winifred." Peninsula Bible Church Web site (www.pbc.org), The Ray C. Stedman Memorial Library Index, Archives of Elaine Stedman. July 30, 1996. Database online.

_____. *Spiritual Warfare*, Peninsula Bible Church Web site (www.pbc.org), Ray C. Stedman Memorial Library. Discovery Publishing, Internet Edition 1999. Database online.

_____. "Unsheathing the Sword." *Eternity*, March 1986.

_____. "Why I Am An Expositor." *Theology, News and Notes*, XXXII, no. 4, December 1985.

OTHER PUBLISHED WORKS

Ahlstrom, Sydney E. A *Religious History of the American People*, vol. 2. Garden City, N.Y.: Image Books, a division of Doubleday, 1975.

Bailey, Ronald H., and William K. Goolrick, ed., *The Home Front: U.S.A.*, World War II. Alexandria, Va.: Time-Life Books Inc., 1978.

Brokaw, Tom, *The Greatest Generation*. New York: Random House, 1998.

Chafer, Lewis Sperry. *Grace*. Findlay, Ohio: Dunham Publishing, 1947.

Dallas Theological Seminary Web site (www.dts.edu). Dallas, Tex. "A Rich Tradition: A Brief History" section. Database online.

Isserman, Maurice, and John Bowman, gen. ed., *World War II*. New York: Facts on File, Inc., 1991.

Kraus, C. Norman. "Dispensationalism," Mark A. Knoll, ed., *Eerdmans' Handbook to Christianity in America* (Grand Rapids, Mich.: William B. Eerdmans Publishing Company, 1983), 327–330.

Marty, Martin E. "The Electronic Church," in *Eerdmans' Handbook to Christianity in America.* Grand Rapids, Mich.: William B. Eerdmans Publishing Company, 1983.

Rocky Mountain College Web site (www.rocky.edu). Billings, Mont.: "College History & Heritage" section. Database online.

Rowdon, Harold H. "Hudson Taylor," Dr. Tim Dowley, ed., *Eerdmans' Handbook to the History of Christianity.* Hertz, England: Lion Publishing, 1977.

Shearer, Doug. Quote on "The Rogue River Fellowship" section, Peninsula Bible Church Web site (www.pbc.org), The Ray C. Stedman Memorial Library.

Skinner, Betty Lee. *Daws.* Grand Rapids, Mich.: Zondervan, 1974.

Stedman, Elaine. "Body Language." Discovery Paper #8157. Peninsula Bible Church Web site (www.pbc.org), The Ray C. Stedman Memorial Library. Message given on March 8, 1998. Database online.

Stedman, Ray C. *Body Life.* Glendale, CA: Regal Books, 1972.

_____. *Authentic Christianity.* Palo Alto, CA: Discovery Books, 1975.

Swindoll, Charles. "The Picture of Integrity: Ray Stedman." *Insights Newsletter*, vol. 2, no. 6, December 1992.

"An Unruly Time (1960–1980)," Mark A. Knoll, ed., *Eerdmans' Handbook to Christianity in America,* Grand Rapids, Mich.: William B. Eerdmans Publishing Company, 1983.

Whitworth College Web site (www.whitworth.edu). Spokane, Wash.: "About Whitworth" Heritage section. Database online.

UNPUBLISHED WORKS

Burnside, Joanie. "A Stone's Throw: Peninsula Bible Church 1948–1998." 1998. Photocopy.

Forsyth, Bev. Unpublished document. 1992. Photocopy.

Stedman, Ray. "The Desperate Need for Biblical Truth in Our Churches." n.d. Photocopy.

_____. "The Purpose of Preaching." March 1986. Multnomah Ministries, Portland, Ore.: Audiotape CB6003.

_____. "Spiritual Survival." n.d. Photocopy.

Swindoll, Charles. "Of Servants and Mentors." n.d. Photocopy.

Whitcomb, Wade. "Passing of the Torch: A Homiletical Biography of Ray Stedman." 1998. Photocopy.

Books by Ray C. Stedman

Adventuring Through the Bible: A Comprehensive Guide to the Entire Bible. Grand Rapids, Mich.: Discovery House Publishers, 1977.

Authentic Christianity. New York: Jove, 1977; Portland, Ore.: Multnomah Publishers, 1984; Grand Rapids, Mich.: Discovery House Publishers, 1996.

The Beginnings. Waco, Tex.: Word Books, 1978.

Behind Suffering: Expository Studies in Job. Waco, Tex.: Word Books, 1981.

Birth of the Body: Acts 1-12. Portland, Ore.: Vision House Publishers, 1974.

Body Life. Glendale, Calif.: Regal Books, 1972; Grand Rapids, Mich.: Discovery House Publishers, 1995.

Death of a Nation: Jeremiah. Waco, Tex.: Word Books, 1976.

From Guilt to Glory: Hope for the Helpless. Portland Ore.: Multnomah Publishing, 1985.

Folk Songs of Faith. Glendale, Calif.: Regal Books, 1973.

God's Final Word: Understanding Revelation. Grand Rapids, Mich.: Discovery House Publishers, 1991.

God's Loving Word: Exploring the Gospel of John. Grand Rapids, Mich.: Discovery House Publishers, 1993.

Growth of the Body: Acts 13-20. Portland, Ore.: Vision House Publishers, 1976.

Hebrews (IVP New Testament Commentary Series). Ray C. Stedman et al. Downers Grove, Ill.: InterVarsity Press, 1992.

Highlights of the Bible: Poets and Prophets (Genesis-Nehemiah). Glendale, Calif.: Gospel Light Publications, 1979; Glendale, Calif.: Regal Books, 1980–1981; Grand Rapids, Mich.: Discovery House Publishing, 1997.

How to Live What You Believe: A Life-Related Study in Hebrews. (Bible Commentary for Laymen). Glendale, Calif.: Regal Books, 1997.

Is This All There Is to Life: Answers from Ecclesiastes. Grand Rapids, Mich.: Discovery House Publishers, 1999.

Life by the Son: Expository Studies in 1 John. Waco, Tex.: Word Books, 1980.

Living Peacefully in a Stressful World: A Strategy for Replacing Stress with Peace. Ray C. Stedman et al., Discovery Enterprises, 2000.

Man of Faith: Learning from the Life of Abraham. Portland, Ore.: Multnomah Publishers, 1986.

Nehemiah. Joy of Living Bible Studies, 2002.

Power Out of Weakness: Expository Studies in 2 Corinthians. Waco, Tex.: Word Books, 1982.

Psalms of Faith. Glendale, Calif.: Regal Books, 1989; Joy of Living Bible Studies, 2001.

The Queen and I. Waco, Tex.: Word Books, 1977.

Reason to Rejoice: Love, Grace, and Forgiveness in Paul's Letter to the Romans. Grand Rapids, Mich.: Discovery House Publishers, 2004.

Revelation. Joy of Living Bible Studies, 2003.

Our Riches in Christ: Discovering the Believer's Inheritance in Ephesians. Waco, Tex.: Word Books, 1976; Grand Rapids, Mich.: Discovery House Publishers, 1998.

The Ruler Who Serves: Mark 8–16. Waco, Tex.: Word Books, 1985; Grand Rapids, Mich.: Discovery House Publishers, 2003.

Secrets of the Spirit. Old Tappan, N.J.: Fleming H. Revell, 1975.

The Servant Who Rules: Exploring the Gospel of Mark 1–8. Waco, Tex.: Word Books, 1976; Grand Rapids, Mich.: Discovery House Publishers, 2002.

Solomon's Secret: Enjoying Life, God's Good Gift. Portland, Ore.: Multnomah Publishers, 1985.

Spiritual Warfare: Winning the Daily Battle with Satan. Grand Rapids, Mich.: Discovery House Publishers, 1999.

Talking with My Father: Jesus Teaches on Prayer. Waco, Tex.: Word Books, 1975; Grand Rapids, Mich.: Discovery House Publishers, 1997.

Triumphs of the Body: Acts 21–28. Portland, Ore.: Vision House Publishers, date unknown.

Understanding Man: How We Got to Where We Are. Portland, Ore.: Multnomah Publishers, 1986.

Waiting for the Second Coming: Studies in Thessalonians. Grand Rapids, Mich.: Discovery House Publishers, 1998.

What More Can God Say? A Fresh Look at Hebrews. Glendale, Calif.: Regal Books, 1977, 1985.

What on Earth Is Happening? What Jesus Said about the End of the Age. Grand Rapids, Mich.: Discovery House Publishers, 2003.

What's This World Coming To: An Expository Study of Matthew 24-25, the Olivet Discourse. Glendale, Calif.: Regal Books, 1986.

ABOUT THE AUTHOR

—⊸⫘⫘⊸—

MARK S. MITCHELL has been the teaching pastor at Central Peninsula Bible Church on the San Francisco Peninsula since 1986. He is a graduate of Denver Seminary and Gordon-Conwell Theological Seminary. He and his wife, Lynn, have three children—Anne-Marie, Kimberly, and Matthew—and live in Los Altos, California. His thriving ministry is an outgrowth of Ray Stedman's ground-breaking Peninsula Bible Church in Palo Alto, California.

NOTE TO THE READER

THE PUBLISHER INVITES YOU to share your response to the message of this book by writing Discovery House Publishers, Box 3566, Grand Rapids, MI 49501, U.S.A. For information about other Discovery House books, music, or videos, contact us at the same address or call 1-800-653-8333. Find us on the Internet at http://www.dhp.org/ or send e-mail to books@dhp.org.